UNIVERSITY LIBRARY
W. S. U. - STEVENS POINT

Organizing and Operating Special Classes for Emotionally Disturbed Elementary School Children

Organizing and Operating Special Classes for Emotionally Disturbed Elementary School Children

Thomas E. Stone, Ph.D.

Parker Publishing Company, Inc.

West Nyack, N.Y.

©1971, by
PARKER PUBLISHING COMPANY, INC.
West Nyack, N.Y.

*All rights reserved. No part of this
book may be reproduced in any form or
by any means, without permission in
writing from the publisher.*

Library of Congress
Catalog Card Number: 78-130032

Printed in the United States of America
ISBN—0-13-642017-6
B & P

To my wife, Emilita, who lived through it.

A Blueprint of the Program

The role of the public school has expanded to include the total development of the child within the educational mainstream, irrespective of physical, intellectual, or emotional handicaps. The school is, in a sense, the heart of the community and has a responsibility to increase its involvement as a member of the community team. One educational approach gaining recognition is the identification and placement of emotionally disturbed children in smaller class settings where they can gradually develop the inner organization for reality task functioning.

If these intelligent, emotionally disturbed children are not placed in special classes, they will have increasing difficulty functioning in regular class—and outside the school. By providing smaller structured team-teaching settings with a closer one-to-one relationship with the teacher, the human catalyst to inner growth, these children can begin to captain their own ship in the mainstream of society.

This book sets forth, one educational brick at a time, the school team steps necessary to organize and implement these special classes in the elementary schools. The identification, dynamics, screening, and placing of the disturbed child into special designed class are followed by a graphic picture of the program in operation, the gradual farming out of students back into regular class, and the range of reality situations a program like this faces, including ways to resolve difficulties that may arise.

This book provides elementary public school systems with the practical educational guidelines for setting up special classes for emotionally disturbed children, selecting the teachers, and carrying through with a curriculum, necessary materials and equipment, teaching techniques, parent-teacher conferences, and a summer transition-adjustment class program.

To help the emotionally disturbed child in his total organization is to serve every child in his regular class, the classroom teacher, and special teachers, since these children drain the time and energy of the regular class teacher due to the varying nature and depth of these disturbances.

The preventive-developmental focus, intrinsic to the program, serves to build a basic personality foundation in preparation for increasing reality demands and the stresses of preadolescence and adolescence. It is an early, comprehensive community attack on the problems that face society, ranging from drug taking to personality breakdown.

These classes are a crucial doorway to an organized life for the emotionally disturbed child and have far-reaching consequences, both for his future goals and for the total school program. There is no realistic alternative.

Thomas E. Stone, Ph. D

ACKNOWLEDGMENTS

I wish to make special acknowledgment to the following people who worked with me, as a team, in the development of the program and the writing of the book:

An Elementary School Principal	Mr. Warren Hochberg, M.S.
A Coordinator of Emotionally Disturbed Classes	Mr. William Langan, B.A.
A Teacher of Emotionally Disturbed Children	Mr. William Gilmer, M.S.
A Psychological Services Office Manager	Mrs. Edith Woods

I also wish to thank:

Mr. Robert Stone for his help on the book.

The Three Village Central School District No. 1, Setauket, New York under the dynamic leadership of Dr. Francis J. Roberts, Superintendent of Schools, for providing the opportunity to develop this program.

Dr. Ruth Rabinovitch, Consulting Psychiatrist, Glen Cove, New York, who worked with the program and emphasized the importance of early placement in the transition-adjustment classes.

Dr. Richard Reuben, Consulting Pediatric-Neurologist, Roslyn Heights, New York, who was important in clarifying the diagnostic picture.

Miss Laurie Legendre, Reading Specialist, who made invaluable contributions to the program and to the book.

Mr. David Abramovich and Mr. Robert McKee, who typify the transition-adjustment class teacher in action.

Mr. Roscoe J. Denton, Jr., photographer, for the staged pictures.

Table of Contents

1. THE PROBLEM-AN ANSWER • 17

Where the Problem Begins • Profile of the Disturbed Child • The Child Drains the Teacher and the Class • The Value of the Special Class • Parents of Emotionally Disturbed Children Are Not to Blame • Transition and Adjustment • Some Technical Dimensions • How to Use This Book • How the Child Looks at the Special Class • Team Communication—A Key to Success • Curriculum, Techniques, and Materials

2. IDENTIFYING THE EMOTIONALLY DISTURBED CHILD • 31

Clues to the Emotional Disturbance • Early Attempts to Make the Best of It • The Need for Diagnostic Action • How to Attack the Problem at a Preschool Level • Preschool Help to the Family • Action Steps in the School • The Individual Testing Process • Evaluating the Test Results

3. THE DYNAMICS OF THE EMOTIONALLY DISTURBED CHILD • 43

Causes of Emotional Disturbance • Effects on the Family Life • Portrait of a Disturbed Five-Year-Old Boy • Developmental Interferences • The Illusion of

Environmental Cause • The Blamed and the Blameless • The Role of the Public School • Goals for Disturbed Children • The Parents Must Understand

4. HOW TO ORGANIZE A DISTRICT TRANSITION-ADJUSTMENT CLASS PROGRAM • 54

Selecting the Program Director • A Model for the Transition-Adjustment Class Program • The Director's Responsibilities • The Director as a Team Member • The Director and the Principal • The First Step—Documenting the Need • Setting Up a Transition-Adjustment Class Program • Selecting the Transition-Adjustment Class Teacher • Points on Transition-Adjustment Class Organization • The Principal's Ship • The Transition-Adjustment Classrooms • Getting the Youngsters to School • The Role of Transportation • Class Acceptance • Initiation of the Program • Parents as Part of the Team • Advantages of Summer and Secondary Transition-Adjustment Class Programs • Summarizing

5. PROCEDURES FOR TRANSITION-ADJUSTMENT CLASS SCREENING • 73

Preparing the Referral Form • Setting Student Priorities • The Psychologist's Evaluation • The Post-Evaluation Parent Conference • Transition-Adjustment Class Priority • The Parent and the Program • Informing the Student

6. CURRICULUM • 83

The Importance of Motivation and Attitude • The Need to Build Interest • Other Aspects of the Transition-Adjustment Class Curriculum • Case History of "The Child Who Wouldn't Talk" • The Elementary Transition-Adjustment Class Curriculum • Reading • Pressure from Parents • How Parents Can Help • The Right Materials at the Right Time • The Reading Specialist • Handwriting • Spelling • Mathematics • Science • Evaluating Student Progress • Reporting to Parents • Notes on a Junior High School Transition-Adjustment Class Program

7. ESTABLISHING A PHYSICAL EDUCATION PROGRAM FOR TRANSITION-ADJUSTMENT CLASSES • 107

Physical Objectives • Mental Objectives • Socio-Emotional Objectives • Time Allotments and Class Composition • Individual Attention and Special Help • Class Organization • Program of Activities • Difficulties Likely to Arise • Summing-Up

TABLE OF CONTENTS

8. THE IMPORTANCE OF ART EDUCATION IN TRANSITION-ADJUSTMENT CLASSES • 121

Art and Breakthroughs • The Value of Working with Wood • The Fascination of Clay • A Choice of Materials Can Be Liberating • The Goals in Art

9. MATERIALS AND EQUIPMENT • 129

Power Tools Before Hand Tools • Specifications for Power Tools and Their Use • Power Machinery • Power Machinery Implementation • Some Simple Power Tool Projects • Directions to Make a Paper Tray • Woodworking Equipment • Supplies for Woodworking • Construction Materials • The Role of Play Materials • Other Materials Helpful for Learning Activities • Special Academic Materials • Miscellaneous Materials • Budget Area Considerations • Conclusion

10. TEACHING TECHNIQUES • 142

The First Weeks of the Transition-Adjustment Class Program • The Acting-Out Child • How a Puppet Got Through to a Withdrawn Girl • The Errand as a Technique • A Day in the Transition-Adjustment Class • Homework Is Checked • Science and Music • The Individual Work Period • Time for Lunch • The After-Lunch Session • The Final Period • The Advantages of Team Teaching in the Transition-Adjustment Classes • The Individual Study Area

11. FARMING OUT • 160

Reentry Procedure • Touching Bases with the Child • Selecting a Teacher • The Farming-Out Trial Period • The Farming-In Procedure • Case Study of Ron • From the View of the Transition-Adjustment Class Teacher • The Diary of Ron Continued • The Transition Back • A New Start

12. THE SUMMER TRANSITION-ADJUSTMENT CLASS PROGRAM • 174

The First Summer • Factors That Weigh in Favor of a Summer Program • Who Should Be Enrolled in a Summer Program? • The Summer Staff and the Facilities • The Summer Curriculum • The Day's Schedule • Points to Consider

13. THE TRANSITION-ADJUSTMENT CLASS TEACHER • 180

As Seen Through the Teacher's Eye • The Training Variable • As Seen Through the Principal's Eye • Teaching—A Many Faceted Affair • As Seen Through the Director's Eye

14. THE PRINCIPAL LOOKS AT THE TRANSITION-ADJUSTMENT PROGRAM • 188

The Principal as Team Leader • The Team Discusses a Special Boy • The Principal Works with the Parents • The Principal's Role with the Child • How to Handle Problems That May Arise • The Principal and Farming-Out • The Principal as the Building Coordinator

15. DIFFICULTIES TO BE ENCOUNTERED AND HOW TO APPROACH THEM • 196

An Initial Obstacle • Parent Apprehension • The Long Struggle to the Mainstream • The Problem of Space • Transportation • The Substitute Teacher and the Transition-Adjustment Class • Other Hurdles to Program Acceptance

16. FUTURE DIRECTIONS • 204

APPENDIX • 209

INDEX • 245

ONE

The Problem— An Answer

The emotionally disturbed child is an increasing concern in education.

The entire school staff is puzzled by these children who do not respond to teaching techniques and remedial measures, and who are out of step in regular class with patterns of behavior that can include:

distractibility	blank expression
tuning-out	temper outbursts
inappropriate peer interaction	destructiveness
odd mannerisms	unpredictability
disruption	variability in performance
difficulty in handling independent tasks	surprising streaks of information
inability to accept direction	excitability
inaccessibility	silly laugh
short attention span	disorientation
academic blocks	imaginary tales
go-go jet propulsion	rudderlessness
frozen silence	

These patterns vary from child to child but are parts of the disturbed mosaic. They can present a serious problem to the classroom teacher, music, art, and physical education teachers, reading specialist, speech therapist, learning specialist, nurse, and principal.

This book details the characteristic behavior patterns and underlying dynamics of the emotionally disturbed child. It outlines the philosophy and goals of special classes for emotionally disturbed children. And, it provides school systems with the step-by-step educational procedures to set up and operate special classes for emotionally disturbed children.

Entailed is a coordinated team effort by administrators, special teachers, nurse, school doctor, reading specialist, speech therapist, and psychologist. They work together to provide services to the classroom teacher, the hub of the educational wheel, so that *all* children can benefit from the educational process.

The key to learning is a preventive-developmental focus. It centers on the early organization of children for realistic, productive functioning in society. The preventive program yields a narrowing of adolescent difficulty through the early development of inner strength, discipline, and control.

WHERE THE PROBLEM BEGINS

A preventive-developmental, school-community team effort is a root attack on the following mental health facts of life: [17] *

- One in every ten persons is suffering from some form of emotional illness.
- Mental illness is an important factor in many physical illnesses.
- Emotional disturbance is an important factor in seventy-five percent of all accidents.
- Five million persons are alcoholics, affecting twenty million family members, with two hundred thousand new cases estimated each year.

Mental illness is a crucial factor in criminal behavior, work inefficiency, delinquency, broken homes, suicide, and narcotics addiction.

"More than 10 percent of the nation's 70 million school-age children suffer some form of emotional disturbance, according to the National Institute of Mental Health (NIMH)."[14]

Four million children under the age of 14 are in need of treatment

---

*The reference numbers that appear throughout the text pertain to the bibliography at the end of the book.

for emotional difficulties. One million or more children have severe emotional disturbances which require special class placement.[17]

"Only 10 percent of the nation's school systems have any kind of programs to aid children with mental handicaps—and most of these concentrate on mental retardation, not emotional disturbance."[14]

In a recent Westchester County, New York, survey, it was found that "only one out of every 1400 children needing care between two and five years of age are being treated either in clinics or by private psychiatrists. Comparable ratios reported are one out of 170 between ages 6 and 11; one out of 110 between 12 and 14, and one out of 90 between 15 and 18. In the whole population between ages 2 and 18, one out of 160 are treated."[9]

Dr. Gilbert Kliman, Project Director of The Center for Preventive Psychiatry, White Plains, New York, concludes that "the battle to prevent or halt lifelong mental illness at the earliest stages is being lost by default." He points out that "the percentage of children detected by the survey is comparable to the percentage of those children who will ultimately require hospitalization for mental illness."[9]

Little wonder some school systems are starting at a preschool level where they can concentrate on the early identification of children with difficulties, utilizing team resources, and working with nursery schools, doctors, and community facilities.

The New York State Board of Regents has proposed public school classes for four-year-olds by 1970 and three-year-olds by 1978. Some school districts already provide evaluation and testing of young children to clarify their difficulties and to determine preventive measures. Some locate placement outside the district for these children with atypical problems; for example, a private preschool day-training center for emotionally disturbed children.

There are presently in the elementary schools a large number of intelligent children with deep emotional difficulties. These students struggle from grade to grade. Their difficulties interfere with learning and social acclimation in regular class. If they are not identified and placed in special class, they will have increasing difficulty in preadolescence and adolescence.

Many will fall by the educational wayside, dropouts from society. They will not fulfill their creative potential, and they represent a prohibitive toll in human resources.

By providing smaller, structured class settings, with a closer one-to-one relationship with the teacher, who is the human bridge to inner growth, these children can be gradually organized for assimilation back into the educational mainstream.

In smaller groups geared to their total development, they are able to build up inner stability and self-regulation. They are able to deal with outer reality and to develop the tools and techniques to achieve realistic goals.

PROFILE OF THE DISTURBED CHILD

One disturbed child who had been floundering in regular class wrote:

> Onece there was a little buck and it swame in a little pand it was aloun. It did not look happy at all he didn't have no freud. It just swims in the old pounb.

Another wrote:

> When you kick a boy make sure he is dead. Look at his body, has he bled?
> Instead of going out and playing with all the boys, I stay inside and make a whole lot of noise.
> It was a nice try, but I'm afraid you're going to die.
> When you see my ugly face, You got a ship and left the human race.
> If I were you I wouldn't go south, Or you'll walk into a monster's mouth.

In their art, clay work, written and verbal expression these children mirror their deep fears and disorganizing conflicts that upset the learning applecart.

After placement in a class for emotionally disturbed, a gifted boy wrote a story about a person who found a cat one winter's night:

> It was getting darker, and so I thought I'd better get this poor animal a place for the night. So what I did was I put him under my coat and took him into the railroad station under the benches. I said, 'Good night, Tiger,' and he went fast asleep under the bench. The next day I went up to the station and he was waiting for me. I had bought something for him—FOOD! Boy, did he go for that! He was gobbling it up as if he hadn't eaten in days. He probably hadn't. My relationship to him grew fonder. *(The cat left.)* My best guess is that he lived with another family in some other town, and he wandered

THE PROBLEM—AN ANSWER 21

off as cats will do. But that pound of cat food was what he needed to make the long journey home. I hope he made it.

Emotionally disturbed classes increase the odds that the child will make the "long journey" successfully.

THE CHILD DRAINS THE TEACHER AND THE CLASS

In placing the emotionally disturbed child in special class, every other child in his regular class benefits. The regular classroom teacher and special teachers become more productive because these disturbed children have drained their time and energy in a task doomed to defeat due to the emotional disturbance.

Therefore, setting up classes for the emotionally disturbed in the elementary schools is a psycho-educational move that not only salvages the disturbed child but also reverberates through the entire school system. A few special classes can service hundreds of regular class teachers and thousands of students—students who would not otherwise receive the maximum learning experience because an inordinate amount of time and energy must be devoted to the disturbed child by the regular class teacher.

Teachers are baffled, bothered, and bewildered by these disturbed students. These children respond differently. They continually *try* the teacher. They do not learn up to expectation.

Even when the child is not a pervasive disturbance, the teacher is haunted by the child's inability to learn. She is likely to blame herself. Unless one has taught a disturbed pupil in regular class it is difficult to grasp the emotional and physical burden the teacher endures.

The other students in the regular class quickly observe that the disturbed child is different. Many tolerate him. They do not complain that he gets away with odd patterns of behavior. It is as if a part of them identifies with the disturbed child. Still, their learning can suffer when the disturbed child is poking, distracting, and upsetting the class routine. Some children, with difficulties of their own, torment the emotionally disturbed child, trigger off his antisocial actions, and aggravate him to the point of blow-up.

A substitute wrote the following note to a teacher of an emotionally disturbed class. It illustrates the stress these children produce:

Whee. I survived; no scratches or bruised shins, but my nerves sure had a workout. These kinds of jobs I can do without! And what kind of day was it? It was a day that Bob ran out and hid in the art room. Jack climbed the fence when we were out. All the boys hopped out the window at one time or another until I realized I have to live without fresh air. Hank and Bob did stints in the office. Airplanes flew all day. The basket was full of them. The prime object for teasing, abuse, dirty comments, and threats was poor Mary.

Well, after a day like today I bless the fact that my kids are fairly normal and that there are people like you with patience and understanding to handle children with problems like they have.

THE VALUE OF THE SPECIAL CLASS

When the disturbed child makes progress in special class, the parents respond with a sense of well-being. After years of frustration, a forward movement is sparked between child and parents.

One disturbed pupil, after years of non-productivity in school and disruption at home, was able to return to regular class after one year in special class. Art was an important outlet for this particular child. Assimilation back into regular class started in art. His drawings changed from weird, distorted creatures to human figures. He was easier to handle at home. His parents were able to feel proud about his growth and achievement, a rare experience for parents of disturbed children.

One parent of a disturbed boy wrote to his special class teacher:

> This year we see such a change in his personality. He has learned to get along with other children, enjoy their company and even seek their friendship instead of being a "loner." He feels this is due to your understanding and teaching ability.

PARENTS OF EMOTIONALLY DISTURBED CHILDREN ARE NOT TO BLAME

The more the data is analyzed, the more it appears that the disturbance developed at an early age, irrespective of environmental experience. The causes often appear to be intrinsic interferences in development rather than extrinsic experiences.

Everyone is an "experiment in nature," a gestalt of constitution, a milieu of experiences. Equally important is the unique way in which one reacts to life happenings—often "experiments in fate" (hospitalizations; divorce; birth order in the family; separations during wartime)—with his particular heredity. To single out the parent as the one "at fault" in the total configuration, is a naive oversimplification.

The parents of an emotionally disturbed child are faced with a crisis in living that can be understood only if one has lived day in and day out with such a child. The unpredictability, the explosive potential of a hand grenade with the pin out, and the fierce contrariness—all necessitate constant surveillance. This understandably exhausts the parents and increases family tensions. It presents them with as severe a test as a parent can face and takes a toll on the other children in the family.

Rather than the parents' creating the child's emotional disturbance, the disturbed child creates emotional anguish in the parents and ignites latent problems that rise to the surface and magnify parental conflicts.

TRANSITION AND ADJUSTMENT

Transition-adjustment class is one term a district can utilize for emotionally disturbed classes. These classes also serve as a stepping stone for more severely disturbed children ready to transfer from private schools for emotionally disturbed. For them, the public school special class is the next step towards reality functioning in the human matrix.

Awareness of the importance of transition-adjustment class programs was demonstrated by the New York State Legislature which in 1964, amended Article 89 of the Education Law to provide (as of July 1966) the educational services for emotionally disturbed children already available for physically handicapped and mentally retarded children. At age five, the entrance age for kindergarten, with the cut-off date determined by the district, New York State schools are responsible for providing proper educational placement for all children regardless of their difficulties.

Transition-adjustment classes at the elementary level, particularly for children five to seven, are the essence of preventive-organization. In addition, special classes at the junior high school level meet the challenge of organizing students with serious emotional disturbances who are on the threshold of adolescence. They also provide continuity for children already in elementary transition-adjustment classes who are chronologically ready for junior high school but still need the smaller group setting.

With transition-adjustment classes part of the warp and the woof of the school system, the students can be gradually assimilated back into the educational mainstream. The alternative, to set up special classes outside the school milieu, isolates the disturbed child from the very setting within which he must gradually learn to function.

Add summer transition-adjustment class programs and you provide continuity and structure for children already in these classes. You also present a headstart opportunity for children set to enter a transition-adjustment class in the fall. Without a summer program, many of these children do not become involved in organized activities because there are few programs geared to their needs. As a result, they tend to revert to former modes of behavior.

In the summer program there are play activities, sports, arts and crafts, stories, songs, dances, field trips, reading readiness materials, and academic experiences for those who are ready. They are directed by transition-adjustment class teachers and college-student aides.

In setting up district special classes for emotionally disturbed children, a summer program can be considered an integral part of the total educational picture.

SOME TECHNICAL DIMENSIONS

By "emotionally disturbed" is meant a pattern characterized by:

1. Pervasive difficulty in inner organization and integration from an early age which impairs the child's ability to:
    - Climb the developmental ladder;
    - Transform primitive impulses and drives into higher sublimatory channels of functioning (for example, reading, arithmetic, hobbies, sports, abstraction, concept formation);
    - Utilize creative capacities in everyday achievement.
2. Merging of imagination with reality, at times, so there is no clear differentiation between the inner and outer world. Frightening fantasies take on the color of reality, haunting and striking terror in the mind of the child.

These grave difficulties in inner organization, and separating imagination from reality, are profound psychological roadblocks that hold the child back from finding himself in regular class in spite of high intelligence.

The degree of emotional disturbance varies in the individual child. It ranges from children who function at a mentally retarded level and are placed in special classes for the mentally retarded by mistake (the emotional disturbance masking the higher capacity), to children in regular class who are on the fringe academically and socially. The latter's need for special classes may be no less critical than the former's as they can manifest serious breaks in functioning with the biological stresses of adolescence.

An emotionally disturbed child is defined under the New York State Education Law as a "person under twenty-one years of age who has been determined to be emotionally disturbed as a result of an examination made by a qualified psychologist and a qualified psychiatrist, or by an approved clinic, and who is not capable of benefiting through ordinary classroom instruction, but may be expected to profit from a special educational service or program as determined by school authorities."

HOW TO USE THIS BOOK

This book will delineate the standard operating procedures for screening pupils for placement in a transition-adjustment class. These procedures are covered from the moment the child is referred for school difficulties to the final decision for special class placement.

The role each member of the school team, including the consulting psychiatrist, plays in the evaluation and placement is detailed. Tools and techniques for ruling out mental retardation are presented. Is a neurological factor suspect? If so, the child is referred to a consulting pediatric-neurologist to rule out primary brain dysfunctioning. (This term is used instead of brain damage when there is no clear indication of injury, damage, or defect in the brain.)

Together with the identification of emotionally disturbed children, and school team procedures for placement in special class, this book examines the role of the parent as part of the team. Parent conferences provide data on the early developmental history and present functioning. They also provide the opportunity to discuss the transition-adjustment class program so that the attitudes and feelings of the parents regarding placement can be expressed.

These parental attitudes are critical. Children are not placed in a transition-adjustment class without reaching agreement with the parents, because the long range goal of total organization for life functioning is not possible if the parents do not understand and accept the aims and directions of the special class program.

It is not necessary for the child to be involved in outside treatment as a prerequisite for placement—although with trained, involved therapists it can be a useful facet in the child's total development.

Disturbed children need the small group organization over a long period of time to gradually assimilate back into regular class. The transition-adjustment class program provides an educational-therapeutic fabric; a cloth of ongoing continuity, structure, flexibility, and close pupil-teacher rapport.

How to set up these transition-adjustment classes is described. The administration and building staff are a crucial force in the development of the program. Transition-adjustment class programs are system-wide. They are coordinated through the psychology department, pupil personnel services, or another administrative branch. In school districts with limited services available, the program has to be tailored to the reality situation.

The classes are housed in an elementary school. In this building, the special class teachers are directly responsible to the principal as captain of the ship. The system-wide director of the transition-adjustment class program works closely with the building principals as part of a coordinated team.

As in regular class, the transition-adjustment class teacher is the educational protagonist at the heart of the program. The training, experience, and personality of the teacher will be examined in this book along with his part in the development of the program in the building. If the special classes are to catch on in the school setting, it is important for the transition-adjustment class teachers to hit it off with the rest of the school personnel, including secretaries, custodians, and cafeteria aides, The involvement of regular teaching and non-teaching personnel is necessary for the eventual assimilation of the disturbed child back into the mainstream.

HOW THE CHILD LOOKS AT THE SPECIAL CLASS

Children entering the transition-adjustment class program have the opportunity to visit the classroom, meet the teacher, and have their questions answered before they start in the class.

The disturbed child has been referred to as "he" purely for expository purposes. The problem knows no sexual barriers.

However, bear in mind that the sex-linked factor has many threads: girls are developmentally twelve months ahead of boys at six years of age and eighteen months ahead by nine. Seventy-eight percent of stillborn fetuses before four months of age are boys; in the first year of life more deaths are boys. In later life, boys are more prone to brain-injury, and to diseases like muscular dystrophy, blindness, limited vision, and deafness. Studies indicate that more than two-thirds of the children retained, sixty-seven to seventy-eight percent of those referred for reading disabilities, three to four times as many stutters, and sixty-seven percent of those with emotional problems all are boys.[1]

Transition-adjustment class men teachers are important in working with disturbed boys and providing a masculine identification. (Schools need more elementary men teachers, particularly in the primary grades, for boys often have little contact with male figures.) Women teachers can do the job as well, particularly with younger children. The important variables are dedication, empathy, and a structured approach.

When disturbed children are placed in special class, they invariably feel relieved. The losing battle is over. They have been in a situation over their heads, and have had to endure frustration, defeat, and apartness. They know they are different. The rest of the class knows they are different—and may treat them so.

Each day is an exercise in disaster.

In the transition-adjustment class, they have the opportunity to organize themselves and to meet success more often. They find self-hope and a fledgling feeling of confidence more readily. Like a shattered army, they have the opportunity to regroup their forces, to regain their motivation and desire, and to begin to function independently. They gradually meet the challenge of reentry into reality space through inner self-development.

The race is no longer on one leg.

The moment of truth takes place when the disturbed child walks into a special class. He finds seven or eight other children with difficulties similar to his own. Some are more withdrawn, some are more outgoing. In this sense, it is a heterogeneous setting.

The children are of different ages. There is about a three-year age span in his class. One class, for example, may have students five to seven years of age; another seven to nine, and another nine to eleven or twelve. It depends, of course, on the actual age range of students assigned to the class and may, at times, have to cover more than a three-year span. The classroom will optimally have toilet facilities (particularly for the younger children), locker space, and access to the playground.

There may be two or three classes near each other, but the rest are better placed throughout the school district as part of the mainstream concept.

The child is provided with transportation to and from school in a special bus. His day is four-and-a-half hours; usually from 9:00 or 9:30 a.m. to 1:30 or 2:00 p.m. This is the optimum period of time he can mobilize his resources for learning; past this time his concentration wanders and he begins to lose control.

He finds a flexibility not present in regular class. He is no longer pressure-cooking. There is also structure, and he soon realizes that he has to begin to play the game by the rules.

He meets stimulating opportunities, rare in regular class, ranging from work with a jig-saw, drill press, or sanding machine to photography, guitar lessons in class, and a punching bag; from Tri-Wall materials to the Bell and Howell Language Master and the Controlled Reader Jr.; from tape recorders to expanded physical activities, science projects, and ceramics.

He gets closer help and instruction from a teacher who struggles with him every inch of the way in his reading, writing, and arithmetic. He may get help from pre-student and student teachers from nearby universities who provide the close relationship that is the developmental cornerstone of the program.

Learning is geared to realistic achievement at a level at which he can cope with the work. The student gradually learns to trust and believe in the teacher. He begins to want to learn and achieve.

Out of this closer one-to-one teaching matrix, he slowly develops discipline, frustration-tolerance, respect of others, and initiative. Then the time comes to move out for a regular period in arithmetic or music, the "farming-out." He is hesitant. The first move is difficult. But he gradually makes his way at his own pace.

Team teaching (two adjoining classes) is an integral aspect of the transition-adjustment class program. It provides flexibility in grouping. For example, an older child might fit in better with a younger group in reading or physical education. The student also has the chance to work with two teacher-parent figures, and if he becomes explosive in one class he may calm down in the second without destroying the "teachable moment" in the first.

The reading and speech specialists, science coordinator, and art, music, and physical education teachers work closely with the special classes.

Sports and physical activities are important. They build:

aggressive outlets	assertion
confidence	peer collaboration
taking constructive direction from adults	the ability to withstand stress gracefuuly
espirit de corps	independence
perseverance	discipline
frustration-tolerance	a sense of enjoyment

while developing muscular skill and a good feeling about one's body.

By and large, the development of the disturbed child in the transition-adjustment class basically rests on the shoulders of his teacher.

TEAM COMMUNICATION—A KEY TO SUCCESS

There are periodic school team conferences with the transition-adjustment class teachers, special teachers, science coordinator, learning specialist, speech and reading people, nurse, principal, psychologist, and others directly involved with the student. In these team sessions, the progress of individual children and the development of the building program are discussed. There are district-wide meetings of the transition-adjustment class teachers with the director to coordinate the development of the school system's transition-adjustment class program. Parent-teacher conferences are regularly scheduled, and the parents may see the teacher, and other members of the school team, at any time.

CURRICULUM, TECHNIQUES, AND MATERIALS

As the transition-adjustment class program unfolds, this book will describe a flexible curriculum, materials, and equipment. It will provide individualized instructional techniques and ways to maintain cohesive control in the class.

It will spell out measures to provide constructive release of aggression, and the dynamic interaction that takes place among the children and the teacher.

Chapters ahead will describe the task of each member of the school team, the step-by-step farming-out process from special to regular class, and a summer transition-adjustment class program.

Transition-adjustment classes can serve as excellent field training experiences for teachers specializing in the area of the emotionally disturbed, and will kindle the interest of student teachers in working with these children.

Difficulties that arise in setting up and organizing a transition-adjustment class program will be explored in such areas as parent acceptance of the class, the agonizingly slow development of some students, school team communication, student-teacher reaction patterns, transportation, space and budget considerations, teacher criteria, school district support, and the use of these special classes as a "dumping ground."

With these special class programs the school assumes more of a role in the community. The school psychologist is appropriately titled a "community psychologist." The school direction is toward the total development of the child. The child's right to learn and take his place as part of the human society is recognized, whether he is mentally retarded, physically handicapped, emotionally disturbed, or afflicted with brain dysfunctioning.

Also, the community role grows because the school undertakes responsibilities not shouldered by other institutions in society. The home, mental health clinics, reading clinics, and private therapists may not have been able to resolve the child's difficulties due to a combination of interfering factors; for example, a reading or mental health clinic may be too far away, or the waiting list too long; the parents may not be able to afford private professional services; or the emotional disturbance is too deep to be helped by short-term measures.

This book provides guidelines for public school systems in the country to use in organizing and carrying out transition-adjustment class programs. For the emotionally disturbed child, it is a crucial doorway to an organized life. His realistic functioning in the mainstream has far-reaching consequences both for the total school program and for his future goals in society.

There is no realistic alternative.

TWO

Identifying the Emotionally Disturbed Child

Those of us who have worked in the schools have become increasingly aware of the number of intelligent children who are not able to make it in regular class. Even if provided with the finest of teachers and a flexible curriculum geared to the individual child, these children just don't learn.

One minute they seem to be catching on; the next, they seem to lose it all. They appear to try, but learning does not fall into place.

This is the description of one student who was referred for psychological evaluation:

> George is far below other members of his class in all academic areas. Although he has repeated second grade, he is unable to cope with third-grade material and the responsibilities that go along with it. He has not managed to grasp essential concepts learned in first grade.
>
> He is very erratic in his behavior in relation to learning. He is very difficult to motivate and his attention span is extremely low. He appears to learn in spurts, where he will try very hard and is able to grasp the concepts, and yet he will fall back to the point where all previous learning is completely blocked out. His independent work habits follow the same pattern. A typical response of George, particularly in the earlier part of the year, was to continually raise his hand to answer a question and yet, when called on, a blank expression would come over him as if he had no knowledge of what it was he was responding to, nor the answer.

Reading presents particular problems, and since it is so pertinent to other areas it has hampered him greatly. He has just recently moved into a second-grade reader. Since he lacks the powers of concentration, and to some extent lacks confidence, he is poor at drawing conclusions. He also has difficulty with sound symbol relationships.

He appears unable to retain what he has learned, even to the point where, when asked a question twice in a row, he will attack the problem with the same difficulty as he did with the first and seems to see no relationship between the questions.

Under direction he is able to manipulate objects very well, although, even on a solely concrete level, he still has difficulty understanding exactly what it is he is doing. He shows remarkable interest and ability in science and also a great sense of imagination.

I would like to have him tested to find out his best educational level and to possibly discover some emotional problem which may not have readily been determined these past years and which may be the cause of his lack of concentration and disinterest.

His reading teacher noted the following:

At present George is able to read at a second-grade level. This may seem like great progress, but his performance is very erratic. Sometimes the smallest words can hamper him. For a period of time during the winter he was doing quite well, concentrating on his work, very motivated; his handwriting was extremely neat and he was gaining in self-confidence. Now when called on he seems to be in a fog.

In general, his ability to express himself is poor. Sight vocabulary and comprehension are also poor.

An evaluation was made. The results showed that this was a student with superior intellectual potential. The blocks to his learning were emotional in nature.

This chapter details the procedures for ruling out other possible causes and zero-ing in on the emotional factors.

CLUES TO THE EMOTIONAL DISTURBANCE

Not only do disturbed children have severe obstacles to learning but their difficulties also radiate out to every facet of school life.

Their behavior includes:

- Impulsive hitting out

IDENTIFYING THE EMOTIONALLY DISTURBED CHILD

- Breaking or taking other children's possessions
- Running away
- Disrupting class routine
- Defying the teacher
- Poking and teasing other students
- Not standing in line
- Throwing food in the lunchroom

Their behavior can be at the opposite pole:

- Withdrawal into a shell
- Ghostly appearance
- Lack of communication
- Distance from teachers and classmates
- Averted look
- Backing away if a friendly hand is placed on the shoulder
- A wall of silence
- A separate island.

Peculiar manifestations may accompany the behavioral puzzle: strange noises, silly laughter, vacant, tuned-out look, odd facial gestures, grimaces, restless, go-go jet-propelled behavior in class, jiggly bodily movements at the seat, distractibility, clownishness, wild, improbable stories, and inappropriate actions that the other pupils laugh at in disbelief.

The experienced classroom teacher who has mapped out the learning program for the year is aghast at the havoc wrecked by one child who is out of kilter with the learning goals and educational directions for the class. She is faced with the need to provide a disproportionate amount of time and energy in managing one child at the expense of the group. She is forced to remind him continuously to raise his hand if he has something to say, to stay in his seat, not to mark his neighbor's paper, to pay attention to page 24, and please not to make those funny noises.

EARLY ATTEMPTS TO MAKE THE BEST OF IT

In desperation, the teacher allows the disturbed child more freedom from the rules so that she can concentrate her efforts on the other students who are primed to learn. Better to let him roam—if he doesn't bother the other students; to sit in his seat playing with a piece of clay or string—as long as he is quiet.

The other children notice and ask, "How come he can do that

when you tell us we can't?" It becomes harder for the teacher to maintain consistent discipline if one child sets his own rules. His behavior may trigger off others in the class who have a potential for acting up.

It is interesting to see other students in the class accept his ways because they realize, as he does, that he is "different." Some accept his deviant actions with an attitude of "Don't pay attention to Tim; he's just acting silly again." They may try to help him to get out the right book or to have his pencil ready. His behavior strikes a responsive cord within themselves and, through this identification, they try to help.

Of course, the opposite can take place. They experience their own unresolved conflicts through him and encourage his odd behavior, or they become increasingly resentful at the interference in their own learning or in the ways in which he bothers them. Some may pick on him or use him as a scapegoat. Others may say, "Does he really belong in school?"

The classroom teacher is torn by her desire to help the child learn and by her responsibility to the rest of the class. She may have him sit next to her desk where she can keep an eye on him and try to work on a one-to-one basis. She may have him come in after school for individual help.

Frustration begins to build within her as he does not respond or show appreciation. She doubts herself. She is irked that all she has put into it, above and beyond the line of duty, has not produced results. There is no feeling of satisfaction or accomplishment.

Exhausted at the end of the day, she takes the problem home with her, wrestles with it in her mind, and feels defeated that she has not been able to reach him as she had hoped. Her total teaching performance becomes colored by an insoluble reality situation.

It weighs on her mind and interferes with her total teaching.

THE NEED FOR DIAGNOSTIC ACTION

If the disturbed child is not able to cope with reality tasks, to produce on his own, to "cut the mustard," then it becomes necessary to act promptly to determine the causes and possible solutions for his inability to function in the regular school setting.

The problem is of even more serious proportions than appears within the classroom. School is a model for later life functioning; it encourages the development of inner discipline, organization, self-reliance, and inner strength as an ongoing preparation for the inner and outer stresses of preadolescence, adolescence, and adulthood.

The child will be facing potential danger in the future if he is not able in the years before preadolescence to:

- Develop inner cohesiveness and integration.
- Take charge of his impulses so that he is captain of his own ship.
- Independently handle age-appropriate reality tasks with confidence and assertion.
- Utilize intellectual and emotional resources creatively and constructively.
- Relate to peers on a give-and-take basis.
- Deal with reality without escaping into various subterfuges.
- Accept reasonable limitations imposed by parents, teachers, and other authoritarian figures.
- Withstand frustration and accept long-range goals at the expense of immediate satisfaction.

It is clear that the so-called "quiet period" preceding preadolescence is a sleeping volcano if inner personality knitting has not accompanied each of the merging developmental stages.

One observes with increasing alarm the direction young children are heading when they do not get set for later life: depression; breakdown; suicide; destructive outbursts; high school, college and job failure.

In short, without corrective steps, the school system will not head off potentially serious trends in personality development.

One sees a six-year-old boy developing a paranoid feeling that everyone is against him; a five-year-old girl terrified by scary creatures that haunt her day and night; a young boy who in adolescence will gravitate towards drugs and destructive outbursts; a young girl who will not be able to cope with her sexual impulses in adolescence and may become pregnant; and a boy with a brilliant mind who will never learn to read well.

What is the role of the school in the preventive-developmental mosaic? The school is a central force in the community. In this role, the school team is concerned with the total growth of every child as a foundation for everyday functioning in society—irrespective of the handicaps he or she may have.

In its expanding community involvement, the school finds it must concentrate on early identification and corrective measures as part of a preventive mental health effort.

HOW TO ATTACK THE PROBLEM AT A PRESCHOOL LEVEL

One important step is to provide prekindergarten school district evaluation services. The school psychologist works with nursery schools, doctors, and community resources in identifying preschool children with developmental difficulties, and with parents of three-and four-year-old or even younger children, who have reason to be concerned with the progress of their child.

If the psychological evaluation suggests a deeper emotional interference, the parents can be referred to the consulting school psychiatrist for further evaluation and confirmation of the psychological findings.

If the test findings, symptom picture, developmental history, or psychiatric evaluation raise the question of brain dysfunctioning, the parents can be referred to the consulting school pediatric-neurologist to clarify or rule out the neurological factor.

The term "brain dysfunctioning" is used rather than "brain damage" because, as Dr. Richard Reuben, Director of the Pediatric-Neurological Unit of the New York University Medical Center, points out, the latter term implies an injury, damage, or defect in the brain, and an underlying anatomical basis, when, in point of fact, this data is often difficult to confirm.

The question of "brain damage" may actually refer to a disorder in function. "Brain damage" does not add to one's knowledge of what goes on in the brain, and has a final implication of anatomical damage with only a residual to work with. However, since many "brain damage" syndromes show spontaneous improvement or may be outgrown with age, Dr. Reuben suggests the term "developmental delay" or "brain dysfunctioning" when there is no definite evidence of anatomical lesion.

The symptom picture is now set into reality perspective in terms of a functional disorder with implications for improvement.

With regard to the use of the electroencephalogram (EEG) as part of the neurological evaluation, Dr. Reuben points out that it is open to question since, with major syndromes like epilepsy and cerebral palsy, where there is a severe defect in brain functioning, the EEG is frequently normal. Thirty to forty percent of those with temporal lobe seizures, for example, showed a normal electroencephalographic record although induced drowsiness and sleep did bring out a more characteristic epileptic pattern in most. It is apparent, therefore, that since the EEG may not record abnormal patterns when there is gross evidence of brain injury, it is of questionable value in the minimal syndromes when there is no definite indication of brain damage.

Besides, the range of normal of EEG variations in any one child is great. There is no stable pattern for the variations in children. They are less consistent, less organized, and more subject to change than in adults. Also, EEG recordings measure only that part of the brain which is one-eighth of an inch below the electrode. It is not clear what these recorded patterns have to do with the rest of the brain. Dr. Reuben concludes that the more one knows about the EEG, the more conservative one becomes about its use. An extensive neurological examination, together with the past history, may be the best tools for determining neurological dysfunctioning, with the EEG recommended only for specific cases.

PRESCHOOL HELP TO THE FAMILY

Preschool recommendations to parents may include ways to structure the child's home environment, and nursery school as an organizing experience. One four-year-old child, too disturbed to function alone in nursery school, had another adult, obtained by the parents, stay with the child in nursery school and provide the one-to-one structure he required while still gaining the benefits of the group situation.

Early identification of the emotionally disturbed child can lead to placement in a private day setting for emotionally disturbed children.

Emotionally disturbed children, identified prior to kindergarten through school district psychological services, can be placed in district transition-adjustment classes on reaching public school age (when they do not require a private center for more severely disturbed children).

Preschool meetings with parents can help to identify children with potential difficulties before they reach school age.

When kindergarten registration takes place in the spring for fall entrance, one useful procedure is to have members of the school team present (psychologist, speech therapist, principal, teacher, nurse) to identify children with potential difficulties, and to have the parents fill out a form that would detail pertinent background data and present functioning within and without the home. The school clinical observations and written information can then be utilized to determine proper placement for the child prior to kindergarten. A parent conference, when indicated, can clarify the personality picture and determine further diagnostic steps and corrective measures.

ACTION STEPS IN THE SCHOOL

The payload for a preventive-developmental approach is the school team. This means a coordinated effort by art, music, and physical education teachers, administrators, nurse, school doctor, reading specialist, speech therapist, and psychologist. The team provides services to the classroom teacher. She is the backbone of the educational framework; in the final analysis, she has to carry the ball.

The "moment of truth" takes place in the classroom.

In her core role, the teacher has a central part in the identification of emotionally disturbed children. Experiencing day-by-day relationships with each child in his work, in how he gets along with others, in reports from the lunchroom and special teachers, and in talks with the parents, she has an overall grasp of his capacities, limitations, difficulties, and rate of progress. Her observations can be fortified with standardized group aptitude and achievement tests together with previous cumulative record folder data. These help in her evaluation of each student.

When the teacher is concerned with the direction of a particular child, she can talk with previous teachers and school specialists who have worked with the child.

Her next likely step is to discuss her observations with the building principal who may have additional data on the student. As the administrator, it is his responsibility to decide on the next move. This may be a team conference with the school members involved to pool the data, followed by a request for further evaluation by other team members not already involved—for example, reading or speech specialists.

A next step may be psychological testing after discussion with the parents. The evaluation includes measures of intelligence, visual-motor coordination, personality and, perhaps, achievement.

Intelligence tests not only provide a score but tap the underlying potential to learn. For example, the student may obtain an intelligence score of "101," but would be capable of "130" if there were no interfering blocks. Or, a more dramatic example: a girl may have been placed in a mentally retarded class because she obtained an intelligence score of "73" when, in fact, the emotional disturbance masked higher underlying capacity.

Most children referred for school psychological testing have at least average, and usually above average, intellectual potential. It is rare indeed that a child in regular class who shows a primary mentally retarded condition is referred for testing. Year after year the psychologist sees children who do not attain near their maximum intellectual capacity due to varying degrees of emotional interference, with some instances of brain dysfunctioning.

THE INDIVIDUAL TESTING PROCESS

For school children from four to seven or eight years of age, a good measure of intelligence is the Stanford-Binet Intelligence Scale, Form L-M. A new addition is the Wechsler Preschool and Primary Scale of Intelligence (WPPSI) for children aged four to six-and-a-half. For younger children, and those not able to function high enough to obtain a score on these tests, another useful measure is the Merrill-Palmer Scale of Mental Tests, with test items starting at eighteen months and going to six years of age.

From eight to fifteen years of age, one can continue to use the Stanford-Binet, but there are many excellent features to the Wechsler Intelligence Scale for Children (WISC) that weigh in its favor, particularly at the older age levels. This is a matter of personal preference to the psychologist. The WISC, which also can be used from age five up, has the advantage, like the WPPSI, of a verbal and performance scale score (as well as a total score like the Stanford-Binet), with various subtests within the verbal and performance areas.

For intelligence testing from ages sixteen and above, the Wechsler Adult Intelligence Scale (WAIS) is generally used.

The nine Bender-Gestalt designs and human figure drawings provide a measure of visual-motor and emotional development. The drawings also indicate intelligence. An achievement test, like the Gray Oral Reading Paragraphs, provides a quick measure of reading recognition important in that reading is basic to learning. The Wide Range Achievement Test is another useful measure to determine the reading and arithmetic level.

The Rorschach is the best single measure to tap personality dynamics and to determine the diagnosis and prognosis. The Children's Apperception Test (CAT) and Thematic Apperception Test (TAT) are more structured projective measures that utilize pictures as stimuli for fantasy, rather than the amorphous quality of the inkblots. By the unstructured nature of the Rorschach, deeper analysis is possible since it can be utilized as an "emotional x-ray."

However, there are important qualifications to the use of the Rorschach:

1. The Rorschach as a personality tool is only as effective as the training, theoretical knowledge, and experience of the tester.
2. Since most testing is on children referred for various difficulties, there is limited Rorschach data on children not referred for evaluation.
3. Rorschach findings must be compared with clinical observations to obtain an overall picture of personality functioning.

EVALUATING THE TEST RESULTS

Once the school team has accumulated and discussed the available data on the child, outside resources involved with the child are contacted with parental permission: reading clinic, private therapist, mental health clinic, private tutor or speech therapist, family physician, hospital, foster home placement agency, and pediatric-neurologist.

The more information one has, the more the pieces of the human puzzle can be fitted together to determine the degree of the symptoms, contributing causal factors, and corrective measures.

In determining a diagnosis of emotional disturbance, it is necessary to rule out primary mental retardation and neurological dysfunctioning. The psychological battery, including both intellectual and projective measures, clarifies whether the child is basically retarded or functioning as a pseudo-retardate. The potential may be mirrored, for example, on the WISC subtest scores each of which is a measure of intelligence, or the WISC intra subtest scatter, the Stanford-Binet by the student's ability to pass an item at or above his age level, and by the quality of the Rorschach percepts.

If the psychological findings point to possible brain dysfunctioning, or if, for example, the developmental data includes a convulsion, serious head injury, or periods in which the child appeared to blank out, a pediatric neurological evaluation is recommended.

Slowness in visual-motor coordination may not be necessarily due to a neurological factor. It may be part of the emotionally disturbed picture or due to a maturational lag. The pediatric neurological examination can help to clarify the diagnosis.

The data on the child is supplemented by conferences with the parents. It is important at some point to have both parents present. Through their eyes, one gets a view of how the child is functioning at home and outside of the home. One also learns more about parent attitudes and what concerns them about their child's behavior.

Parent conferences provide an opportunity to obtain a thorough developmental history from the time of conception on so that preschool patterns can be clarified along emotional, social, physical, and intellectual lines. The developmental history is an important tool in understanding present behavior patterns. An example of a "Developmental History" form is in Appendix A.

With emotionally disturbed children it is generally possible to establish developmental interferences in the first few years of life. When they are not as obvious, when the parents state the trouble started when the child first went to school, one can point out that it was precisely when the child had to function on his own, independent of the parents, that the underlying problem rose to the surface. One may find in such a case that the child is closely attached to the mother, or a sibling, or will not leave the yard to go and play at a friend's house.

It is the link with parent, the stability provided by the home, that makes it possible for some children to skim along in the preschool years. However, it is when the disturbed child is faced with kindergarten and the nitty-gritty learning tasks that increase with each grade level that his problems may crystallize. When he must operate on his own power, self-start separate from the parents, and cope with reality, the child who has not developed the basic personality foundation in the preschool years will begin to have trouble keeping up with the group. Frustrated and discouraged, he will face increased difficulties in preadolescence. Then, in adolescence, additional biological stresses will take their toll.

Summarizing, the identification of the disturbed child involves:

1. At a prekindergarten level, school district services:
   a. Psychological evaluation.
   b. Psychiatrist, social worker, and other school personnel working with community nurseries, doctors, and agencies.
   c. Parent conferences to determine the home picture, developmental history, and parent concerns.
   d. Referral for a psychiatric or pediatric-neurological examination when further evaluation is indicated.

2. At spring kindergarten registration:
    a. Observation by the school team of children set to enter school in the fall.
    b. Form to be completed by parents to provide further data on their child.
    c. Parent conferences prior to kindergarten entrance.
    d. Further evaluation (psychiatric, pediatric-neurological, vision-hearing) when indicated.
3. At the elementary school level:
    a. Classroom teacher observations.
    b. Cumulative record folder and group testing data.
    c. Observation by other members of the school team: school nurse, special teachers, reading specialist, speech therapist, social worker, learning specialist.
    d. Administrative findings.
    e. Psychological evaluation.
    f. Parent conferences.
    g. Data from outside resources.
    h. Psychiatric, pediatric-neurological, vision or hearing data when indicated.

THREE

The Dynamics of the Emotionally Disturbed Child

When the data is collected from the school team, community resources, and parents, it is natural for teachers and administrators to raise basic questions on the nature of the emotional disturbance, its causes, the depth of the disturbance, the degree to which the emotionally disturbed child can change, and future educational goals.

Before these special classes are set up, one needs to understand the dynamics of the disturbed child and the prognosis for success of a transition-adjustment class program.

The emotionally disturbed child withdraws into an imaginary world, a world in which imagination and reality merge. Terrifying, built-in fears of "ghosts," "witches," "devils," "monsters," and "dragons" plague his existence.[4]

Along with the unrealistic thinking trend, there is basic disorganization in personality development. Instead of inner integration and knitting there are unconnected islands and dikes with holes—a "Chinese Wall," with breaks in the foundation.

These children have not been able to structure a concept of themselves as separate and independent. They have not been able to concentrate and function independently with learning tasks in spite of high intelligence. In the moment of reality they falter, break step, tune-out, let loose, panic, fall apart. Like a man asked to run a race on one leg, they are doomed to defeat.

With the lack of stable inner growth, these children are not capable of self-regulation and adaption to the environment. There is no sense of where they stand with themselves or with the outside world. There is no rooted feeling of identity. They are not able to take charge, but are at the mercy of their feelings and drives. Facing reality crises is like crossing a bridge which suddenly breaks beneath them.

Of course, there are individual differences in emotionally disturbed patterns. Some of the children are not far out of reality, have developed areas of inner strength and control, or have brilliant capacities that mask the emotional disturbance. Some have friends; are good at sports; read well. Some can enter the science sphere and outdistance the teacher. Some function in regular class—more or less; less as the work becomes harder, as adolescence starts to erupt, as making a living and cutting a niche in society are the next reality hurdles.

CAUSES OF EMOTIONAL DISTURBANCE

When did the disturbed pattern emerge? The more one probes the past and documents what went on in the early years of life, the more one comes to the realization that the disturbed behavior has its roots in the beginning stages of life.

There are indications of early uneven, erratic peculiarities and lags in the developmental process.[15]

In talking with parents of disturbed children one finds varying patterns: As an infant the child did not want to be held. He was not cuddly. He did not hold on when carried. He did not reach out. He was content to stay by himself, a "playpen baby." He did not smile back. He shied away from human contact. Emotional lifelines from the parents were tossed aside or bounced off an invisible barrier. In his island fortress, the child was remote, impenetrable, isolated.

It was not necessarily the mother who rejected the child, but the child who rejected the mother.

Some of these children may not cry or let their needs be known; they may scream without signaling or gesturing as to what is bothering them. As infants, they may have been colicky, cried in spite of comforting attempts on the part of the mother, or continued to vomit, regurgitate, or have diarrhea without observable cause. They may sleep long hours, appear apathetic, or fail to imitate their parents' actions.

Other disturbed children react in a different fashion. They cling to the mother. They do not want to be let down. They are afraid if the mother is not in the same room. They hold on to an old toy. Any kind of change throws them into a panic. Routines have to be set; moving from one house to another is a major crisis. They may not want to leave the home. When there is separation in nursery school or kindergarten, they show disorganized behavior and are not able to follow through with everyday procedures.

Infantile manifestations may include over-sensitivity, tenseness, nervous reactions to noise, light, touch, and other stimuli. There may be later fears ranging from getting a haircut to animals and "monsters" in the dark. These children are often extremely alert to every nuance of what goes on about them with a kind of fearful apprehensive expectation.

With some, there may be a history of allergies, bronchitis, difficulty in breathing, asthmatic-like conditions, and eczema.

Disturbed children may show charged-up, jet-propelled behavior at an early age. They are into everything, destructive, and difficult to manage. The parents are faced with a constant struggle for control. There may be ingrained oppositional moods, aggressive outbursts, temper tantrums at the drop of a hat, violent upsets, insatiable demands that are never satisfied, and an inability to withstand frustration.

EFFECTS ON THE FAMILY LIFE

It is little wonder that the negativism, unpredictability, fierce contrariness, and explosive potential of the disturbed child wear out the parents. They hardly have a moment of rest.

The constant surveillance, day and night, required in the management of a disturbed child drains the physical and emotional energies of the parents and presents a potential lifetime burden to them. Rather than the parents causing the disturbance in the child, the reverse may be more to the point. The disturbed child ignites latent pathological trends in the parents, triggers marital conflicts, hinders the effort and attention due other siblings, and creates havoc in the family structure.

It is helpful for the school team to be aware of the pressure that parents of emotionally disturbed children undergo so that they can understand the home picture in working with them.

Parents of emotionally disturbed children do not have the opportunity to be proud of the early accomplishment of developmental milestones. These children are slow in many areas of growth. They do not show the anticipated degree of emotional responsiveness or feeling tone. As a result, the parents are deprived of the satisfactions that accrue to parents of nondisturbed children.

PORTRAIT OF A DISTURBED FIVE-YEAR-OLD BOY

Here is the description of a disturbed five-year-old boy by his mother:

> He is very bright, affectionate, high-strung, extremely tense and hyperactive. His behavior is becoming increasingly difficult to control even when he is relatively calm. There seems to be *nothing* that can effectively restrain his actions, especially when he throws tantrums and gets violently angered.
>
> A worrier, he eats and sleeps very poorly. He has frequent nightmares, wets his bed, and is extremely easily annoyed and angered. I'm afraid he might hurt himself or someone else in a burst of temper. There have been several close calls already.
>
> He seems overly concerned with death and killing and has threatened us and himself. He speaks a great deal about killing someone or something, half under his breath, saying he is going to kill that old window, or T.V., or baby doll, or whatever he happens to be glancing at; almost whispering it to himself and increasingly so since his grandmother's death recently, and since Martin Luther King was killed. He heard a little about it on T.V.
>
> He can't get enough affection. He craves it tremendously and is worried we'll leave him.
>
> His behavior is erratic and unpredictable. Frequently during the day, he will burst into a rapid stream of silly nonsense intermingled with baby talk; then says later, "I couldn't stop, Mommy."
>
> He also seems to react exaggeratedly to situations and sometimes inappropriately.
>
> Many times during the day, no matter where we are, and without any apparent reason, he will suddenly begin laughing loudly and nervously, keep this up for five or ten minutes, and begin running wildly all over the house, throwing things, knocking down or climbing all over whoever might be around, and screaming at his sister, three, to get out. The sudden loud nervous laughter is always the start of his wild behavior. Sometimes I can head him off and get him diverted; often we fail.
>
> He refuses, or ignores, most of our requests which finally become commands no matter how reasonable or routine.
>
> When scolded or punished, he reacts violently and often gets very silly, almost hysterical; screams, threatens, kicks, runs and throws,

uses bad language, and may, when furious enough and we can't calm him down or lose our own tempers, run upstairs, stripping off all his clothes and hide, or run outside screaming he's going to run away. Once I let him go but had to rush after him when he headed for the big street, and forcibly bring him back.

His nursery school teacher said he was a withdrawn child but had improved tremendously during the school year. He loves learning of any sort. However, he finally refused to continue going to school saying nobody liked him when questioned. He thinks he is "bad" and children don't like him. It's true they won't play with him for very long. After calling him silly or loud mouth, they leave him alone for the most part. He seems hurt by this yet unable to help himself.

After one of his spells of violent anger, when he is finally calmed again, he cries, climbs all over me, hugging me repeatedly, asking me if we still love him, telling us he loves us very much, and saying "I wasn't really being bad, was I, Mommy?" very worriedly. "I was just being silly, wasn't I, Mommy?" I've noticed he also frequently complains of a stomach ache afterwards and has told me he feels "bad inside."

As far as we know he's very healthy. He has hurt his head on several occasions jumping off the bed and hitting it on the radiator in a wild outburst, and having to go to the hospital to have it taken care of. He also had a large lump, the size of an egg, on the back of one side of his head at birth, but I was told this was due to his position before birth and would disappear and it did. However, it occurred to us to wonder if there might possibly be some physical cause for the problem.

(A pediatric-neurological evaluation was negative.)

He is unusually bright and asks thousands of questions, talks constantly, very loudly, and is very demanding and bossy usually although, on occasion, he can be very sweet, calm, and willing to share his toys. However, he always has to feel he's the boss of each and every situation.

He is very independent much of the time, but then will refuse to do so much as put his own clothes on, saying, "I don't know how," or some other excuse.

Ordinarily, it seems he has a great deal of difficulty adjusting to any new or unusual situation, much more so than the usual child.

He is a perfectionist and frequently, for example, wants to move all the furniture around his way.

He demands to stay with us all the time. He is capable of being very helpful if approached right, but he always wants to have everything of his bigger and better.

Sedatives prescribed by pediatricians have slowed his activity down somewhat, but his behavior remains demanding and erratic, and it's like living with a volcano that often suddenly explodes unexpectedly.

Being reasonable with him, scolding him, making him sit on a chair by himself for a little while, ignoring his behavior and praising him when he is good; *nothing* seems to work. We try not to expect too much of him but frequently even calm routine requests will set him off in anger.

We're all becoming increasingly exhausted and irritable, including Mathew himself, and believe something must be done to improve the situation.

He can't seem to let anything stay just the way it is. He has to change everything all the time, and can't leave anything alone no matter who it belongs to, where we were, and we can't stop him from doing this either, unless we force him. This prevents him momentarily but sets off more fireworks.

(Mathew is now in a transition-adjustment class and in therapy once a week. His acute behavior symptoms here cleared up and he is gradually showing better organization and control.)

DEVELOPMENTAL INTERFERENCES

With emotionally disturbed children one notes interferences at various steps up the developmental ladder: difficulties in feeding, in weaning, in taking solids. These children may later be finicky, picky eaters. There may be sleep interferences. The child tosses, groans, cries out, screaming in his sleep, or gets up at night. There may be head-banging, rocking, or hair-pulling.

Disturbed children may be slow in walking or talking. They may be silent and speak all at once at four, or speak at one and stop until two and one-half. Speech may be fuzzy, babyish, or with a slur. They may speak with little animation or hardly communicate.

Toilet training may be late with "accidents" and bed-wetting past the age-appropriate times. At five or six, they may still not ride a two-wheeler or throw a ball as well as their peers. They may seem clumsy and rough in their movements.

These children may show peculiar gestures, make funny noises, laugh inappropriately, show confusion in time and space, appear deaf, have difficulty tuning in on how others feel, show preoccupation with gadgets, become easily defeated, and have a concrete black and white attitude that precludes the subtleties of many life situations.

The most disturbed of these children may never leave the early autistic shell of the first few months of life where there is no concept of a human world outside. These children will usually need educational placement in a private center for emotionally disturbed.

Other disturbed children perceive the mother as a figure outside themselves but are not able to learn to function as an independent entity in the world of reality.[11] These are the children one generally sees in the public schools who will need special class placement.

THE ILLUSION OF ENVIRONMENTAL CAUSE

Since the deviations, disturbances, and interferences in development start early in the child's life, and affect significant areas of the child's functioning in families where the other children normally progress, one begins to question whether nonenvironmental factors are not significant in the emotionally disturbed pattern.

It is true that the developmental history may show surgical operations and hospitalizations that appeared to be triggering forces in the crystallization of the disturbed picture. Emotional reactions to early separations, and the feelings and fantasies around pain and operations, can never be underestimated in their total impact on personality development. Too many cumulative traumas impair personality growth.

(If hospitalization is medically indicated, it is important for the parents to stay with the child in the hospital, perhaps through the latency period up to nine or ten.)

Whether these "experiments in fate" bring to the surface pathology lurking beneath, or serve as the primary agent in the manifestation of the disturbed pattern, is a moot question. However, it is clear that, as one works with disturbed children over the years, one sees more and more indication of the early appearance of the disturbance. It is as if the child was born with the disturbance or with a predisposition that manifests itself under inner or outer pressures.

The parents are aware of the pervasiveness of the disturbance, either consciously or unconsciously, mirrored, for example, in their strong denial or refusal to recognize the problem.

Parents may state, "He was different from the day he was born." "I knew there was something wrong but I could never put my finger on it." "He didn't seem to develop like the other children."

The disturbed children themselves have a feeling of being

"different" that comes through in projective testing where the figures they see on the Rorschach, for example, are "not born right" or are "broken" and "did not grow."

THE BLAMED AND THE BLAMELESS

If one hypothesizes that the emotional disturbance is rooted in early difficulties in development, intrinsic in nature, one must consider the implication: the parents are not to blame for the disturbance in the child. In the earlier literature, the responsibility for the disturbance was placed on the parents' shoulders. However, in the sixties, the focus shifted to an awareness of early inner developmental difficulties divorced from the way in which the parents handled the child.

It has been fashionable through the years to put the onus on the parents while disregarding the variables that go into the personality configuration. The triangle of development, the "experiment in nature," is composed of constitutional factors, milieu experiences, and, very important, the unique way in which each child reacts to what is going on about him with his hereditary potentials. Each child varies in constitutional strengths and limitations, and in the way in which he perceives and defines the set of circumstances and experiences he undergoes.

To conclude that if the child has a problem it must be due to how the parents handled him is to lose sight of the total warp and woof of growth, and to disregard the constitutional, the chance, the accidental, and the uncontrolled inner reactions of the child that are out of the parents' hands.

There is another point to consider: parents have had a childhood of their own which influenced their own reactions in later life. If they are not aware of these unconscious attitudes, how can they be "blamed" for behavior that follows from these hidden childhood roots? In the long run each person is responsible for his own course of action; to go through life feeling it's all the parents' "fault" is not only psychologically incorrect but reflects a childhood hangover. As long as one can "blame" somebody else, he does not have to assume the responsibility for his own actions—or grow up.

If one accepts that the parents may not be primarily responsible for the disturbed pattern in their child, one can help them grapple with the guilt that hangs over them like a ubiquitous cloud; one can empathize with the terrible distress that has been part of their daily lives.

THE DYNAMICS OF THE EMOTIONALLY DISTURBED CHILD   51

Unless one has an emotionally disturbed child, or has spent a great deal of time with one, it is difficult to feel what these parents go through. They are told they do this and that "wrong." They see other children in the neighborhood developing normally and bringing pleasure to their parents. They undergo a continuous ordeal—with little opportunity to share what they go through with anyone else.

These parents are not in a position to resolve a deep disturbance which was not necessarily of their own making.

THE ROLE OF THE PUBLIC SCHOOL

One approach to the problem of the emotionally disturbed child has been to establish district special classes where, in a smaller group setting with more one-to-one structured help, the child can be gradually organized for assimilation back into the educational mainstream.

A close relationship with the teacher is the key to development. The program provides a total therapeutic-milieu experience.

GOALS FOR DISTURBED CHILDREN

Once one has considered that the emotionally disturbed child was disturbed from an early age, irrespective of how the parents handled him, certain projections follow based on observations of these children. The underlying emotionally disturbed pattern will not change in important respects; the core is there for life. The job is not to remold the deepest layers of personality, because these children will always be odd or different in some ways, off to themselves to some degree, and removed from certain areas of human interaction. Rather, the job is to help these children organize themselves for life functioning in spite of the emotional disturbance; to build over the disturbed core the outer structure that will provide them with the tools and strength to join and function in the mainstream. One is not out to change the bedrock personality substratum but to bring these children closer to reality and to organize them for age-appropriate tasks. The goals are directed towards getting these children back into regular class which, in itself, is a microcosm of society.

One student who transferred into the district is a case in point. He had been unable to learn in the preceding school and was a constant disruption at home. The parents were at the end of their rope. After transition-adjustment class placement, and gradual farming out to special and academic subjects, he was able to attend regular class on a full-time basis one year later (though two years below his chronological age placement), make friends, and successfully attend his religious confirmation. However, projective data before and after the special class placement did not show significant differences in the basic personality picture. The emotionally disturbed pattern was still there, but he could now live with it and cope with the demands of reality.

THE PARENTS MUST UNDERSTAND

The parents are entitled to know the facts about their child's disturbance and what the future has to hold.

These findings cannot be presented to the parents in one conference. The teacher and principal help to clarify the child's difficulties in functioning in regular class. The school psychologist works with the parents to understand more about the inner troubles the child is experiencing and the need for special class placement.

It is hard for the parents to grasp the nature of the disturbance, and the transition-adjustment class recommendation may place them under deep anxiety. Therefore, ongoing parent conferences are necessary. Empathizing with the difficulties they face with their child, and pointing out that the disturbance may not be of their making, can help to develop a common bond between the parents and the school team in the long hard pull to reality organization.

The parents have a right to know that, while the goals are geared towards gradual functioning in society, the child may be different in some ways.

One must be honest and tell them that one can never be sure how adolescence will hit him; how far along he will go in his schooling, in making a living and functioning on his own; that he may never get married; that he may keep more to himself even though he achieves in the regular setting.

To put the cards on the table prepares the parents for the timetable of the future.

When it comes to placing a child in the special class, the parents must be aware of the implications of the move. It must be made clear that the class is for emotionally disturbed children and define what is meant by emotionally disturbed.

It must be pointed out to the parents that the child will lose, as rule of thumb, two years of regular class in the organizing process for realistic functioning.

It must be made clear to the parents that what the program is attempting to do is to shore up a bulwark for the flood of adolescence, and to get the child set now for the stresses of reality.

Unrealistic expectations and bitter disappointments follow if these facts are not presented to the child's parents.

FOUR

How to Organize a District Transition-Adjustment Class Program

To organize a transition-adjustment class program for emotionally disturbed children in the elementary public schools requires a total team work approach involving the district principal or superintendent, other central administrators, and the building staffs.

The key person is the district principal. As the chief administrator, he has the final word on the direction of district programs. He makes the decisions on budget and space priorities, and he is responsible for the overall execution of the master plan.

If the transition-adjustment class program is to succeed, the district principal must be behind the concepts, goals, and implementation of the program. This is a district-wide activity; without the district principal's support there is no viable program. His approval will set the tone for district acceptance of the program and will provide the administrative backing that is necessary for its development.

The district principal works closely with the board of education. The board is an integral part of the school team since they represent the community and are there to determine, with the district principal, school policy. The district principal's support is a crucial factor in their acceptance of the program.

SELECTING THE PROGRAM DIRECTOR

Who will organize the transition-adjustment class program? Since the area is emotional disturbance, the logical department is psychological services, or pupil personnel services in larger districts. If these services do not exist in smaller school systems, it will be the responsibility of another department, or an administrator who has the interest, knowledge, and experience, to set up the program and follow it through.

Pupil personnel services, under a director, generally coordinates district-wide psychological services, guidance, nurses, speech, attendance, reading in some districts, and special classes. With the director of pupil personnel services at an administrative level, he will be in a position to organize and carry out the transition-adjustment class program.

Within a school district, each principal has his own priorities. He faces problems unique to his building situation and develops his own ideas on how best to meet educational goals. His area of special interest may range from the gifted, to science, to a developmental reading program, or to regular class groupings on a more homogeneous basis.

Therefore, it is essential that a transition-adjustment class program be district-wide. It operates within the rules and regulations of the specific building where the principal is the head, yet is centrally coordinated by the director who is responsible for the development of the program and the standard operating procedures.

These procedures cover such matters as:

Organization of the program
Screening procedures
Placement of children
Daily class schedules
Curriculum
Gradual assimilation of children back into regular class (farming out)
Building and district-wide team meetings
Parent-teacher conferences
Materials and equipment budget
Consulting services (psychiatric; pediatric-neurological)
Transportation
Housing of the classes
Teacher screening

A MODEL FOR THE TRANSITION-ADJUSTMENT CLASS PROGRAM

In districts where the responsibility for the transition-adjustment class program rests with the director of psychological services, a non-administrative department head position, it is best if the director is directly responsible to the district principal in line with the district-wide coordination of the program.

Since there are many districts without pupil personnel services, the model presented is one that functions through psychological services, the director having district transition-adjustment classes as part of his department.

Through his office, the director coordinates placement of children in special classes outside of the district as well. The mentally retarded, physically handicapped, and brain dysfunctioning children are served through such resources as Boards of Cooperative Educational Services (BOCES) which are regionally-located throughout New York State to serve districts that have not set up special classes due to such factors as the small number of children within each special class grouping, or the reimbursement which makes it more economical for the district to place children in BOCES operated programs.

THE DIRECTOR'S RESPONSIBILITIES

The teacher is the key to the learning and growth of each child in regular class. This is just as true for the transition-adjustment class—perhaps even more so. Therefore, it is important that the person in charge of the transition-adjustment class program have an important hand in who will be the teacher of the class.

The building and central administrators are involved in the screening process. However, it should be the director's responsibility to make the final recommendation to the district principal on the teacher for the class. The director has the responsibility for the program, including the recommendation of the teacher who will be the single most vital factor in the development of the disturbed child and, in a larger sense, the development of the total program.

The steps toward placement of a student in the transition-adjustment class are initiated by the building team. They pool their information to obtain a clearer picture of what is interfering with the child's functioning. When the disturbed child is not able to follow through in regular class, it becomes apparent that the transition-adjustment class is the only realistic alternative.

The director is involved in the final decision on placement. If the director heads up psychological services, he has had more experience in the field of the emotionally disturbed and, in setting up the program, is closer to the concepts and goals that are the foundation for the operation of the transition-adjustment classes.

(When the director of pupil personnel services is the person in charge of the transition-adjustment class program, he is interested in the findings of psychological services since they have had more experience with disturbed children.)

There are a number of emotionally disturbed children in the public school setting who are not identified. They drift through elementary school at great expense to themselves and to those who work with them. Therefore, the job of the district director of psychological services is to first demonstrate the need for district transition-adjustment classes at the elementary level.

THE DIRECTOR AS A TEAM MEMBER

The cornerstone of a transition-adjustment class program is close collaboration with teachers and administrators on the part of the director and the other psychologists in his department. By putting his shoulder to the educational wheel as a member of the school team, the psychologist helps the teacher carry the ball to the students.

The school psychologist can learn as much from the teacher as the teacher can learn from the psychologist. It is the teacher who lives day by day with students for a third of their waking life. It is the teacher who is in the front line of education, involving herself with the learning of each child in her class in a process better known as "blood, sweat, and tears."

The psychologist is there to service the teacher through recommendations relevant to the reality situation. He can provide further data through parent conferences in which he works with the parents on ways to help the child outside of school.

The psychologist's respect, empathy, and willingness to work with the teacher will lead to acceptance of the psychologist as a member of the school team. The teacher will appreciate the psychologist's down-to-earth approach, and the awareness on his part of the difficult task she faces in the teaching process and in working with a disturbed child in the regular class setting.

With mutual respect established between the teacher and the psychologist, based on everyday grass-roots experiences, the teacher will line up behind a transition-adjustment class program which she realizes has, as one goal, to make it possible for her to teach without serious disruption and without exhausting her phsyical and emotional energies.

THE DIRECTOR AND THE PRINCIPAL

The principal is captain of his school ship. The working relationship between the principal and the psychologist is critical to the success of the transition-adjustment class program. In building matters, it is important that the psychologist touch bases with the principal every step of the way. The psychologist who has worked long at the school game will be aware of the importance of close cooperation with the building principal.

The building principal, in turn, will appreciate the willingness of the psychologist to work within the framework of the school and its chain of command. He will also respect the psychologist to the degree to which he contributes as a member of the school team. Once there is confidence and respect on the part of the principal for the work of the psychologist, the groundwork is set for the development of the transition-adjustment class program.

As with the regular class teachers and the principal, the special teachers in art, music, science, and physical education, the speech therapist, school nurse, and reading specialist will turn to the school psychologist as a member of the team when he earns his position by his contributions and willingness to work cooperatively. These school team members are valuable contributors to the development of the transition-adjustment class program.

The director of psychological services works closely with central administrators in charge of such areas as curriculum, instructional services, and business. Their view of the worth of psychological services will play a large part in their contribution to the development of the district transition-adjustment class program. Here again, touching bases with the administrator in charge of an area of education is a prerequisite for mutual cooperation.

Not to be overlooked as part of the school team are the school secretaries, teacher aides, bus drivers, and custodians. Each, in his own way, is helpful to the transition-adjustment class program. Many a custodian has come up with the necessary equipment when it was needed, or served as a friendly figure to a disturbed student. The school secretary is an important cog in intra-school communication lines, in taking messages, in obtaining cumulative record folder data, and in praising the student on the note he brings to the office.

Certainly, the secretary for psychological services is an integral part of the department.

THE FIRST STEP—DOCUMENTING THE NEED

The director of psychological services and his staff first establish themselves as contributing members of the school team by their evaluation of individual students referred for school difficulties. The next step is to determine how to help the referred student within the school framework.

When team members get together to discuss their observations on a child and the psychological evaluation, the data may point to severe difficulties in functioning in regular class. The problem comes into sharper focus as these students continue to have increasing difficulty in the later grades, and particularly as they approach adolescence.

It is the job of the director of psychological services, in this model, to document the need for district transition-adjustment classes through specific data on disturbed children. These are the children who the teacher, principal, and other members of the school team, in the various elementary schools, agree require a district transition-adjustment class setting.

The next step is to summarize the data on each child, including his name, address, phone number, birthdate, and building area. This data is presented to the district principal and other central administrators to substantiate the need for the transition-adjustment classes.

In discussion with the district principal and his assistants, it is important to sketch the concepts, goals, and implementation procedures for the proposed transition-adjustment classes. Before the transition-adjustment class program is presented to the central administrators, the director must first lay the groundwork with the building principals so that they will support the program when the district principal raises the question of its value in the educational priority order.

Once the district principal places himself behind the transition-adjustment class program, he will, at some point, discuss the program with the members of the board of education to inform them of the new direction proposed within the school. He will explain the total program to the board. He may have the director present at one of the board meetings to discuss the details of the program and to answer questions that might be raised.

The funds for the transition-adjustment class program, and the possibilities for expansion, rest on the support of the district principal and the board of education. The board must be aware, for example, of the gradual assimilation goal of the disturbed child from special to regular class, or they may not weigh this variable over the cost factor since the district program may be more expensive than special class placement outside the district.

If the teacher is the football player who carries the ball; the psychologist and other members of the school team, those who help in the blocking; and the administrators, the managers and coaches—then the board of education, representing the community, are the owners who provide the ball park and put up the money so the team can play.

The board of education, presented with the reality data, will generally be sympathetic to the aims of a transition-adjustment class program, particularly when they have respect for the district principal who is presenting the need for the classes. If they have confidence in the chief administrator, they will have reason to believe that he, as the educational expert, has good reasons for proposing the program.

It may also be appropriate, in the judgment of the district principal, to explain the proposed transition-adjustment class program to interested community groups like parent-teacher associations. These meetings will help to gain their understanding and backing for the program.

Once the school members have been involved—from regular class teachers to other members of the team, including the building principals, the district principal and his assistants, and the board of education—the time is ready to put the transition-adjustment class blueprints on the building line.

SETTING UP A TRANSITION-ADJUSTMENT CLASS PROGRAM

First, how many classes will be formed? Initially, it is suggested that two classes be organized, in adjoining rooms or close by. Two classes provide a potential for team-teaching. They should, if possible, be located in a building where the principal is involved in the goals of the program. The active participation of the school principal will have much to do with the acceptance of the program by the teachers in the building.

Since the school personnel in the building will, in one way or another, be involved in the transition-adjustment class program, it is crucial to orient them to what the classes are all about and the important role each of them will play. This can be done through:

1. Building meetings prior to setting up the classes.
2. Building meetings once the classes are organized.
3. Smaller team meetings with those who directly participate in the transition-adjustment class program. The smaller team meetings would include the principal, art, music, and physical education teachers, speech and reading people, and the nurse.

SELECTING THE TRANSITION-ADJUSTMENT CLASS TEACHER

The teacher of the class is the primary force both in the development of the disturbed child, and in the acceptance of the program in the building through his relationships with the rest of the staff. The teacher is a kind of public relations person who sells the program by his actions, personality, and willingness to be part of the school team.

Based on experience, it can be assumed that approximately seventy to eighty percent of the disturbed students in the class will be boys. Therefore, there are definite advantages in having men teachers. Boys need a masculine figure to identify with; since many have difficulty controlling their impulses, the man teacher is also in a position to exert physical restraint when it is necessary. A woman teacher provides a mother figure particularly with girls. A mother figure may also be a constructive identification for some boys in the light of their background.

How is the teacher for the class chosen? As there are no set requirements for teaching a transition-adjustment class, much depends on the overall appraisal of the candidates. Factors to be considered are experience, training, bents, feeling attitudes, ways with children, interest in the field of emotionally disturbed, and ability to work with the school staff. Disturbed children are a severe challenge. They require the involvement of the teacher in a backbreaking, slow, arduous task. Progress is measured in inches rather than yards, and often unrewarded and unappreciated by outside standards. These children must strike a special chord in the teacher who is to undertake this Homeric educational odyssey.

It is advisable that the teacher of emotionally disturbed children have a "break" every three years or so, and teach a regular class for one year so as to realign his bearings in a regular class setting.

The teacher of emotionally disturbed children should be certified in elementary education. He should volunteer for the position. And, he should have a firm, structured framework. These special classes are similar in concept to regular classes; out of structure is developed the organization for realistic functioning. New York State recommends teacher certification in early childhood, elementary or secondary school education, and additional work in the field of emotionally disturbed.

In choosing teachers to initiate the program, it is well to have experienced people in the field of emotionally disturbed who are master teachers, dedicated, concerned, able to reach children and to command their respect, and who have proved themselves in action on a caliber with Vince Lombardi's old Green Bay Packers. This is a high order of excellence—but it is clear that the teacher is the backbone of the program, and so must be as highly qualified as possible.

When two competent, experienced teachers of emotionally disturbed children are available through careful recruiting, who can work well together and with the building staff, the program is ready to go. Once the district program has developed and expanded, there is no reason why interested regular elementary school teachers in the district cannot fit the bill as teachers in the transition-adjustment classes—though this may not always be the case.[2] After all, the master teacher in the regular class will carry the same attributes and charisma into the special class and will continue to run a tight educational ship.

It is not always possible to find experienced teachers in the field of emotionally disturbed to start a program since this is a relatively new direction in education. A regular class teacher may have the know-how to initiate the transition-adjustment class program as well as a teacher with a master's degree in the area of emotionally disturbed, since intangible personality factors weigh the teaching scales.

In the school system, one will find teachers whose interests go towards emotionally disturbed children, who may have had some experience in the past with these children, even in a summer camp, or who have taken some courses in this area and are willing to take on the challenge of the new program. If the teacher is from the building in which the class is to be housed, and has a good working relationship with the staff, the program's development is enhanced.

Teacher candidates may also be recruited from graduate college programs for emotionally disturbed children.

One of the experienced transition-adjustment class teachers can be assigned the role of coordinator of the program once the program has been expanded, for example, to six elementary classes. The coordinator, who also continues teaching a class, is directly responsible to the director of psychological services. In this capacity, the coordinator will organize periodic meetings with the transition-adjustment class teachers, as well as team building meetings; he will follow up on the progress of students in the program, observe the other teachers (with a substitute provided for his class during this period of time), and coordinate other aspects of the program

Teacher pay is usually based on the regular teacher salary scale. In some districts, there may be a differential ranging from two to five hundred dollars. The coordinator receives an increase, similar to that for department heads in a building, for his additional duties and responsibilities.

Prestudent and student teachers from nearby colleges and universities provide additional help while these teachers-to-be, in turn, receive valuable experience in working with emotionally disturbed children. Student teacher participation strengthens the program without a corresponding increase in cost.

POINTS ON TRANSITION-ADJUSTMENT CLASS ORGANIZATION

The suggested model of two classes, close by, provides for teaching within each classroom along with flexible grouping for team teaching There is the advantage, also, of two teacher figures. When there are two classes near by, a student can be moved from one to the other to blow off steam when the occasion arises.

One transition-adjustment class in the district is a start when there are not enough disturbed children identified to form two classes, or when there are other limitations such as finances, space, teacher availability, or acceptance by the school district.

It is important, as in any new venture, to attempt no more than you can handle. It is better to develop a program gradually with the important variables under control, and iron out the wrinkles, than to rush into a new educational enterprise before establishing a firm foundation. Over-extending the program can boomerang and destroy much of the good work that has gone into the initial stages.

In organizing a district transition-adjustment class program, one can learn more about the operational workings through visits to nearby districts that have these classes. Talks with the special class teachers and administrators clarify the realistic picture. One can learn more about their experiences, progress, and problems. Data from other districts running special class programs for emotionally disturbed children can be sifted, together with information from state education departments, to determine their applicability to the school district.

THE PRINCIPAL'S SHIP

An important factor is the building chosen for the program. One principal may look forward to having the program in his building while another may wish to use the available space for other purposes. The enthusiasm generated by the principal will set the atmosphere for his building staff. If the principal is not in favor of the classes, he may place a damper on the program. It is better, therefore, to have the classes situated with a principal actively interested in the transition-adjustment concept. However, when reality factors necessitate placement in a building where the principal is lukewarm, the program can still succeed if the standard operating procedures are spelled out, and the teacher of the class and the director work to develop the program with the principal and his staff.

It is the job of the transition-adjustment class teacher to follow the rules in the principal's ball park. His hours in the building will be the same as those for the regular teachers. It is his responsibility to attend meetings called by the principal and to follow through with building routines. His participation as a building member helps to bring about a closer working relationship with the other teachers. This is especially important when his students will be gradually farmed out to regular class on a part-time basis.

THE TRANSITION-ADJUSTMENT CLASSROOMS

Space should be ample. There should be a bathroom if possible, certainly for younger children. Also, there should be an outside play area and gym nearby if it can be arranged. Where space is at a premium it is possible to "double-team," that is to have two classes in one room on an overlapping schedule.

One class can run, for example, from 9:00 a.m. to 1:30 p.m.; the other from 11:30 a.m. to 4:00 p.m. The overlapping period can be spaced through separate lunch hours and special subject scheduling. Overlapping has potential advantages as well: group flexibility in team-teaching, and, with a man and woman teacher, a mother and father figure.

Disturbed children are not able to concentrate and follow through on a full day schedule. They reach a point of diminishing returns. The optimum time is four and a half hours, with the academic work scheduled early in the day. Once the children are assimilated back into regular class on a part-time basis, their day can be gradually lengthened to go beyond the transition-adjustment class hours. It is a long, hard pull to organize emotionally disturbed children in the transition-adjustment program and prepare them for "farming-out."

Physical education, art, science, and music are integral parts of the program as they are in regular class. These areas are important channels to growth, and play a crucial role in the creative expression expression and personality development of disturbed children.

Since many of these children are clumsy and awkward and have not participated actively in sports, due, for example, to their poor self-image and fears, physical education has much to offer in terms of their total growth pattern as well as providing pleasure and enjoyment. With two classes, physical education groupings need not be based on chronological age. Other factors can determine class composition: frustration level, degree of muscular development, or ability to participate in group sports.

Art is a creative tool in the development of the disturbed student and a constructive vent for drives and feelings.

Music also serves a useful function. It is an area in which a child who has met defeat in regular class may sing beautifully or show aptitude with an instrument. There is the added benefit of the discipline which goes into the practice.

Science, too, is a practical, concrete way to spark interest and learning in a disturbed child.

Lunch is usually half an hour, in the lunch room as part of the regular school assimilation.

The number of children in a class is generally eight, with an age range of three to four years. Under emergency pressure, classes may have nine students but rule of thumb is eight, or even seven. Once the class has settled down into the routine, and some of the children are farmed out for regular periods during the day, the teacher may be ready to take another student or two into the class.

It is the policy to leave the decision to the teacher as to when another child can enter the class. The teacher is in the best position to know how the class organization is going and when the timing is right to add another student. Implicit in this procedure is the guiding principle that these classes are not "dumping grounds" to get rid of a pupil who doesn't fit in. Rather, they are carefully structured settings in which long-term goals are set into motion for the total growth of each child towards realistic functioning in the lifestream.

Equipment and supplies for the classroom are best coordinated through a district-wide budget set up by psychological services. They can be ordered together for all the classes and delivered to one central place, in this model, the psychology department. The procedure relieves the principal from including these materials in his budget, and eliminates the difficulties that arise in shipments to the building where the special and regular class materials are together. The advantage of a district-wide budget increases as the program grows and there are more classes in different elementary buildings.

GETTING THE YOUNGSTERS TO SCHOOL

Transportation is vital to any special class program. If the children do not get to school, there is no program. Since the hours are different from those in regular class, bus schedules must be set up with the transportation officer. It is important to work closely with the transportation coordinator from the inception of the program, since his cooperation is essential.

The transportation coordinator is an intermediary between the bus company and the school. On the one hand, he is responsible to the district and, on the other, he has to maintain friendly contact with the bus company to carry out his job. Schedules for district transition-adjustment classes present the bus company with additional bus runs. If their contract covers all transportation in the district, the transition-adjustment class bus routes represent more work and expense to the bus company.

Each child must be picked up at a corner near his house and returned there by special bus—usually a bus that transports children to regular class. (Consideration can be given to station wagons, owned by the district, to transport students to and from district transition-adjustment classes.)

Bus drivers are important to the program. Their cooperation and involvement can help to smooth out difficulties that may arise, for example, when a child acts up on the bus.

(Transportation to special classes outside of the district for mentally retarded, physically handicapped, emotionally disturbed, and brain dysfunctioning children may be handled through boards of cooperative educational services (BOCES), or by county or regional transportation. When one or two children are to be transported to an association for retarded children (ARC) day training center, or to a private center for emotionally disturbed children, it is usual to have the taxi companies in the area bid for the contract.)

In New York State, the school district must provide appropriate education, and transportation within a distance of twenty miles, for handicapped children at the age of five, in line with the district entrance age for kindergarten. If there are not proper educational facilities available within the school district, placement is arranged outside of the district.

Amendment to Section 4407 of the New York State Education Law provides tuition up to nineteen hundred dollars a year to private schools, within and without the State, when district facilities or placement in a BOCES program are not available, at the age of five and up, for handicapped children.

(In the not too distant future, states will provide educational facilities for handicapped children three or four or younger as part of an early preventive-developmental approach.)

THE ROLE OF TRANSPORTATION

When plans are drawn up for the transition-adjustment class program, the transportation officer must be involved every step of the way, as another member of the team so that he is aware of the goals and direction of the program. His involvement increases the effort and concern he will put into transporting the students.

When there is an opening in the class due, for example, to a child moving into regular class or out of the district, provisions must be made for a new student to be transported to the class. This is an inconvenience to the transportation officer who must notify the bus company, who, in turn, must reschedule the bus route. The willingness of the transportation coordinator to go along with changes in the bus route is necessary for the smooth running of the program.

Once the students are set for fall transition-adjustment class placement, the best route stations can be determined and discussed with the transportation coordinator so that he can work out the schedule with the bus company. Since this is a district-wide program, students will be attending from all parts of the community. The number of buses needed will depend on such factors as the number of classes, their location, and the home addresses of the students set for a particular class.

As the program grows, it is likely that there will be classes in more than one building. Transportation arrangements are complex since the variables include, for example, age, home school area, and sex of the student or teacher. (You do not want one girl in a class of boys; a girl may specifically need a lady teacher if there is one.) One child may trigger off another and have to be separated, or it may be important to place a disturbed boy in a different school than the one his twin brother attends.

Children are generally placed in their own building area, when possible, so they can be graduallly assimilated back into regular class in their own home ground—though farming out can work as well in another school.

The transportation officer will want to schedule the classes when the buses are not transporting regular class children. It is important to work around this realistic framework as part of a cooperative team effort. A workable class schedule is 9:00 a.m. to 1:30 p.m. with time modifications geared to regular district busing schedules; for example, 9:30 a.m. to 2:00 p.m.

During the summer, the director of psychological services meets with the transportation officer to go over the data on each child and the school he will attend. The bus stops for each route are determined. A letter is then written to the parents by the director stating approximate times each child will be picked up and returned home each school day, the corner, the classroom number and elementary building, the teacher, and the request that the parents call if they have any questions on transportation.

During the school year, as problems arise on transportation, the parents can contact psychological services or transportation. It is important to work closely with the parents at the beginning of school for they become discouraged, upset, and bitter when the bus is late or does not appear. These problems are compounded when the district is on an austerity budget and bus transportation is burdened.

It is generally best to have the children ride the special bus even if they attend a transition-adjustment class in their own school area and can walk or ride the regular bus. This provides continuity in bus scheduling and a minimum of changes. Exceptions may arise, for example, when a student in the transition-adjustment class is able to attend class for the rest of the regular school day and then goes home on a regular bus if the building is in his school area. When the class base is in another elementary school area, parents are often willing to pick up the child at the end of the regular school day.

The transition-adjustment class teacher will meet the school bus in the morning. He will also see to it that the children get on a bus in the afternoon. This way, he also gets to know the bus driver. With his cooperation, there is more chance the driver will wait if the child is not at the designated corner, or speak with the teacher about a pupil who is acting up on the bus rather than calling the bus company.

The district transportation coordinator is involved with every step of the transportation picture. Since the director will also be working with the transportation officer on all handicapped children in the district who will be attending special classes, within and without the district, and providing him with the necessary data he requires, a mutual working relationship will tend to develop that will carry the program forward.

CLASS ACCEPTANCE

The question may be raised as to whether the child will be made a scape-goat by his peers when he is placed in a transition-adjustment class. There are two points to consider: One, in regular class he was seen as "different" by the other children. There is much to be gained by organizing him in the transition-adjustment class so that when he gradually returns to the regular class he will move into the mainstream in behavior and academic functioning. Two, in preparation for the program, the involvement of the school staff will serve to clear the way for acceptance of the class.

The operation of the transition-adjustment class program within the elementary school is also a factor in its acceptance. Children in the transition-adjustment class may run audio-visual aids in regular classes and assemblies. Children in regular class may visit the special class and observe the use of power tools or science projects. And there may be farming in: a child in regular class who has difficult moments may visit the transition-adjustment class at set times during the week.

INITIATION OF THE PROGRAM

During the spring preceding the initiation of the fall transition-adjustment class program, the director, transition-adjustment class teacher or teachers of the classes, and principal of the building in which the program will be housed can meet with the building staff to discuss the goals and operating procedures for the program, and can follow up with a meeting at the beginning of the school year. Periodic team building meetings can then be held during the school year.

The director, or coordinator of the transition-adjustment class program when one is appointed, can schedule district-wide meetings for all the transition-adjustment class teachers to discuss procedures, student progress, and specific questions that may arise.

The director will report to the district principal and central administrators on the development of the program.

As the district-wide transition-adjustment class program nears the end of the year, plans are made for each child for the following year. Alternatives include:

1. Continuation in the transition-adjustment class for the following year on a full-time basis.
2. Part-time farm-out areas for students to continue in the transition-adjustment class.
3. Regular class placement.

By the time the student is ready for full-time regular class, he will have been farmed out during the school year for most of the day, in preparation for the fall regular class.

When a student is placed in a farm-out class, part-time, or a regular class, full-time, he is placed at a level where he can succeed. For example, a student may be placed in a regular fifth, rather than sixth grade, when he is ready for full-time assimilation, because his arithmetic is at the fifth grade level. The parents and child may balk at the placement at first. When the recommendation is followed out, however, the reasons for the lower grade placement become apparent: the opportunity to accomplish the task at hand and to gain a core of confidence in coping with reality; to get acclimated to every facet of regular class functioning; and to provide a year of foundation growing in preparation for junior high school and the preadolescent to adolescent transition period.

When a student is ready for regular class on a full-time basis, the transition-adjustment class teacher will meet, at the end of the year or the beginning of the fall, with his new regular class teacher and building principal to provide data and suggestions on working with the student. The director, coordinator, and transition-adjustment class teacher will follow up on the progress of the student during the school year in regular class.

There is also a follow-up with the outside therapist or other agencies who may be working with the student.

PARENTS AS PART OF THE TEAM

It is essential that the parents are aware of the concepts and purpose of the transition-adjustment class program and are in accord with the placement of their child in the class.

During the school year, there can be four regularly scheduled parent-teacher conferences, with the second and fourth including a written report specifically designed for the program, as well as other conferences when they are indicated. At the end of the school year, the recommendations of the school team are discussed with the parents regarding the fall placement.

Communication lines are always kept open between teacher and parents. They can call or come in to clarify such concerns as: "Why is my child not getting homework?" "Why is he getting hit by some other pupil in the class?" "Why is he playing and not getting work?" "Why isn't he in regular class subjects more of the time?"

Face-to-face conferences are preferable to telephone conversations. The meeting, generally in the school rather than in the parents' home, is the key to maintaining two-way cooperation. The conferences provide the teacher with information on outside events that might explain the behavior of the student in school.

The director of psychological services is available to parents on matters that trouble them. If it concerns the teacher and the student, it is suggested that they first have a conference with the teacher to air their questions if they have not already done so. If necessary, another meeting can be arranged with the director, coordinator, teacher, and principal if indicated, to discuss questions on the parents' minds. It is important to deal with the parents' doubts, through the parent-team conferences, before they escalate.

ADVANTAGES OF SUMMER AND SECONDARY TRANSITION-ADJUSTMENT CLASS PROGRAMS

A transition-adjustment class summer program for five weeks—for example, from 9 a.m. to 12:30 p.m. with one trained teacher and college student aide for every eight children—provides the continuity and structure for children already in a transition-adjustment class. For children set to enter a transition-adjustment class in the fall, it is a springboard organizing experience.

In the summer program, children are provided with organized play activities, sports, arts, crafts, science, and academic experiences. Teachers are available for parent conferences after 12:30 p.m. A written summary of each child's progress is presented to the parents at the end of the summer session.

It is difficult for parents to deal with a disturbed child in the summer when there are no structured settings available. Many of these disturbed children will not fit into a regular day camp program.

At some point, organization of a junior high school transition-adjustment class is a consideration. The setting up of a secondary transition-adjustment class program is an exacting challenge: to organize disturbed students in the midst of the preadolescent to adolescent transition, and to help them to assimilate gradually back into regular class. Close team cooperation is the prerequisite for the development of the program. The teacher, as in the elementary transition-adjustment class, is the prime factor in the direction the program takes and the improvement the student makes.

A junior high school transition-adjustment class not only serves students in regular sixth grade going on to seventh grade, and students presently in the junior high school who are having increasing difficulties in functioning, but also students in the elementary transition-adjustment program who chronologically fit a secondary setting but are not yet ready for departmentalization.

It is helpful to have the teacher of the secondary transition-adjustment class teach one regular class period in the building in his specialty, as a way of joining in with the regular school staff—a suggestion of Dr. Francis Roberts, Superintendent of Schools.

SUMMARIZING

The organization and implementation of a district elementary transition-adjustment class program involves a carefully structured teamwork model with a director and standard operating procedures to determine the need for the classes, the screening process, the operation of the program, the selection of the teachers, farming out, transportation, and the role of the parents. The organic development of the program includes a summer transition-adjustment class setting and classes at the junior high school level.

FIVE

Procedures for Transition-Adjustment Class Screening

Placement in a district elementary transition-adjustment class is the last step in the screening process. In the basic model presented, the coordination of the screening procedures is the responsibility of the director of psychological services.

Students are generally referred for psychological evaluation by the classroom teacher. The referral may also be initiated by the principal, reading specialist, nurse, speech therapist, special teachers, school social worker, the parent, family pediatrician, clergyman, and other community resources. In some instances, a student may refer himself. Community, home, and school are interweaving threads in the fabric of the child's life space. Student difficulties arising outside the school are an integral part of the total configuration and a concern of the "community psychologist." Parents as taxpayers are entitled to school services they support financially.

PREPARING THE REFERRAL FORM

Whatever the source of the referral, it is standard operating procedure to have the classroom teacher fill out the referral form obtained from the principal's office. The classroom teacher, as the central member of the school team, is in the best position to provide data on the reality picture and initiate the referral.

The form includes pertinent data on the student, reasons for the referral, and parent awareness of the referral. There is space for additional information to be completed by other members of the school team who are involved with the student.

The form is routed through the school nurse since information on vision, hearing, operations, hospitalizations, injuries, illnesses, diseases, convulsions, and physical handicaps is important in the total evaluation.

The referral is processed through the principal for his signature as the final link in the building chain of command.

Before the form is written up by the classroom teacher, she will generally discuss with the principal her reasons for the referral. The principal may also ask the teacher to write up the referral based on information he has received in school or from the parents. If other members of the school team wish to refer a student, they will discuss the referral with the classroom teacher and the principal.

If the parents or family physician make a request for an evaluation directly to the psychologist, he will discuss the request with the building principal. The principal or the classroom teacher will then fill out the referral form.

When the completed referral form reaches the principal's desk, it is his decision whether to sign and pass the form on to psychological services for evaluation at that time. When the referral has been initiated by a professional source outside the school, or by the parent, it is standard procedure to follow through with the evaluation as a community service.

However, if a parent requests an evaluation because, for example, she feels her child is bright and academically far enough ahead to skip a grade, this is the principal's decision to make. His conference with the parent will clarify the next educational step.

When the parents request an evaluation, a conference with the psychologist may resolve their questions, or other measures may be indicated first so that an evaluation is unnecessary.

SETTING STUDENT PRIORITIES

The principal gauges which referral forms to sign and pass on to the psychologist. He is aware that psychological services cover the total district and a priority order is essential. In some instances, the principal may feel there are ways in which the classroom teacher, and other members of the school team, can help the student first before calling in the psychologist. He is aware that there are other students in his building who may have more serious difficulties that demand immediate attention.

The psychologist carries his weight as a member of the school team when he processes the principal's priority referrals within a reasonable amount of time. When emergencies arise, he must be ready to provide "instant service." He is available when he is needed most.

The elementary school priority order of evaluations filter out those students who generally do not have serious difficulties in functioning. With few exceptions, the referrals that reach the psychologist's desk deal with above-average capacity students who have serious emotional disturbances.

(Student referrals processed at the secondary level also show serious emotional difficulties. Inner personality knitting has not developed in the earlier developmental stages, and the sleeping volcano begins to erupt during the preadolescent to adolescent transition when the biological catalyst balances the scales in the direction of impulsivity and disorganization.)

Before the completed referral form has reached the psychologist, signed by the principal, the parents have been contacted, generally by the teacher, on the proposed evaluation. While it is not legally necessary in New York State, for example, to get parental permission for a school psychological evaluation, it defeats the purpose of the team approach to go against the parents' wishes and examine the student without their cooperation. If they are opposed to the evaluation, testing their child will only complicate any attempt to resolve the present problems.

In the final analysis, parents must make the decisions on their own children. If they are not ready to accept the evaluation, they are not ready to explore ways to change the disturbed pattern. At a later time, they may be more willing to have their child tested in light of continued difficulties.

Therefore, the policy is set that no student will be evaluated by psychological services unless the parents are in favor of the referral.

Even when parents request a referral, or are in favor of the psychological evaluation, it is hard for them to face the seriousness of their child's condition when the data is discussed with them.

THE PSYCHOLOGIST'S EVALUATION

Once the referral form has been completed by the classroom teacher and the school team, signed by the principal, and the parents notified, the referral form is sent to psychological services with a priority ranking. The completed form, logged in by the psychological services secretary, serves as a record of the referral and is kept in the psychological folder. The principal may wish a duplicate copy for his file.

Since psychological services are district-wide, they are coordinated through the director. He will assign referrals after consultation with his staff. Due to limited personnel, the psychologists service referrals in all of the buildings, on a priority order, rather than limiting themselves to a specific school or schools. A central psychological office is preferably located in one of the schools where it is part of the school team rather than situated in a separate building.

Before the psychologist evaluates a student, he may wish to talk with the classroom teacher and principal first to obtain further data. With time a factor, the student may be evaluated first, followed by the team conference.

Once the student is evaluated with a psychological battery, the data is analyzed and a report is written. A copy of the report is personally handed to the principal, or his secretary, in a sealed envelope to insure confidentiality, rather than sending the report through interoffice mail.

There is no mention made on the cumulative record folder that the child was tested by the psychologist.

A team conference is arranged with the teacher, principal or assistant principal, nurse, and other involved school members, to share the data and to determine helpful steps within and without the school framework. It is important for the psychologist to get a clear idea of how the student functions in school, and to check the psychological findings against the clinical observations of the school team. The psychologist contributes his analysis of the roots of the difficulty, the underlying seriousness of the personality picture, and ways to help in school.

When there is a question of a brain dysfunctioning factor, a recommendation for a pediatric-neurological evaluation will be discussed with the school team and followed up in the parent conference. If placement in a transition-adjustment or brain dysfunctioning special class is a consideration, the neurological fee may be paid for out of the psychological services budget. It is well to have the parents discuss the recommendation with the family pediatrician.

THE POST-EVALUATION PARENT CONFERENCE

The next step, after the team conference, is to have the teacher or principal notify the parent that the student has been seen by the psychologist. It is suggested to them that they call the psychologist for an appointment to discuss their child. This procedure places the initiative for the conference on the shoulders of the parent rather than "drafting" the parent by a call from the psychologist.

The parent-psychologist conference should include both parents if it is possible. It may help to schedule an early morning or late afternoon appointment so that both parents can attend. In some instances, an evening appointment will be necessary. When only one parent can be available, usually the mother, the door is left open for a later conference with both parents. The parent-psychologist conference provides the opportunity to discuss the school picture with the parents, to determine home functioning, to gather the developmental history, and to discuss useful measures to help the child at home and at school.

The parents may not have a clear picture of the school pattern and it may be helpful to have the teacher join the conference to clarify reality points. There will be an ongoing follow up with the school team and the parents on how the student is progressing.

In the school team conference, analysis of the psychological and school data may point to severe interference in regular class functioning, with greater difficulty anticipated as the demands for independent, self-starting operations increase. If this is so, the classroom teacher, principal, other members of the school team, and psychologist consider the need for placement in a transition-adjustment class.

TRANSITION-ADJUSTMENT CLASS PRIORITY

Once the school has recommended placement in a transition-adjustment class, the student candidate is assigned a building priority order, based on a team decision between the director of the program and the building principal. When there is an opening in a transition-adjustment class, the director determines the district-wide priority order after consultation with the building principals.

A student is not placed in a transition-adjustment class if the principal and director are not in agreement. However, with the team concept in operation, and the main concern the student, the placement order is mutually resolved. The principal respects the director's experience in the field, and the depth of the psychological findings. The director, on the other hand, respects the principal's observations on the student's functioning, and the school team findings.

If a psychologist other than the director has evaluated the student and followed through with the school team, he will discuss the recommendation for transition-adjustment class placement with the director prior to the psychologist-parent conference. The building priority order will be set by the psychologist, the director, and the principal.

What determines the placement priority order? Operationally, it is the degree to which the student is not able to function in regular class. The disturbance may show itself in disruptive behavior, marked withdrawal, and academic failure. For the administrator, high priority goes to the student who acts out his difficulties, upsets the balance of the regular class, interferes with the learning of other children, and drains the energies of the teacher.

There is, of course, flexibility in setting a priority order depending on the individual set of circumstances. Emphasis is directed towards placement of younger disturbed children so as to organize them before their underlying difficulties magnify and interfere more with reality functioning.

There is one guideline that weaves a thread through the program: *Every effort is bent to maintain the student in the school setting regardless of the seriousness of the emotional disturbance.* Exemption and home teaching remove the child from the mainstream and defeat the purpose of education. In removing the problem from the school, the emotional disturbance is swept under the educational rug. Only in the school environment can the student develop his capacities for productive functioning. Every child has the right to be part of the human scene, if it is at all possible, and only through the human matrix of peers and interested adults can he realize his potential for human interaction.

Therefore, the more disturbed children are likely to be placed in the transition-adjustment class program since they have greater trouble coping with school. However, since these students will take longer to be assimilated back into regular class, a program can not be based on an arbitrary cut-off date of, say, two years. Rather, the goal is long-term organization of the child, to his limits, in preparation for adolescence, educational requirements, and making a living.

A point may be reached where the special class program has done all it can, academically, socially, and emotionally for the student, and the next realistic goal is preparation for a vocation at the secondary level.

In the conference with the parents, where the recommendation is to be placement in a transition-adjustment class, it is important for both the parents to be present. In laying the groundwork for the recommendation, it is helpful to go over the developmental history carefully, to explore the parents' perceptions of the child's difficulties and assets, and to clarify his school performance.

THE PARENT AND THE PROGRAM

When the placement recommendation is made to the parents, the facts are presented honestly.

The class is for emotionally disturbed children. By emotionally disturbed, we mean a child who, from an early age, has not been able to organize himself for reality functioning. Along with this difficulty in organization, the child tends to "tune out;" to go into a world of his own where reality and imagination merge. In his imaginary world, the child builds up fears that make it more difficult for him to cope with everyday tasks. As he gets older, and the work gets harder, he will have increasing difficulty with school work, independent functioning, and reality task concentration. If he does not get organized now, he will not be prepared for the preadolescent changes around nine or ten; for the transition into adolescence around twelve, thirteen, or fourteen; or for later adolescence. He needs to develop a basic foundation for later life functioning. The school team believes the best way to achieve this goal is through placement in a transition-adjustment class.

If an opening is not immediately available, no guarantee is made as to when the student can be placed in the class. It is generally better to alert the parents to the recommendation even if placement is not available, so that they have time to consider the placement possibility for a later date.

The parents are often shocked at the recommendation. They know their child has problems but they did not believe they were that serious. They are concerned by the term "emotionally disturbed"; they will grasp at straws to substantiate their view that he is "not really disturbed," or that he has made "wonderful progress over the summer."

What determines the placement priority order? Operationally, it is the degree to which the student is not able to function in regular class. The disturbance may show itself in disruptive behavior marked withdrawal, and academic failure. For the administrator, high priority goes to the student who acts out his difficulties, upsets the balance of the regular class, interferes with the learning of other children, and drains the energies of the teacher.

The parents will ask questions about the transition-adjustment class program which are explained in detail: hours, curriculum, transportation, farming out, teacher, number of children in the class, age range, and building assignment if that is set. The parents will air serious doubts and misgivings about the placement.

They are told that, on the average, their child will lose two or more academic years in the organizing process for later life functioning. Parents are disturbed at the thought of their child below his grade level, and a two-year or more academic loss is difficult for them to take.

The parents are told that, as part of the placement procedure, the child will be seen by the consulting psychiatrist, a service provided by the school. Consulting psychiatric fees are part of the psychological services budget.

If the parents agree to the evaluation but the psychiatrist lives outside the school district, they will often get lost going to the appointment, and not show up at all, or they will arrive too early or late due to unrecognized resistances or feelings of being "drafted." In practice, it is better to have the psychiatrist come to the school and see the students, after reviewing the school and psychological data.

During school hours the students can be brought from class, after clearing with the parents, or, during the summer, appointment times with the psychiatrist are arranged with the parents at the elementary school where psychological services are housed.

The parents will need time to think about the placement and will turn it down, more than half of the time, for a number of reasons ranging from the fact that they don't want their child treated "differently" to the belief that he will "snap out of it" in regular class.

However, if they are interested, the next step *before* placement is to have the parents visit the class. This can be arranged in the summer as well, if there is a summer transition-adjustment class program. The visit to the class is scheduled by the director after clearing with the building principal and the transition-adjustment class teacher. (In the planning year for the program this is not possible since there is no district class to visit.) The parents, who up to this point were in favor of the class, may now declare that their child is not like "those other children" and refuse placement.

No student is placed in a transition-adjustment class without the consent of the parents. It is difficult enough with the parents' collaboration; it would be disastrous without it. The program has long-range, total developmental objectives. To attempt to place a student without the parents as part of the team in the long, arduous struggle to the goal is to court failure. Parents may require more time to become aware of the depth of the disturbance. As their child continues to have increasing difficulties in the classroom, they may be more likely to accept placement a year later—though this is not necessarily the case.

Once the parents are in favor of placement, and crucial doubts have been resolved in their mind, the student is placed on the priority waiting list for the building. The district coordinator also considers other candidates with serious disturbances; children who may have moved into the district during the school year, for example, from a special class for emotionally disturbed students. The preventive direction of the program also requires high priority for younger-aged emotionally disturbed children.

Before placement, a full physical examination is recommended, including a blood test and urinalysis, booster shots brought up-to-date, and a complete vision and hearing evaluation.

INFORMING THE STUDENT

When an opening is available, the parents and the regular class teacher explain to the student that he is going to be placed in a smaller class where he can get more help with his difficulties. Parents often anticipate a negative reaction on how the child will accept the class due to the externalization of their own feelings. Actually, most students welcome the chance to find themselves in the smaller group, and are only too aware of their inability to carry the ball in regular class. Any doubts or worries the student may have about the change may be helped by having him visit the class and talk with the transition-adjustment class teacher prior to the move.

When a student is placed in a transition-adjustment class the date for transfer is set, after touching bases with the sending and receiving principals, and after transportation is arranged through the transportation officer. The cumulative record folder is sent to the new class. The regular class teacher confers with the transition-adjustment class teacher to fill in the school picture.

The parents are told where and approximately when the child will be picked up by the special bus to and from home, and arrangements are made for close parent-teacher cooperation through regular school conferences.

The screening process has led to the final step of placement in a transition-adjustment class. The student is now in a setting geared to his total educational development.

SIX

Curriculum

The term *curriculum* generally evokes concepts related to academic achievement. However, when applied to transition-adjustment classes, the term *curriculum* assumes much broader dimensions.

It goes beyond the academic and reaches into the personality of the individual. It attempts to restructure the individual in such a manner that he will develop a reality-based self-image that conforms to the real world around him.

As one teacher aptly put it, "In order to rehabilitate these children, it is necessary to create an atmosphere not of mere tolerance or even acceptance. It is incumbent upon the transition-adjustment class teacher to create an atmosphere which says to each student: 'You are an essential part of society. We want you. We need your talents, whatever they may be.' "

The curriculum encompasses more than is generally implied in the word. The transition-adjustment class teacher, in conjunction with other team members, assesses each child's needs, assets, and liabilities. This appraisal includes physical, psychological, emotional, social, and academic factors. On the basis of these findings, always subject to reevaluation and change, he prescribes a curriculum tailored to the individual.

THE IMPORTANCE OF MOTIVATION AND ATTITUDE

The transition-adjustment class approach to teaching incorporates all the techniques enlisted in any well-constructed curriculum. The regular class teacher is primarily concerned with the sequential development of skills that will lead to successively higher levels of achievement and ultimately to a competence proportionate to the child's intellectual capacity.

All good teaching requires student motivation and the development of learning attitudes. The time and effort expended by the regular teacher on these two factors are determined by the characteristics of the individuals who make up the group. In the regular class, the development of motivation and attitude can be considered to take no more class time than it does to teach the subject and, in many instances, less time is required.

On the other hand, with the students who comprise a transition-adjustment class the teacher is concerned with motivation and the development of positive attitudes from the time the child enters the class until the time he leaves. In fact, these attitudes are the prime avenues by which the disturbed child can begin to grapple with the learning process.

A student usually enters the transition-adjustment class with a background of academic failure. Former teachers describe his attitude as "lazy"–"no interest"–"could do better if he tried." In many cases, the child enters the transition-adjustment class as non-functional or borderline-functional in academic areas after years in regular class. In addition, he may have been retained once.

It is not a reflection on either the regular class teachers or the regular class program that he failed to learn. Most transition-adjustment class children have been unsuccessful because of interferences in the learning processes. These result from inner emotional difficulties which have, in turn, created a system of negative attitudes toward school in general and learning in particular. Even the disturbed child reflects on his poor learning orientation: "I can't"–"I can not do it good enough"–"Who needs it?"

For most of their school lives, these children have met with nothing but frustration and defeat. It is no wonder that their attitudes toward school and teachers are negative. The following conversation is typical of the "teacher is an enemy" attitude of these children:

> **Student:** You're a real nice guy.
> **Teacher:** How do you know, Jim?
> **Student:** Well, every other teacher I had, I'd find a pole or a tree and I'd beat it and beat it and I'd say, "Take that and that

you rotten_____. (Here he used a string of curses.)
Teacher: How does that show that I'm a nice guy?
Student: Well, I haven't done it to you yet.

A youngster who had been unable to talk in a school setting for many years, showed his first indication of a desire to speak by writing notes to the teacher: "Mr. Lincoln is crap, crap, crap!" This was the first time he was able to express his hostility toward the world of adults. It was the first time he felt secure enough to express his anger without fear of reprisal.

This is the heart of the transition-adjustment class curriculum: to create an atmosphere conducive to self-expression within the framework of a structured setting that is flexible enough for such expression and at the same time firm enough for the maintenance of discipline and learning.

THE NEED TO BUILD INTEREST

The term that best describes the transition-adjustment class approach to teaching is "An Interest-Centered Learning Program."

Initially, the major emphasis is placed upon interest rather than academic achievement. This does not imply that academic areas are neglected. Interest, drive, and motivation are tools to help re-establish the student in the learning area. For most of these children, whose inner disturbances made learning difficult or impossible, failure in school has served to compound their problems. It is only when the wish to learn school subjects arises in the individual that he can begin to apply himself.

At first, the attempts to learn are half-hearted because the student anticipates defeat. However, when small successes, highly praised by the teacher, indicate to the student that he is capable of accomplishing tasks, his application to his studies increases. Concomitantly, his work improves as his sense of self-worth develops. There is mutual reciprocity between emotional attitudes and academic achievement.

One student, Andy, age twelve, had a pervasive record of negative behavior and lack of achievement. But then Andy became fascinated with the tape recorder. At first, he would record only weird, animal-like sounds. Bored with this, he began to make up words. He would go on and on in his "foreign language." Then, in conjunction with another boy, he started singing soul songs. Later they began to record impromptu stories. Not satisfied with the results, they began to write scripts.

Andy could neither read nor write nor spell, but he did have an excellent imagination. He would dictate to his partner who was more skilled in this area. In order to have his own copy and to make his own creation, he laboriously copied from the original, a goal inspired by his teacher. It was in this manner that Andy began to learn the letters of the alphabet, to write, to want "to spell right," and to develop a desire to read.

Interest, involvement, success, sequential skill development, competence—this was Andy's story. Andy achieved his objective through the unique opportunities available in the small class setting.

OTHER ASPECTS OF THE TRANSITION-ADJUSTMENT CLASS CURRICULUM

In addition to flexibility within structure, motivation, and development of positive attitudes, there are additional premises which are basic to the transition-adjustment class curriculum:

1. Success in any area is the prime motivating force in the development of a continuum of successful achievement in that area. It is the jumping off point for participation and accomplishment in unrelated activities—either new, or those in which the child had previously experienced frustration.
2. The transition-adjustment class teacher's attitude must be one of unwavering optimism. This means that the child's previous performance, academically and behaviorally, is discounted. He is given an opportunity to "start from scratch." His records are scrutinized only for the purpose of determining more about his past experiences so as to understand more about his present difficulties. The transition-adjustment class teacher is the catalyst in the rehabilitative process, providing every available opportunity to reinforce the rebuilding. He is the watchdog who prevents past mistakes from repeating themselves. He is convinced that the child will succeed and he encourages the child with his enthusiasm.
3. Any teaching-learning situation involves a relationship between the person imparting and the one receiving knowledge. In working with transition-adjustment class children this relationship serves as a crucial force. Indeed, success or failure hinges

largely on the rapport developed between the student and the teacher.
4. In a regular class, progress is generally measured in terms of class norms. In a transition-adjustment class, progress is measured in terms of what the student did yesterday against what he does today. Sometimes the gains are measured in inches and must be searched out and praised. The fact that Jim yelled out only six times today compared to seven times the previous day, does not appear to represent much of an advance. But when you consider that in the beginning, Jim was constantly interrupting the group, it is clear he is putting out a great deal of effort and is on the way.

CASE HISTORY OF "THE CHILD WHO WOULDN'T TALK"

The following study reflects the philosophy of the transition-adjustment class curriculum, and its implications, in a practical context.

Name: Ben
Age: 9 years
Grade placement: 4th (retained once in 2nd grade)
Functional achievement: None
Major characteristics: Although Ben spoke at home, he never uttered a word, not even a sound, in the school setting.
Procedures: After eighteen months of setting the stage, the teacher decided that the optimum time had arrived. The stage setting involved the implementation of the transition-adjustment class philosophy. Ben's refusal to speak was never alluded to by the teacher as an attempt to get him to speak. Ben's improvement pattern was initiated via the use of power tools. Both his adherence to the safety rules and the articles he produced were exceptional. He was made the teacher's assistant. He taught other members of the transition-adjustment class, and children from regular classes, how to use the machinery. But he never spoke a word. He moved from this area into participating in mathematics and penmanship.
Stage-Setting: The teacher assumes a cool attitude toward Ben and a friendly one to the rest of the group. The daily arithmetic assignment is given out but Ben is not permitted to participate.

Ben sits at his desk crying; the teacher pretends not to see him. Other children call his crying to the teacher's attention. The teacher tells them to do their work.

The teacher goes over to Ben's desk, cups the boy's chin in his hand, and exerts gentle pressure on his jaw and mouth. Looking straight down into the boy's tearful eyes, the teacher bursts out with staccato comments—remarks other children often used to tease Ben. These are all in question form:

"Are you the little nut in the back of the room?"

"Are you the creep who can't talk?"

After each question, the words "are you?" are repeated two or three times. The process lasts several minutes. The teacher returns to his desk, leaving Ben to his own devices. Shortly after, the teacher gives Ben permission to do his arithmetic.

Although Ben starts his assignment after the other children, he completes it first. He angrily puts the paper on the teacher's desk. The teacher ignores his anger. Ben's face is filled with anticipation. The teacher checks the paper and smiles slightly.

> Teacher: Ben, come here, please.
> *(Ben comes to his desk.)*
> Teacher: That's a very beautiful paper, Ben. It is very neat. The writing is very good. You have only two problems wrong and you did it quickly. You couldn't do this last year could you, Ben?
> *(Ben shakes his head.)*
> Teacher: Ben, could you write last year?
> *(Ben shakes his head.)*
> Teacher: Do you know how to write now?
> *(Ben nods his head.)*
> Teacher: You learned how to hold the pencil. Then you put your mind on forming the letters. Then you did a lot of practicing. Remember how many lines of *I*'s and *B*'s you had to make before you learned how to write?
> *(Ben nods his head.)*
> Teacher: *(Pulling out a pile of papers)* Look at these, Ben. *90*'s and *100*'s in spelling, arithmetic, sentences, and writing. No "nut" in the back of class could do this kind of work. Could he?
> *(Ben shakes his head.)*
> Teacher: Ben, Can you talk?
> *(Ben nods his head.)*
> Teacher: Ben, talking in school is going to be just like writing only instead of using your fingers you will use your lips. You will put your mind to it and you will do an excellent job, just as you do in writing. Do you want to try now?
> *(Ben nods.)*

The teacher and Ben go into a private room. The teacher seats Ben and hands him a printed paper. The teacher cups the boy's chin in his hands and exerts a gentle pressure on his jaw and mouth.

> Teacher: Let's read, Ben.

> *(Ben's little face screws up. Tears start to roll down his cheeks. His lips start to move and the teacher relaxes his pressure.)*
>
> **Ben:** M-m-m-m-my. *(The first word was out!)*
>
> The teacher hugs Ben tightly. He tells him how brave he is. All the tensions caused by pain, fear, and a sense of betrayal ease. The teacher continues to hold him as he says:
>
> **Teacher:** Was it hard, Ben?
>
> **Ben:** Yes.
>
> *The teacher begins to read and Ben repeats after him:* "My name is Ben. I am a good boy."
>
> Before going back to class, the teacher apologizes for being "mean" and embarrassing him.
>
> In front of the group, the teacher asks: "Would you like me to get ice cream for the class, Ben?"
>
> "Yes," he answers.

Ben's hesitant "Yes" in front of the group to whom he had never spoken before was only the beginning in a series geared to provide him with the chance to develop and reenforce his confidence in talking. Several weeks later, a well-earned commendation was presented to him with appropriate ceremony:

> TODAY IN CLASS BEN PARTICIPATED IN OUR VERBAL MULTIPLICATION TEST. HE GOT 100%. HE READ 15 PAGES IN HIS LIBRARY BOOK. THIS WAS DONE IN CLASS. IT IS NOT EASY FOR BEN TO DO THESE THINGS AND YOU MUST BE PROUD OF HIS DETERMINATION AND COURAGE.

Ben was subsequently farmed out, and returned eventually to regular class where he is doing well.

THE ELEMENTARY TRANSITION-ADJUSTMENT CLASS CURRICULUM

Competence in reading, writing and arithmetic, some knowledge of science, art, music, and physical education, and social involvement are skills and abilities almost mandated by society.

Rather than presenting a comprehensive curriculum guide, techniques and recommendations based on actual experience are described.

READING

Once physical disabilities have been ruled out as causative factors in reading retardation, the transition-adjustment class teacher attempts to determine the type of conditions and modes of approach that will lead the child to successive stages of skill development.

In building a program for these children, one should bear in mind the fact that they have the potential necessary to learn to read. The prerequisites for the development of the reading curriculum are attitude, experiential background, relationship between teacher and child, and the selection of an individual technique for each student. Experience has shown that these children will usually respond and show progress in their reading skills when these requirements are met.

During the initial period in the transition-adjustment class program, an assessment is made of the student's ability and attitude toward reading. The sum total of his experiences at home, in school, and among his peers, weaves a pattern that leaves him favorably inclined towards reading, antagonistic toward it, or simply indifferent.

Through observation of the student in the transition-adjustment class, conferences with previous teachers, and information from the cumulative record folder, the reading pattern is clarified.

The home situation is another facet to the educational diamond that is sharpened through conferences with the parents. Once the parents feel the interest and concern of the transition-adjustment class teacher for their child, they will generally report and discuss the child's experiences at home in an open manner.

PRESSURE FROM PARENTS

Parents worry over their child's academic weaknesses and, in particular, his reading ability. They may expect too much from their child. The parent-teacher conference helps to alleviate the pressure the parents are consciously or unconsciously exerting upon their child. At the conference, the teacher gains insight into their attitudes, and works to reduce their concern over the child's learning problems. The child's reading level is explained to them along with techniques and materials to help the child improve his reading skills.

In one parent conference, the pressure placed upon the child by his father was brought to light through discusssing the procedures they followed at home to help their child in his reading. The father was upset over his son's failure to read at the level of other children his own age. It was embarrasing to visit relatives and friends and have the child's disability brought to light. In an attempt to remedy the situation, he "worked" with his son several evenings a week. The father was a college graduate and in a professional field. His son was an only child. As a result of the conference, the father realized he had been overly demanding throughout the child's life. The mother did not push her son in any area but felt that she had been overly permissive in her approach to handling him.

Through open and candid discussion the parents agreed that there was a difference in the way each handled their son. They felt the boy's confusion had been due in part to a lack of consistency. The parents had the opportunity to discuss their views frankly with each other, and with another adult who was involved with their child.

As to the reading session, the father admitted he became impatient and yelled at his son when he did not perform up to snuff. The mother stated that she would leave the room because she became upset whenever this happened.

The conference benefited both the parents and the teacher and, indirectly, the child. The teacher suggested that the father give up his "academic sessions" with the son and spend time with him in a more relaxed, friendly way. To try to teach him at home only turned the child against learning.

HOW PARENTS CAN HELP

At the other extreme, one sees parents who do not provide an atmosphere that generates an interest in reading on the part of the child.

The parents and the teacher can work together to develop the child's interest through enrichment experiences that include movies, plays, trips, museums, and similar activities. The parents can capitalize on an excursion by readings before, and discussions after, the trip.

It may help the child to have a place of his own for his books, and to receive them as presents for his birthday and other special occasions. A children's book club, and trips to the local library, in which the child uses his own library card, serve as motivating factors. Reading to the child before bedtime and discussion of stories and books with him are encouraged, as well as reading books of his own choosing.

These home activities not only help the child with his reading but also develop healthier family relationships.

THE RIGHT MATERIALS AT THE RIGHT TIME

The reading materials and equipment used in the transition-adjustment class program are the ones available in any classroom. The key lies in choosing the correct materials and methods at the appropriate stage of the child's overall progress.

Basal readers are of little value, particularly in the initial stages. The children associate past failure with these books and their comments illustrate their feelings:

> I had that book last year.
> Not that creepy book again!
> That's a second grade book. That's for babies.

Aside from these past associations, the basal reader may present the student with a greater work load than he is prepared to handle. The size alone may frighten him.

One of the most constructive techniques, one which incorporates the areas of language arts, including oral and written expression, and penmanship and grammar, has been the use of *experience booklets.* These booklets contain stories dictated by the student to the teacher. If the child is not at ease dictating to the teacher, he may dictate on the tape recorder and allow the teacher, at a later date, to transfer the story to his booklet. Most of the children, however, enjoy telling stories and relating experiences to the class so that the teacher can copy them down as they are telling them to the class. These stories are based on the child's own activities and interests. They may be true or drawn from the child's imagination.

The teacher will record these stories and type them prior to placing them in the booklet. A primary typewriter is used for the younger children's stories. In those situations where the student copies his own stories, they are placed in the booklet prepared by the child under the teacher's guidance. The student may make illustrations to go along with the story, or add a page of relevant pictures cut from magazines. The student reads the stories from time to time with the teacher and the class and, if he wishes, with his parents. Many times the children like to read their stories to visitors who are observing the class. The children are proud of their booklets and become enthusiastic over this approach to reading.

CURRICULUM 93

To take further advantage of the interest they show in their experience booklets, the children are encouraged to make permanent tape recordings of their stories. They play the tapes from time to time for the entire class, or plug in earphones so that they can enjoy the tapes alone. Each child has his own tape which is stored in the teacher's desk.

A piece of equipment useful in reading is the Bell and Howell Language Master (Figure 6-1). This machine is available, with cards, for developing various skills. Each card has a strip of dual tape on which the child hears the instructor pronounce a word or phrase. The student then turns to the adjacent side of the tape to record his own response.

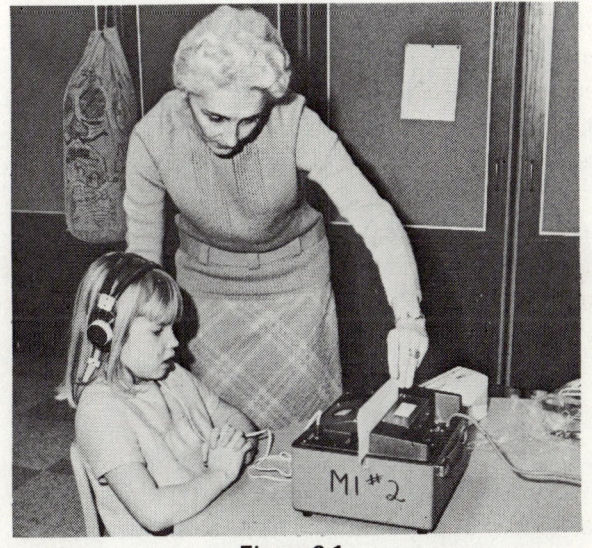

Figure 6-1
The Reading Specialist Utilizes the Language Master

Children with severe difficulties in auditory discrimination and sight word acquisition can use the word picture cards to help them develop a sight vocabulary. On blank cards, available from the distributor, the teacher can write down words which are new to the child or ones which cause him trouble.

Another machine helpful in the reading program is the Controlled Reader, Jr. (Educational Development Laboratories, Huntington, New York). It is basically utilized to increase speed in reading and to develop comprehension. It sharpens attention span and such basic skills as left-to-right scanning. The Junior model is geared for individual children and small groups.

Weekly Reader Practice Books, particularly the Science Reading Adventures, are valuable for independent work. These stories are short, interesting, and simple enough for the students to follow on their own without becoming overly confused. These workbooks can also be used in small group, teacher-directed activities.

Phonics are tailor-presented to each student. Along with teacher-prepared materials, which coincide with their present reading, commercially prepared ditto workbooks are utilized. Permanent type workbooks are rarely used as the students lose them, destroy them, or find them uninteresting.

The McGraw Hill New Practice Readers are also helpful. These stories are short and the topics varied and interesting. The work assignments are short, and if the preparatory stage has been worked out with the students, they can generally handle the assignments independently.

Basal readers are used when and if the teacher feels the child is ready to handle them. If the team is preparing a child for farming out, his basal reader assignments are correlated with the regular class program.

In addition to these materials and techniques, there is a wide variety of games, for example, "Spill and Spell," as well as experiences in the total language arts area that stimulate and motivate these children as they do in any regular reading program.

THE READING SPECIALIST

It is essential to the program to have the building reading specialist actively involved with the transition-adjustment class. Frequently, if a child has been a pupil in the school in which the transition-adjustment class is housed, the reading specialist has already diagnosed the child's reading problems. She is aware of the reasons for the child's placement in this class and she can follow up with the teacher on his progress.

If the student is new to the reading specialist, she tests the child at the request of the transition-adjustment class teacher when he feels the child is ready. The reading specialist generally administers the following measures:

1. Tests for balance, body image, laterality, and dominance.
2. Tests for auditory and visual discrimination.
3. Phonics test.
4. Informal reading inventory.

CURRICULUM

Once the team decision is to provide reading help, the reading specialist works closely with the transition-adjustment class teacher. Together, they plan the method, techniques, and materials to be used with each child. Constant reevaluation is part of the program.

Experience shows that the nonreader is often deficient in visual-auditory areas. For this reason, the Frostig Program for the Development of Visual Perception (Chicago, Illinois, Follett Educational Corporation), the Newell C. Kephart *The Slow Learner In The Classroom* (Columbus, Ohio, Charles E. Merrill Books, Inc.), and the G. N. Getman *How To Improve Your Child's I.Q.* (Laverne, Minnesota, Announcer Press) are materials frequently utilized. Short work periods, five to ten minutes, are adhered to—with varied approaches.

As soon as the child displays visual and auditory skills, he is introduced to a structured phonics approach. While phonics are stressed, the sight method, tracing technique, structural and configurational work analysis, experience approach, and programmed learning are included as well.

The consonants, arranged in unvoiced and voiced categories, are introduced first. Concrete materials are part of the teaching scene. For example, when introducing the first unvoiced consonant, *p*, a clay, wooden, or stuffed pig is handled by the students. The teacher draws a picture of a pig and points out that the tail of the pig has the same shape of the letter *p*, the very letter that starts the word *pig*. Henceforth, the letter *p* and its sound are referred to as *Mr. Pig*. Every letter is associated with some concrete object and given a name. The children enjoy learning to use the various names with their associated sounds.

As soon as the unvoiced sounds are absorbed, the short vowels are introduced and blending is begun. Nonphonetic words like *the, said,* and *is* are introduced as sight words, using the Visual-Auditory-Kinesthetic-Tactile (V-A-K-T) approach, if necessary. Quickly the children learn to read simple sentences like "The fat cat sat," or "Tip sat on the cot." At this point, sentence analysis can indirectly begin. The teacher asks, "Who sat on the cot?" He urges the children to answer in complete sentences. The *who, what, where, when, why,* and *how* questions are asked.

Another technique is to have the children describe the picture a particular sentence calls to mind when the teacher writes the child's description on the board or on a piece of paper. In this way, the children visualize the total sentence.

As soon as possible, the child is introduced to books, and reading proceeds along concrete learning paths.

A child will receive individual instruction in reading until the teacher feels he is ready to be moved into a small group in the class.

All techniques used with emotionally disturbed children work only if the proper relationship is established between the student and the teacher.

HANDWRITING

Since handwriting is a basic learning tool, it is an important area to develop. Handwriting can be a cause of deep frustration to the confused, disorganized child. It is usual to find severe difficulty in handwriting skills with students in a transition-adjustment class. As in any learning area, the child is taught from the floor level up. He does not move from manuscript to cursive writing unless the teacher is confident he is ready for the new task. Pressure is not applied.

In helping the children develop their handwriting for practical use, legibility is stressed rather than fancy hoops and loops. They begin with short assignments and learn individually or in small groups.

Instruction on letter formation is given, on the board, to the entire group. Independent work begins once the ability to form the letters has been achieved.

Dittos are prepared so that each child will have his own paper to work with at his seat. Each child, by having his own individual assignment for the day, can complete it without becoming upset if he falls behind the other students. The child will tend to be neater and to achieve at a higher level if he does not feel he is involved in a "race" with his classmates.

Motivating these children to write is a difficult chore. They function best when the writing assignment concerns them or their experiences—though they will respond to activities that involve the class as a whole. However, it is difficult to prepare assignments that are applicable and interesting to the entire class.

The best approach is for the teacher to prepare individual assignments for each student. Each child is given the opportunity to write in the daily class diary. The children can also write for the school paper. Motivation grows when they know that if they do a neat job their work will be placed on a master ditto and run off for the entire class. They also enjoy writing stories for their experience booklets.

The following are some approaches found to be helpful in

motivating good handwriting. They are part of the total language arts program.

A student who is interested in caring for a particular animal in the classroom can copy material and information on his pet. (One student prepared a booklet about gerbils which included his own writing and illustrations.) The need to write legibly becomes evident to the child when he realizes that this information will be made available for the other students and visitors to read. He also has the opportunity to visit other classrooms to show his pets and to read the materials he has prepared.

A class diary is a motivating tool to do well when each child has the opportunity to work in it. The diary is available for all to see and it is read to the class from time to time.

Individual materials completed by the students can be placed on a ditto for everyone to see.

The student, with teacher guidance, can prepare a transparency of his best handwriting for use on the overhead projector. The transparency can then be used to demonstrate to the class the better points of the student's work.

The experience booklets the children prepare on their own have many uses, and one of them is to motivate good handwriting.

Neatness, legibility, and effort will take place once motivation is sparked. Parental help and involvement are important. Parents are requested to have their children make use of their handwriting skills at home. They can accomplish this, for example, by having them help in writing shopping lists, invitations, and greeting cards.

SPELLING

The spelling lists will vary according to the individual levels of the students. Much can be done to make spelling activities fun and interesting to the students.

When the student is writing stories for his experience booklet, he is encouraged to look through his spelling lists for words that he might be able to use in his writing.

Group games encourage students to learn their spelling words. These games would include spelling baseball and charades.

Spelling baseball is scheduled at least once weekly. The class is divided into two teams whose members change from time to time so as not to encourage set rivalries. A diamond is placed on the blackboard. One student will keep score if the group is odd-numbered; the teacher, if it is even-numbered. A student may try for a single (one word correct), a double (two words), a triple (three words), or a home run (four words). Bases are placed in each corner of the room and the batter will move around according to the number of words he has chosen and gets correct. His movement is tracked on the board. Each misspelled word is an out and each team has three outs. Words are presented from the individual spelling lists of the students.

New words are introduced to the group. These words are placed on the chalkboard and examined for spelling, configuration, and meaning. To aid them in grasping the meaning, the teacher introduces antonyms and synonyms they already know, sentences with these words included, and the game of charades. After reasonable exposure, an individual is permitted to go to the front of the room and act out a word of his choice. The child who determines the correct one has the next chance to pantomime his word. If he is not prepared to do so he has the right to pick someone else.

When the children are aware that charades will be played later, it ensures greater attention to the lesson at hand. It lends to the appeal of the game if the teacher participates both as an actor and as a guesser of a wrong answer.

One of the advantages of the game is that everyone has a chance to participate on an equal basis. For example, John, who was a nonreader, acted out a Dr. Jekyll and Mr. Hyde situation. He took an imaginary drink from an imaginary bottle and proceeded to grimace and walk around the room in a grotesque fashion. The immediate response from the class was the correct word, "change." Because of the uniqueness of this approach, John gained self-satisfaction and earned a degree of status from his peers which, in turn, motivated him to participate and succeed in other academic areas.

Difficult words are placed on the bulletin board and the teacher has the children try to spell the words without looking.

Words listed are prepared on dittos with certain letters left out; the students are required to fill in the missing letters.

When oral sentences are indicated, the teacher makes an effort to keep the sentences humorous and to use the names of the students as subjects.

Formal spelling tests are enjoyed by the children as long as they are not too frustrating. Reinforcement is, of course, necessary and must be followed through week to week.

MATHEMATICS

When it comes to mathematics, the "modern math" materials are usually too frustrating or too abstract for the emotionally disturbed child to handle or to understand, due to his limited motivation and his concrete level of development.

The transition-adjustment class teacher begins with simple, structured mathematics using a variety of concrete materials. The child may use blocks, Cuisenaire rods, or a counting frame in his work. Number lines can be utilized with success, though some of the children find them too confusing at first. For the younger child, one can teach addition and subtraction best with materials like the counting frame and counting blocks.

The teacher does not take away their "crutches" too rapidly if he feels the child cannot work without them. The important thing is to develop his interest so that he can perform mathematical operations and try in an area which previously had baffled and upset him.

The teacher can instruct mathematics through games and audio-visual equipment. The use of the overhead projector is valuable in teaching new materials in which the child can follow directions, step by step, with the teacher.

Children who do not want to sit at a desk can do their counting with large blocks on the floor. Number lines can be made there with chalk or tape; many learning games can be played this way. The use of portable chalkboards is recommended so that the children have the opportunity to do their work on the board.

These children seem to enjoy playing card games, and many mathematical facts can be taught by using ordinary playing cards. Various concepts can be introduced and reinforced such as "more and less" and "highest and lowest," for example, in a card game like "War." Games can be played where the children add points to obtain specific sums, like Casino or dice.

There are many commercially prepared games available and a variety of these should be part of the classroom. There are many ideas and activities in the mathematics field that can be found in professional magazines and books.

The basic aim is to get the children to develop a healthier attitude toward mathematics, through interesting presentations short enough to maintain their attention. Long seat work assignments are taboo.

Reinforcement is necessary to maintain skills that have been taught, but drill work should be kept short. Major emphasis is placed on making mathematics meaningful to the child. As in other areas, if the emotionally disturbed child feels learning mathematics has some value to him he is more likely to pursue it. Classroom activities, therefore, are based around the development of an interest in mathematics and the presentation of practical or fun activities in which the child can use what he learns.

Classroom stores, school book stores, woodworking activities, and science projects are all avenues for putting mathematics to practical use.

Parental cooperation is helpful in making mathematics a real experience for the child. The parents are encouraged to have their child utilize in the home mathematics he is learning in school; for example, looking at a timetable, checking the temperature, playing dominoes and handling an allowance.

SCIENCE

Science is an interest-centered activity handled mainly by the transition-adjustment class teacher, taking advantage of particular bents of the students. If there is a science specialist in the building, he can help to stimulate experimentation and learning (Figure 6-2).

With the small number of students in the transition-adjustment class, the teacher and the science specialist can plan group activities

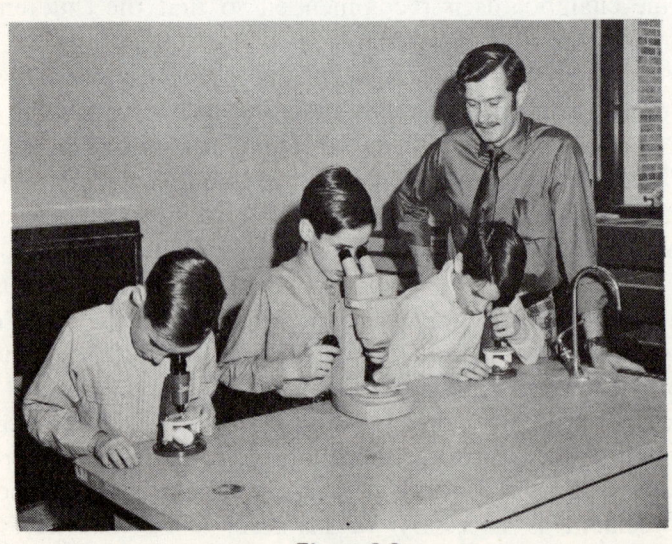

Figure 6-2
Examining Specimens in Science

that will involve all of the children. By having two teachers present, the team approach allows the children ample supervision and direction with special science equipment.

A major focus in planning science activities is to have the child's curiosity in people, animals, and the physical world about him serve as a catalyst to explore learning.

Children are encouraged to start their own collections and scrapbooks in any area they desire (Figure 6-3). Opportunities are provided to experiment within the classroom and to carry out simple experiments at home. Field trips are a series of life experiments that excite their interest in the world of reality.

Figure 6-3
Identifying Rocks Collected by the Children

A variety of materials should be on hand for use in the classroom. Take-apart items should be provided such as old clocks, toys, radios, and motors. These items reduce their tendency to take apart desks and radiators. Two young children, who did not have access to these materials earlier in the year, dismantled practically everything in the classroom with a screwdriver and a wrench. Covers were off electrical outlets, pipes were apart under the sink, closet doors gave way, and students' desks collapsed. These drives were channeled into more constructive activities by the teacher. The children were provided with take-apart items and allowed to help in putting together new equipment in the classroom.

Pets, such as fish, are used to good purpose in the classroom. A class can have two tanks, one for small tropical fish and a bigger one for the larger varieties. The tanks should be placed where they can be observed by the teacher; feeding and cleaning are always supervised activities. The tanks should be checked at the end of each day.

All of the animals in the class should be kept in secure cages. On one occasion a white rat escaped from a transition-adjustment classroom. When the children noticed the uproar it caused among other classes and teachers, the teacher was quick to realize that the situation would no doubt "happen" again. The rat was placed in a locked cage from that time on.

Some children wrote little booklets about their animals and visited other classes to show them and read their observations. After the transition-adjustment class teacher helped them construct a maze for the hamsters and mice, the children expanded on this idea to make a large one out of plywood. They used it to put on a demonstration for other classes and presented it at the school science fair. In the classroom, they built tunnels and houses out of blocks and boxes.

One transition-adjustment class teacher had a pet for each child beside their desks. He obtained them by placing an advertisement in the local newspaper. The students had specific times during the day to take care of them and to play with them. It was interesting to watch the children reach down, whisper, and pet their animals as they worked through the day. All but one of these animals survived the year. One was lost when the boy attempted to give it a bath in the sink. The teacher must be certain that the pets are treated well and are not used as scapegoats.

Nature walks are fun, relaxing, and provide ideal learning situations for the children. With supervision, there should be little difficulty on these outings. There may be walks in the local woods, beaches, or town nature trails. The children are encouraged to observe animals quietly instead of wildly chasing them. They are encouraged to collect rocks instead of throwing them.

On one trip to the beach the children decided to "chip in" their individual collections of shells and make one giant collection. The shells were cleaned, glued onto a large piece of painted plywood, and labeled. The class presented the shells to the principal who, in turn, mounted them for all to see on the entrance bulletin board. This gave the children a feeling of accomplishment and of belonging to the school.

Teaching emotionally disturbed children involves a total approach. One teacher prepared a lesson on how to determine the age of a tree, and other facts about how trees grow. Over the weekend, he cut a section from a felled tree. On Monday, he brought the class to his yard and cut three-inch-wide sections with a power chain saw. The children were supervised. Each child was given his own section to keep. The teacher explained the rings, bark, and other tree parts. The children were thrilled over this demonstration and they treasured their own pieces of the tree.

Science activities can be a way to include the parents. One project was borrowed from the Cub Scouts monthly theme, "When Dad Was a Boy." It was expanded to include granddad. The children were asked, with the help of their parents, to bring in examples of how things have changed over the years. The parents enjoyed the project as much as the children.

Photography is a useful approach. Besides teaching basic facts about cameras and relating it to the eye, it is fun and acts as a motivating tool. The children enjoy developing the pictures, either in the classroom or in the school darkroom. The camera should be readily available for use by the transition-adjustment class teacher or, better still, be part of the class equipment. A 35-mm camera and a Polaroid camera are recommended. The 35-mm is preferable because it allows the children the experience of developing the pictures. Snapshots are taken of classroom activities, nature walks, and special events.

Better relations are built up with the other staff members when the transition-adjustment class assumes the responsibility of recording on film all of the school special events, and taking pictures for individual teachers who are putting on class plays or auditorium programs. The children use snapshots in their experience booklets, class diary, and individual scrapbooks.

Students should be encouraged to take part in the annual science fair. The teacher provides direction but most of the work is completed at home with the help of the parents.

Science presents the transition-adjustment class teacher with almost inexhaustible opportunities for integration with language arts and arithmetic—and exciting, meaningful educational experiences.

(An excellent curriculum guide is *The Illinois Plan For Special Education of Exceptional Children,* Interstate Printers and Publishers, Inc., Danville, Illinois.)

EVALUATING STUDENT PROGRESS

Student progress is based largely on the teacher's evaluation, together with school team observations. Standardized intelligence and achievement tests are generally not administered until the student is farmed out so as not to put him under premature pressure.

Anecdotal records are kept on each student. A simple looseleaf notebook with dividers serves this purpose.

Contacts with outside professionals and agencies are noted. When an outside resource requests school data, with parental consent, the written progress report and anecdotal records are sent together with the psychological data.

REPORTING TO PARENTS

There are monthly school parent-teacher conferences, and more when necessary. In the conference, the student's progress is explained, home data illuminated, and parent questions and concerns discussed.

A written report is presented to the parents at the mid and close of school. It helps to clarify how the student is doing. The report accentuates the positive without giving a false picture that would generate unrealistic hope in the parents.

A copy of the written report is enclosed in Appendix B.

NOTES ON A JUNIOR HIGH SCHOOL TRANSITION-ADJUSTMENT CLASS PROGRAM

The ideal approach to a transition-adjustment class program is to place disturbed children in a small-structured framework at as early an age as possible. This goal is rarely realized. Disturbed children may not be identified early due to a withdrawal pattern. This identification problem is minimized when transition-adjustment classes become an established part of a school system and the school team becomes more aware of the characteristics of the withdrawn child.

Another problem arises when a disturbed youngster is identified but the parents do not accept transition-adjustment class placement.

It may be years later, as the child's behavior and academic work go progressively downhill, that the parents will reconsider transition-adjustment class placement.

Some of the students in elementary transition-adjustment classes show forward gains but still require the security and structure of a smaller setting. Yet, for a variety of reasons, the elementary school is no longer appropriate. These reasons include: physical size and chronological age; the need to relate to peers; and concrete proof they have indeed made progress.

In addition, there may be students who are capable of borderline functioning in regular sixth grade but unprepared for the demands and stresses of junior high school departmentalization and the transition from preadolescence to adolescence.

There are also disturbed students who do not move into the district until they are older.

In order to provide for these students, it is necessary to set up junior high school transition-adjustment classes. The basic philosophy of the program is similar to that at the elementary level: an individually-tailored curriculum; participation in school functions, including extra-curricular activities; frequent parent-teacher conferences; shortened school day (four and one-half hours); total team involvement, and farming out.

Of eleven students involved in a junior high school transition-adjustment class program for one year, ten achieved varying degrees of success; one boy did not improve.

A way to present insights into the value of the program is to describe Jim's case.

Jim was in ninth grade. He had attended private school for eight years. During this period he had maintained a *B+ - A* average. Upon entering junior high school, he developed phobic symptoms. Although he attended school from September to January, he was rarely present in his classes. Jim spent his school day hiding in some corner of the school—the boys' room, the library, or the locker room. Early in February, he was transferred to the transition-adjustment class. He was soon farmed out to eighth-grade English. Shortly thereafter, he started eighth-grade social studies, mathematics, and science. He chose the grade level. Because of his reputation for cutting classes, his attendance was carefully observed. From February to June, Jim had one cut. His final grades were one *C* and three *B's*. Jim used the class as a home base. After each regular class period, he would stop off, talk to the other students, sometimes get help from the teacher, and then go on to his next class.

For most junior high students, the lockers where they keep their books, coats, lunch, and go through the ritualistic opening of the combination, serve as a home base. Other students, especially insecure seventh graders who are trying to orient themselves to the new scene, need what Jim required. The transition-adjustment classroom soon becomes the gathering point for troubled youngsters. They gravitate to the transition-adjustment class where they have a feeling of belonging. The class presents an opportunity for "emotional refueling."

The establishment of transition-adjustment classes on the junior high school level is a necessary extension for some students in elementary transition-adjustment classes who need the junior high setting as a placement for students with difficulties functioning in junior high, and as a way station for insecure new students who need a home base.

SEVEN

Establishing a Physical Education Program for Transition-Adjustment Classes

(This chapter was written by Mr. Joseph F. Governali, elementary school physical education teacher.)

Despite the fact that physical activities afford a prime avenue for bodily expression and reality integration for emotionally disturbed children, little has ever been written on the subject for the benefit of those who seek to establish and conduct such a program.

The program explained below can best be described as a pragmatic approach to physical education for transition-adjustment classes. It has been developed over several years of working with transition-adjustment class students at the elementary level. The program is constantly evolving into something new and, hopefully, something more relevant for this particular group. It can be adopted as a starting point by any school system and shaped to fit the needs of its children.

The objectives which guide this special physical education program are three-fold: physical, mental, and socio-emotional.

(Interwoven among the specific objectives are, of course, the more general objectives of most physical education programs.)

Stated in terms of observable student behavior, these objectives can be specifically described as follows:

PHYSICAL OBJECTIVES

1. Improvement in general body coordination

Many of the children in the transition-adjustment classes do not have the coordination needed to perform many of the more basic movements such as skipping, hopping, running, throwing, catching, and dodging. In some cases, it appears to be a lack of exposure (especially with the younger children); in others, it seems to be the result of fear of failure or fear of physical harm. Some students show a lag in visual-motor development. Under this objective the physical educator works to develop these basic coordination skills so the child will have a foundation on which to build future skills.

2. Improvement in cardio-vascular fitness

The majority of these children appear to lack the endurance and stamina which characterize the play patterns of other children in this age group. Under this objective the physical educator works to develop the stamina and endurance which are necessary for participation in the activities typical of this age group.

3. Improvement in general body strength and flexibility

Too many of these children lack the basic body strength and flexibility that are needed to perform even a moderate amount of physical activity. Under this objective the physical educator works to improve the strength and flexibility of these children, and to motivate them to improve for the sake of their own health, well-being, and enjoyment.

MENTAL OBJECTIVES

1. Improvement in ability to concentrate on a task

Almost without exception these children have an exceptionally short attention span. They lack the basic concentration necessary to succeed at a task. Through games and activities the effort is made to help them increase their attention span and to learn to concentrate on what they are doing.

2. Improvement in ability to become involved in activities

In many cases, these children are participant-spectators. They are in a game but are not really involved in what is happening. They go through the motions of the activity but obtain no satisfaction from it (mainly because they cannot, for some reason, let themselves become involved). Through improving skills and eliminating fears, the physical educator works to help these children obtain satisfaction from physical activities and learn to become emotionally involved in what is going on around them.

3. Improvement in qualities of determination and self-motivation

The majority of these children appear to lack the basic elements of determination and self-motivation which are necessary to succeed in the simplest of tasks. In many cases, they give up even before trying. Through physical activities, the physical educator works to build up inner drive and self-motivation, and illustrates the importance of these attributes to the students.

4. Improvement in ability to understand and comply with rules and regulations

Many of these children lack regard for rules and regulations. In many cases, they do not understand rules, cannot remember them, or cannot see their need and purpose. Through rules and regulations in the gymnasium (sneakers; safety; proper use of equipment) and in various games and activities, the physical educator works to demonstrate the need for restrictions and regulations.

5. Improvement in ability to analyze and understand game strategy (as it applies to elementary grades)

It is difficult for most of these children to analyze a game in terms of the strategy needed to play it most effectively. They play the game wildly and without regard to how they can get the most out of it through a better understanding of the tactics involved. The physical educator works to help the children learn to analyze the simplest of games so they can grasp how to put their efforts to best advantage. From these simple situations, they move to a more developed level in games and sports where the strategy is more complex and intricate.

SOCIO-EMOTIONAL OBJECTIVES

1. Improvement in ability to get along with others

Many of these children have little regard for how other people feel and think. It is probably not that they don't care—rather they are just insensitive to the feelings of others. Many of these children do not have a knowledge of the social amenities needed to get along with others. Through games and activities, the physical educator works to teach them the importance of team work and collaborative effort. He tries to help them to cooperate with others towards a common goal.

2. Improvement in self-control

Almost without exception these children lack self-control. For some, it appears to stem from a lack of regard for other people while, for others, it seems that they are not capable of controlling their overflow of emotions. The physical educator works to provide situations where a healthy outburst of emotion is acceptable and those in which a negative outburst is not acceptable. He tries to point out the differences between these situations and helps the children understand the need for self-control at specific times. Sports and games provide an excellent source from which to draw these lessons.

3. Improvement in ability to accept losing

Many of these children are not able to accept defeat even in its most insignificant form. To some, it seems to be a personal insult to lose. The physical educator works to help them learn how to lose and still derive enjoyment out of the activity. Along these lines, he works to help them learn how to be a good winner.

Although these objectives have been organized into separate areas, they should not be thought of as isolated or separate. There is overlapping and coordination among the various areas and among the objectives in each.

Many of these objectives rely on the attaining of other objectives in order to be fulfilled. For example, a child can not become more involved in activities until he improves his basic coordination to the point where he can derive some pleasure out of performing the necessary skills involved in the game. By the same token, he can not improve in his willingness to comply with rules and regulations until he realizes that losing is not a personal affront. All of these objectives are interwoven and interact with one another to implement the general aims of the program.

TIME ALLOTMENTS AND CLASS COMPOSITION

It is suggested that, as a starting point, the youngest group of children (kindergarten, first and second grade) have three periods of physical education a week, each of twenty minutes duration.

The middle group (third and fourth grade) each have three twenty-five-minute periods a week.

The oldest group (fifth and sixth grade) each have four thirty-minute periods a week.

These are the lengths and frequencies that have been proved best through experience. They can be varied to adapt to other situations in other school systems. These time allotments are exclusive of special help sessions.

One year the composition of each of the classes worked out well in terms of program planning. The oldest group was composed entirely of boys which made it possible to plan a program relevant to boys of their age. The year before, the older group had some girls in it which made program planning more difficult. There were few activities in which both the girls and boys were interested, and the program had to follow a down-the-middle course which, at times, was not satisfactory.

The oldest group should be composed of only boys or only girls. A mixed class at the fifth-and sixth-grade level is not a constructive situation and should be avoided if it is possible.

In the two younger groups, with similar age and interest levels, a combination of girls and boys together in the same class works well.

INDIVIDUAL ATTENTION AND SPECIAL HELP

These children are much in need of special help. They require more individual attention than other children. With regard to physical education, this special attention can come in the form of small group sessions with the teacher.

These special sessions are useful to the physical educator and to the student in a number of ways.

First of all, through these sessions the physical educator can strive to give these children the supportive emotional help they need.

A second important outcome of the sessions is to establish better rapport between the teacher and the child. (This is an important objective when dealing with the children in the transition-adjustment classes. Until they learn to trust the teacher, the students are limited in what they are willing to do.)

Third, the children have the chance to practice and learn skills in which they are deficient.

Finally, these sessions give the child an opportunity to attempt to try those activities which he was reluctant to do with the whole class present.

Although the physical education classes are small, they are still not likely to be small enough, mainly because these children have a hard time working on their own. They need constant supervision. The special help sessions are a necessary adjunct to the program.

(If the physical education class itself were to be kept small enough to provide closer supervision, the question would arise as to whether this would be putting the class period to best use all of the time. As much as they need small group help, these children also need the larger group setting in order to learn to work and get along with other people. The larger group session is a period of maximal activity and interaction among the class members. The special help sessions and group activities combine to form the optimum physical education experiences for these children.)

The smaller instruction group is an absolute necessity if one wants to have the most effective program. These groups should be in addition to the regularly scheduled physical education classes and complement the areas taught in the larger class. They should provide an opportunity for the child to work on those skills in which he is most deficient.

And, they should aim toward promoting a better relationship between the child and the teacher; the student and his peers.

CLASS ORGANIZATION

There are different ways to organize a transition-adjustment physical education class. A method of organization found to offer the best degree of success is described below:

1. The children come into the gym and have a designated line upon which they sit awaiting instructions. *It is very important that they have a specific place to go and that they know exactly where it is.* The gymnasium is a large, wide-open space with few of the physical restrictions of the classroom. Without a point of reference from which to operate (in this case a line on the floor), there is a tendency for the class to lose control as soon as they enter the gymnasium. This point cannot be overemphasized.
2. The class is started with brief exercises. Depending on the age level of the class, exercises usually include jumping in place, sit-ups, push-ups, and running in place. At the beginning of the year, all of these exercises, and any others which are introduced, are performed right on the line to which the children

ESTABLISHING A PHYSICAL EDUCATION PROGRAM

went when they came into the gym. This is helpful in establishing the general class atmosphere. When the class begins with a good deal of organization and structure, the probability of having a constructive class session is greatly enhanced. As the year progresses, the exercises can move away from the starting line and include laps around the gym (with specific rules for passing and staying in line) and locomotor activities the length of the gym. No matter what the exercise activity, however, it is most effective to have the class start and finish on a designated line—again to give the class a point of reference from which to operate.

The exercises serve two purposes. First, they are a warm-up for the day's activity. Second, and probably more important for these children, they give the class sessions a degree of structure which they come to expect and depend upon. They soon realize that before the daily activities start, they are going to have to listen closely and to follow directions. This helps to establish the pattern for the class section.

3. After completing these exercises, the group once again gathers on the designated line. This gives the children a chance to "catch their breath" and to organize themselves. At this point, the teacher will either present an activity to the class or discuss with the children several activities from which they can choose the day's program. The suggested activities are geared toward development of a particular skill or social behavior.

It is important to note here that the needs and interests of these children are not necessarily identical with those of regular class children. As a result, many activities which are enjoyable and relevant to regular class children are not suitable for the emotionally disturbed child. "Not suitable" describes the situation mildly. Many accpeted, conventional physical education activities will simply not work. *Thus, it is important that the children be involved in the decision-making process for their program.* The physical educator determines the particular unit or area of activities for the day. He and the class then decide upon the best course of action to follow in order to work in the chosen unit. Of course, this is an oversimplification of a procedure which requires a great deal of flexibility and which is likely to vary in smoothness of operation during the course of the year.

4. The day's activities begin. If there is a need for equipment, students should be selected to obtain the equipment, and to be responsible for returning it to the equipment room when the period is over. Although this may seem like a trivial detail, it can actually be an important phase of the program. It is another factor which helps give organization and structure to the class session and to the individual who is doing the job. The child's natural reaction as soon as he touches any piece of equipment is immediately to play with it. Learning to get the equipment out and wait for further instructions is an important part of his education. It is also important to get the equipment in and out of the equipment room as quickly as possible in order to allow the maximum amount of time for the day's activities. The selection of student helpers should be done fairly; a good method is to rotate students by means of the class list.
5. After the activity is completed, and the equipment is put away, the students have a particular spot on which to line up before leaving. This is important for orderly dismissal. One person is designated as the line leader (again, on a rotating basis). These children must be given time to get organized, and to remove themselves emotionally from the physical education activities.

PROGRAM OF ACTIVITIES

To determine a particular program of activities it is best to think in terms of specific objectives to meet the needs of each class. An activity which one class may enjoy can be detested by a different class. Each class has to be treated separately. Their likes, dislikes, interests, needs, abilities, and group spirit have to be understood if program planning is to meet with success. Although specific activities cover a broad area, there are some helpful generalizations which can be made by age category.

The younger group (kindergarten to second grade), is more interested in those types of activities that emphasize the individual. As a general characteristic, the transition-adjustment class students lack cohesiveness and a group identity. They do not work well as a team, and the youngest group most exemplifies this characteristic. The only kind of group game which can be utilized is one in which the members of the group act as individuals rather than as team members. For example, these children enjoy simple tagging games, and they work well with the apparatus phase of gymnastics (Fig-7-1).

ESTABLISHING A PHYSICAL EDUCATION PROGRAM 115

**Figure 7-1
Learning How to Climb**

They enthusiastically engage in scooter activities. They find satisfaction in setting up road courses with traffic cones, bridges with boxes and large pieces of cardboard, and tunnels. Within these road courses they operate and maneuver their scooters. They enjoy creating their own games with large cardboard boxes as garages, houses, or forts, and their scooters as cars, trucks, and fire engines.

The games they play have to be simple, easy to understand, and have short directions. The children have a great deal of difficulty playing games where a participant has to wait his turn or where individuals are put out of the game. These types of games should be modified or avoided.

The middle group (third to fourth grade), is interested in basic team games, but again, they have to be the type of game in which the team members work on their own and do not have to function as a cooperating group. In other words, games can be utilized in which each team member is free to play the game on his own and the success of the team does not depend on the interaction of the team members.

They enjoy tagging games, modified games such as kickball and wiffleball, and activities which involve throwing a ball at objects such as Indian pins. They also enjoy the apparatus phase of gymnastics. As with the younger group, games in which players are put out should not be emphasized, although they can handle these types of games better than the younger group, and can also play games in which they have to wait their turn. The games they play should be easy to understand, the directions short, and the rules uncomplicated.

The oldest group (fifth to sixth grade), may become interested in team sports. At the beginning of the year, many of these children will want to play only the simple games they were involved with in the lower grades. These children are usually the least skilled and the most fearful about getting into physical activities. They have not attained the skills which most children have at their age and they are reluctant to show their ineptness. These are the children who need the special help sessions to bring their skills level and confidence up to a point where they can obtain satisfaction from participating with other children their own age. After the initial shock of participating is over, most of these children will enjoy the team sports (Figure 7-2).

Figure 7-2
Building Sports Skills

The boys like to play football, basketball, floor hockey, softball, punchball, and wiffleball. The games, of course, have to be modified and the rules kept to a minimum in order to avoid frustration. (This is especially true in a game like basketball which has intricate rules.) As skills are learned, the rules can be made more stringent depending on the particular group.

To determine specific games for the different groups, one can refer to any good text on elementary school physical education.

These may have to be modified and adapted, keeping in mind the interests of the class. Their needs, rather than any criteria of physical achievement, must dictate the choice of activities.

A problem arises when the majority of the group is ready for an activity, such as a team sport for the oldest group, but one or two are reluctant to try. It is here that the special sessions are valuable in helping these few come up to a skills level which will permit them to play with their peers with enthusiasm. The object is not to make them superior performers, but rather to help them derive some satisfaction from participating.

DIFFICULTIES LIKELY TO ARISE

The following are some of the problems which arise in working with the transition-adjustment groups.

1. Their attention span is very short, which makes it difficult to keep them interested in an activity. The teacher must always be ready to substitute new or different activities for one in which the group is losing interest.
2. The distraction threshold of the group is very low. This causes difficulty when there are extraneous stimuli in the vicinity of the teaching area. It also presents a serious problem when the groups are taken outside where distractions are more numerous.
3. Their interests and abilities are widely varied. It is unlikely that every individual will readily participate in an activity. Each child has to be treated individually, yet encouraged to participate and cooperate in terms of the wishes of the rest of the group.
4. Group cohesion is at a minimum. This means that in most cases there is no established team spirit or consensus. This makes teaching these students different from teaching regular classes. They have to be worked with to develop a collaborative group feeling.
5. A calm, smooth-running class can explode into chaos over a seemingly insignificant incident. The physical educator has to be aware of this; to be ready to step in at the first sign of trouble—and his solution must be a fair one.
6. The level of self-motivation is low. They will do very few things on their own. They need constant supervision. They seem to respond only to extrinsic direction and will initiate little as a

result of inner thrust. (Perhaps to become totally involved creates too large a threat of personal failure if they do not meet with success.)
7. Their frustration threshold is very low. They become easily discouraged and will give up without putting into the task the effort that is required to achieve even moderate success. Encouragement and patience are important on the part of the teacher. With games involving children being put out, special care should be taken to modify the game so that no one is out of the activity for very long.
8. They are reluctant to practice a skill. It is nearly impossible to have the class practice a skill required to participate in an activity effectively. The most that can be done in this area is to have them play the game and interrupt at different points to demonstrate how a particular skill can be performed more effectively, or to explain a particular aspect of game strategy. (The skill is taught, but having them practice it is the difficult part.) This is most often done through a lead-up or low organized game which is interesting to them and, at the same time; helps them learn the skills they need the most. Drill type activities meet with little success.

(Typical physical education evaluations on the students are in Appendix C.)

SUMMING-UP

Activities work best when they are geared to the performance level of the group, involve the whole group (with all individuals active), and comply with their needs and interests (Figure 7-3). Activities which have been most successful are those from which the children derive the greatest satisfaction (which flows from success), and receive the least amount of frustration. This evidently requires a custom-made program in which the children play a role in the planning. Some of the activities which have met with a degree of success are the following:

Low Organized Games

Brownies and fairies	Duck, duck, goose
Squirrels in trees	Cat and rat
Tag	Dodgeball
Midnight	The target
Spider and flies	Guard the castle

ESTABLISHING A PHYSICAL EDUCATION PROGRAM　　　　　　　　　119

Low Organized Games (cont.)

    Flowers and wind　　　　　　　　Boundary ball
    Crows and cranes　　　　　　　　Medical war
    Jump the shot　　　　　　　　　　Dog catcher

Individual Activities
  Jump rope
  Gymnastics
    a) Apparatus (stunts and exploration)
      Rings　　　　　　　　　　　　Balance beam
      Ropes　　　　　　　　　　　　Parallel bars
      Climbing pole　　　　　　　　Mini-tramp
      Horizontal bar　　　　　　　　Side horse
                             Movement to music
    b) Tumbling activities　　　　　　Ball work
      Scooter activities

Team Games
  Football　　　　　　　　　　　　Softball
  Soccer　　　　　　　　　　　　　Wiffleball
  Basketball　　　　　　　　　　　Floor hockey

                Volleyball

Figure 7-3
Gross Motor Development

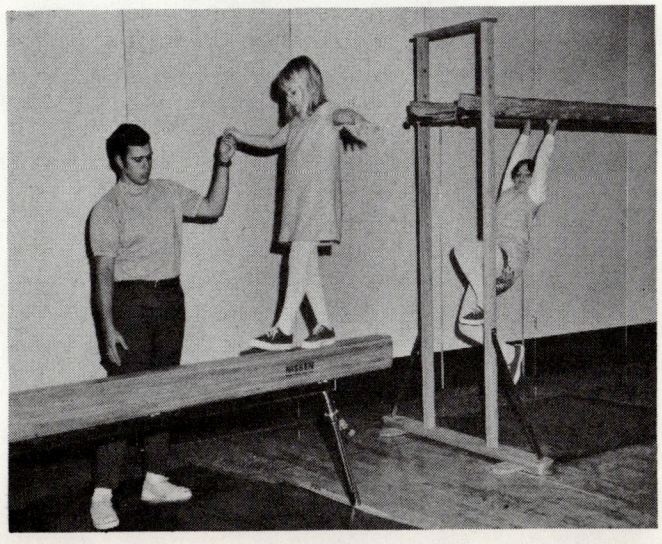

Working with disturbed students over the years, one observes how physical education can be one important door to their physical, mental, emotional, and social growth.

EIGHT

The Importance of Art Education in Transition-Adjustment Classes

This chapter was written by Mr. Edward A. Gargiula, elementary school art education teacher.

Because of its unique nature, it is difficult to experience the full impact of this vital program in art unless you, as a teacher, actually live with it.

At first, there is a fumbling for direction. Later, one's confidence grows. Frustration is a common feeling when working with disturbed children, but soon this turns to gratification as the results begin to show.

With transition-adjustment art classes, the approach and goals are different from regular art classes.

In the regular art program, the child is placed in an environment designed to stimulate motivation and interest in art concepts and media. Hopefully, this will foster within the child an attitude favorable towards art, resulting in a permanent appreciation and understanding, and providing a basis from which further study in later grades can be meaningful.

ART AND BREAKTHROUGHS

In transition-adjustment classes, however, art is used more as a tool; a means to an emotional end. Art can reach out to help these children. It can capture the chaotic enthusiasm of the extravert and soothe his unleashed emotions. It can give voice to the unspoken ideas of the introvert and bring self-assurance.

Donald was difficult to reach. His interests would fluctuate from minute to minute. He would go to any lengths for attention; even when he received this attention he was not satisfied. This child was disruptive and impossible to predict. Donald was discussed at team conferences. No one seemed to have much success reaching him.

While working on a piece of clay in the art room one afternoon midway through the school year, Donald accidentally dropped a pint jar of ceramic glaze all over the table, the floor, and his new shirt and pants. He apparently expected a good tongue-lashing, and seemed very surprised when he did not receive it. The art teacher had him come up to the sink and helped him wash his soiled clothing. This incident seemed insignificant at the time, but from that day onward Donald and his art teacher enjoyed a more favorable relationship. He assumed a leadership role, but not in a bossy way, helping other children in the class with their projects. Although his behavior did not last at this high level, it has never reverted to where it was before the glaze was spilled.

Then there was Laurie, a girl who would never talk to the teacher, and who would rarely speak to any of the other children in her class. One afternoon late in the school year, while the class was working with clay, the teacher noticed that Laurie was flattening her clay into the shape of a pie. Laughingly, he asked her if she was making a pizza. He was expecting the usual silent response, but much to his surprise, Laurie turned to him and said, "Yes, would you like a piece?" He could not let this unexpected conversation stop, and he questioned her about the pizza recipe. She continued to talk, much to the amazement of her classmates. While they were conversing, her classroom teacher heard Laurie talking and could not believe it. Her art teacher asked her to explain the recipe to him, which she did freely. From that time on, Laurie would speak to both of them, although never as freely as she did that first day.

These two examples illustrate situations where breakthroughs were made in the art education program. It is possible that these incidents could have occurred in any other place, at any time, but they did happen in art while the children were involved in a creative process.

An artist speaks by using words, but his work of art speaks because it exists. One can reveal innermost desires, fears, loves, hates, and drives in the art object that he produces. Art is a reflection of the personality of the artist.

Among emotionally disturbed children, there are those who have difficulty making themselves heard. Perhaps they are shy, afraid, or self-conscious of their speech. Art gives them the opportunity to communicate. Through their art work, these children can whisper, talk, or shout without fear.

The students in the transition-adjustment classes have much that has to be said. One must know about each child if he hopes to help him. Record folders, parents, and doctors can supply some of the necessary information, but to hear the root of the problem one must listen to the child.

Each time an art project is completed, the student exposes bits of his inner self. What does the child think of himself, his parents, his teachers? How does the child see himself in relation to others? What does he find pleasure in? What troubles him?

Most children enjoy working with art materials. As the medium is manipulated, the child's feelings can be expressed. He becomes totally involved in a creative experience. And, as he continues to work, he will unfold his real and unreal world before us.

When the child is behind academically but shows some artistic ability, and the rest of the transition-adjustment class team feels the child is ready to begin farming out, it may help to place him first in a regular art class. In this way, he is with new children but the environment is familiar, and he will feel more secure in an area where he can constructively apply himself. He can win the favor and recognition of his new classmates because they will appreciate his ability just as his own classmates did. Once success is achieved in this area, the child can be farmed out into other subjects.

In the art room, the transition-adjustment classes adhere basically to the same rules as do the regular classes. However, allowances are made, based on the individual needs of the class members. For instance, if a withdrawn child begins to act up during class time, his actions are not as likely to be stopped. You might let him go on for a while; then, in a discreet way, settle him down. Always lend encouragement to favorable behavior; that is behavior which is favorable for a particular child.

THE VALUE OF WORKING WITH WOOD

The projects that the children work on are similar to those available to regular classes. However, additional projects are possible because of the small size of the transition-adjustment class, and there are opportunities for greater variety.

Woodworking, for example, would be a difficult project to run in a regular class of twenty-five to thirty students. The amount of tools, wood, materials, cost, and supervision necessary makes this activity impractical at the elementary level. However, with eight children in a class, wood projects are not only practical but are also worthwhile for the students. It enables them to display their mechanical ability, and to create freely in a medium that is not generally associated with elementary education.

Often this activity may justify itself merely for the sake of allowing these children the time and place to let out their frustrations and pent-up emotions. Pounding a nail can serve a far greater purpose than holding two pieces of wood together. Children have been heard giving human identity to the wood that is being hammered with a vengance. Emotions are released in a more constructive way.

The wood and tools are used in the accepted manner. If they are not, the children know that they will not be allowed to continue using these materials. The tools are fine ones. Quality is important because we do not want to create frustrating situations; nothing is more frustrating than a tool that does not perform its function properly.

Many interesting and creative projects have been turned out by transition-adjustment classes. One class created a 3-by 5-foot wood construction that was cooperatively done by all members. They worked on this project during their spare time at the end of art class. After it was painted and ready to hang, they, as a group, decided to present their project to the transition-adjustment class director for his office where it now hangs—admired by all those who see it.

THE FASCINATION OF CLAY

Ceramic clay, like wood, is extremely popular with transition-adjustment class youngsters (Figure 8-1). In fact, working with clay is the most rewarding art activity for these children regardless of the age group. It satisfies artistic-creative needs as well as manipulative-motor skills. Clay, for some, is an art medium that provides an outlet for their feelings. They love to pound it, beat it, hit it, squeeze it, punch it, and even throw it, although the latter activity is kept within bounds.

THE IMPORTANCE OF ART EDUCATION 125

**Figure 8-1
Fun with Pottery Clay**

All children can create with clay, whether it be a foot-high vase or a simple flat plaque with a few lines drawn into it. Since they all achieve success to some degree, they are gratified and develop a feeling of accomplishment.

Regular classes generally have the opportunity to create only one item from the pottery clay during the school year, because of the number of children involved and the work load on the kiln and other equipment. The transition-adjustment classes, however, can have countless opportunities to use this versatile medium.

Once the youngsters demonstrate that they can handle the clay, the tools, and themselves, they are left more on their own to create, at their individual rate of speed, and for as long as their interest will allow. In most cases, the clay holds their attention for many weeks during the school year, with the result that many art objects are created from the pottery clay.

A CHOICE OF MATERIALS CAN BE LIBERATING

For those who cannot work with clay for a sustained period of time, there is a variety of other materials available. The way in which these materials and lessons are given to the transition-adjustment classes depends upon the class and the individual children. There is no set formula that one follows. It is an advantage to have several choices of materials available for the children. In this way they can be drawn to a particular material or combination of materials depending upon what will satisfy their immediate needs.

The transition-adjustment classes are given the opportunity to work with most of the same art materials that are used by regular classes at comparable age levels. Water colors, temperas, and finger paints are explored extensively (Figure 8-2). Although all art materials aid in the development and maintenance of motor coordination, the children have a special liking for the painting media. Colored sticks, pipe cleaners, and wire are among the structural supplies that easily lend themselves to projects that make use of building and manipulative skills.

Figure 8-2
Painting with Tempera

Drawing is a favorite pastime for children and the transition-adjustment classes are no exception. For this two-dimensional means of expression, the boys and girls favor crayons, cray-pas, charcoal, colored chalk, and pencils. The children in transition-adjustment classes use and enjoy a wide variety of art materials. This is done to maintain interest and to provide an atmosphere for expression and accomplishment.

Once they have selected their medium, they usually create what is important for them. Those who are outgoing will seldom take a suggestion. They know what they want to do. A more quiet child, however, might follow the lead of a friend. Rare is the time when a child does not wish to participate at all.

From time to time, a new lesson or material will be introduced to the entire class. The youngsters may not wish to work on this particular lesson immediately, but it is added to the choices they may wish to make in future art classes.

The freedom of choice gives many of the children a good feeling. They can relate to a particular medium, manipulate it, learn to use it correctly, find pleasure in the activity, and develop their inner resources. They can build on this foundation until they are able to broaden the scope and range of materials that they are working with, and to achieve the outlets they are seeking.

About once a month, if the teacher feels that the class is ready, a lesson will be taught in the same manner as in a regular class. This enables the teacher to check their attention span, to see how they will accept and follow specific directions, and to let them know what it will be like when they are farmed out.

Some transition-adjustment classes, because of the personality of the group, can be taught in the fashion of a regular class. However, there are those groups which cannot handle a variety of materials in a regular class atmosphere. They have difficulty following instructions. They need more time to prepare for the rigors of the regular situation. Gradually, they must learn to handle materials within the framework of reality limitations.

An art room is filled with a host of gayly-colored displays that give recognition to work done by students in the various classes. Open shelving holds many unusual and colorful materials. These items serve to stimulate and motivate the art classes.

Many emotionally disturbed children, however, will attempt projects without knowledge of how to use the materials or how to interpret the art concepts involved. A storage shelf will confuse such a child. They do not know where to start, what materials to use, or how to use them. These students can best be instructed in an atmosphere clear of distracting stimuli.

THE GOALS IN ART

Art education is an essential part of the transition-adjustment class program. It is one of the most important areas encountered by these children. Academic subjects do not come easily to most of these students and failure compounds their problems.

One of the purposes of the transition-adjustment program is to give these children self-identity and a feeling that they can achieve.

Art provides a versatile channel for this goal. It provides a creative direction for their drives, and a means to grow and find meaning in the environment.

When materials are offered, there must be something of interest for everyone. Once the child is sparked, whether it be self-motivated or stimulated through the efforts of the art instructor, he will experiment with the material.

As the materials are worked, the creative process is set in motion. Regardless of the end product, a feeling of accomplishment will be experienced.

Once a sense of pride in his art efforts is instilled in the student, he will want to show his work. He will feel more important. He will begin to develop a feeling of self-esteem which can gradually lead to inner aspirations and hope.

When this occurs, the child will be on his way to farming out. This is what the transition-adjustment class program is all about—providing the child with a sense of importance; giving him a chance to find satisfaction; showing him that he can do the task; instilling in him a feeling of worth; and creating in him the desire to rejoin the regular school program.

NINE

Materials and Equipment

The educational world is inundated with every conceivable form of gadgetry touted to promote learning. The materials discussed in this chapter are those with which a measure of success has been experienced over a period of years in working with disturbed children.

Craft activity in itself is not original, nor is it a panacea for reaching these children. However, it is a useful technique in teaching emotionally disturbed children. Carpentry is a pivotal point of the transition-adjustment class crafts program. Both hand tools and power machinery are employed.

In the typical program, proficiency in the use of hand tools and in the completion of hand-finished projects is usually developed. Many programs do not progress beyond the hand tool stage—especially with the younger children. Programs which make use of power tools usually graduate to the more sophisticated machinery after the child has developed skills with the hand tools.

In the transition-adjustment class program the procedure is reversed.

POWER TOOLS BEFORE HAND TOOLS

The novelty of using power tools excites and interests these children. Their use in the initial stages enables the transition-adjustment class students to complete and see their finished product sooner. Working with the power jig saw, for example, makes it possible for these children to prepare their basic materials quicker and more easily than cutting it with hand saws. When preparing a project for finishing, they use the power sander, avoiding the lengthy and fustrating task of sandpapering by hand.

The use of power tools is, in itself, a status-associated activity. The children know they are being given a responsibility and a trust which is something they have rarely experienced in the past.

Another reason for quick introduction and development in this area is its fringe benefits. As the transition-adjustment class students become proficient with power tools, they become "teachers" in the sense that they can help students from other classes in their use.

Regular class teachers, following explanation and orientation by the transition-adjustment class teacher, see the potential for enhancing their own curriculum through the use of the equipment available in the transition-adjustment class.

The teachers may send their students to the transition-adjustment class at a prearranged time for the purpose of making a project in mathematics or science (for example, sun dials, plywood maps, geometric designs, or clocks). The transition-adjustment class students take over at this point. Under the guidance of the transition-adjustment class teacher, they instruct the regular class children in the use of the power machinery. They discuss the safety rules and procedures to follow, and help the students with their initial projects.

Through interaction between classes, teachers gain insights into the transition-adjustment class children and "adopt" them. These teachers become an essential part of the child's development when he is farmed-out. The relationship established between a regular class teacher and a transition-adjustment class child is an important factor in his rehabilitation.

SPECIFICATIONS FOR POWER TOOLS AND THEIR USE

The following is a list of power tools which have been put to good use, and an outline for their implementation.

Power Machinery

- Dremel jig saw, with a 15-inch throat, designed specifically for children.
- Black and Decker ¼-inch electric hand drill mounted horizontally on a stationary stand. It has a 5-inch power sanding disc at-

tachment. This drill can be mounted vertically on a stationary drill press stand. The stand has adjustments which permit raising and lowering of the power drill press.
- Black and Decker orbital finishing sander.

Power Machinery Implementation

I. Goals: The student develops
   A. Positive attitudes toward school.
   B. Concepts of safety, cooperation, responsibility, planning, perseverance, and concentration.
   C. Manipulative skills.
   D. Creative ability.
   E. Satisfaction in being able to perform tasks which are not performed by other classes who do not have this equipment.
   F. The drive to learn in academic areas through practical application; for example, in reading plans, measuring objects, and building projects.

II. Procedures
   A. Introducing machinery to children:
      1. Names of power tools and corresponding hand tools.
      2. Each machine is demonstrated and a comparison between the hand and power tool is made.
   B. Thorough indoctrination in safety (Figure 9-1):
      1. Children are alerted to the potential dangers of machinery. (In order not to create undue fear on the part of the child, it is pointed out that these machines are no more dangerous than other machines with which they are familiar. For example: "A bicycle is a machine. It is used for transportation and pleasure. If a rider goes out on a busy highway or does not pay attention when he is riding, he is putting his life in danger or he may get seriously hurt. Clearly then, it is not the fault of the bicycle (machine) if the rider gets hurt. It is his own carelessness and lack of attention to what he is doing. It is the same with the machinery that we are now going to use.")
   C. Safety guides
      1. For the teacher:
         a) Check all equipment. Look for frayed wires and loose connections. Plug in and see that each machine functions properly beforehand.
         b) Adhere strictly to guides set up for children so that they learn through example.
         c) Supervise closely but with as little teacher interference as possible.

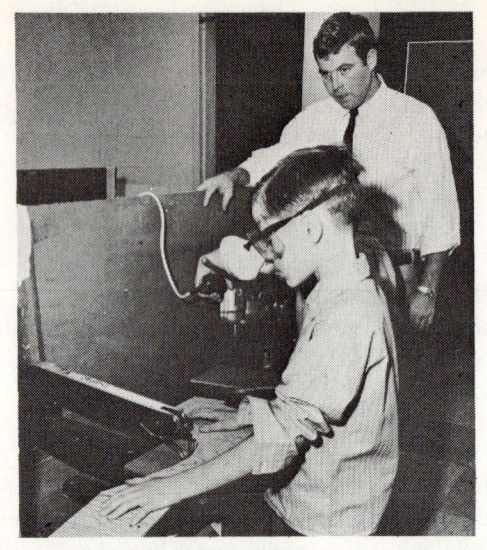

**Figure 9-1
A Woodworking Project**

    d) Set up penalties for those children who violate the guidelines.
2. For the children:
    a) No child is to use the machine without permission.
    b) Articles hanging about the neck must be removed.
    c) Sleeves must be rolled up above the elbow. Watches, bracelets, and rings must be removed.
    d) Hands must always be dry before beginning to operate a machine.
    e) When a machine is in operation two children must be present: the operator and a buddy to watch for emergencies.
    f) Speaking is kept to a minimum and should be only about the task at hand
    g) Safety goggles are always worn.

SOME SIMPLE POWER TOOL PROJECTS

The initial projects are simple to produce. Yet the final product suggests a degree of skill that is gratifying to the children.

For example:

1. The child crayons a picture or a design on a ¼-inch by 6-inch by 6-inch piece of plywood. He cuts it on the jig saw and, within minutes, he is glowing with pride at his puzzle. Another

MATERIALS AND EQUIPMENT 133

variation is to have the child paste a picture on the plywood and cut out the puzzle.

2. The child cuts out a free form name plate from a ¼-inch by 4-inch by 4-inch piece of plywood. A ½-inch by ½-inch piece of pine wood is glued to the bottom edge for support. (See Figure 9-2.)

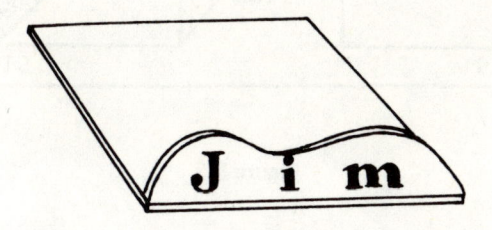

Figure 9-2

3. Creative wood sculptures are made by cutting various shapes out of plywood and gluing them vertically onto a flat base.

There is a variety of plans available from the Dremel Company. However, as the children develop facility with the machinery, they create their own special projects.

Following is an example of a detailed plan made by a student.

Directions to Make a Paper Tray

Materials: ½-inch thick wood, hand saw, hammer, finishing nails, Elmer's glue, sand paper, and clamp.

Step one	-	Cut 4 pieces of wood, 11½ inches by 2½ inches, for sides.
Step two	-	Cut 2 pieces of wood, 9½ inches by 2½ inches, for backs.
Step three	-	Cut 4 pieces of wood, 8 inches by 3/4 inches, for holders.
Step four	-	Cut 2 pieces of masonite, 11½ inches by 9¼ inches, for bottoms.
Step five	-	Apply glue and nail one of the backs to the back of the masonite. (See Figure 9-3.)
Step six	-	Take two of the sides, glue, and nail to the sides of the masonite.
Step seven	-	Set upper level of paper tray aside.

Figure 9-3

Step 5 — MASONITE (BACK, SIDE, SIDE)

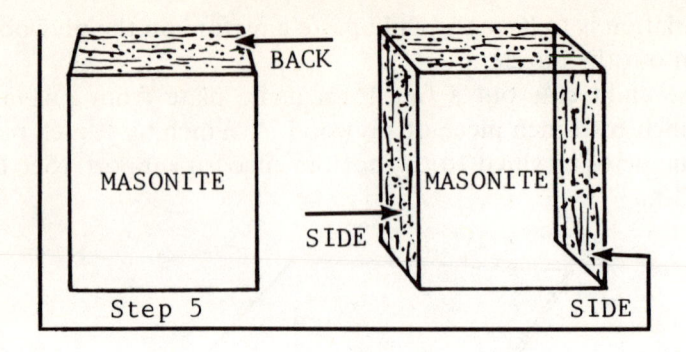

Figure 9-3

Step eight   - Repeat procedure of steps five and six. (Don't forget to put the glue on.)
Step nine   - Glue and nail two of the holders to the sides of the two levels about 2 inches away from both ends. (See Figure 9-4.)
Step ten   - Repeat procedure of step nine on the other side of the two levels.
Step eleven - Sand down completely.
Step twelve - Paint or stain.

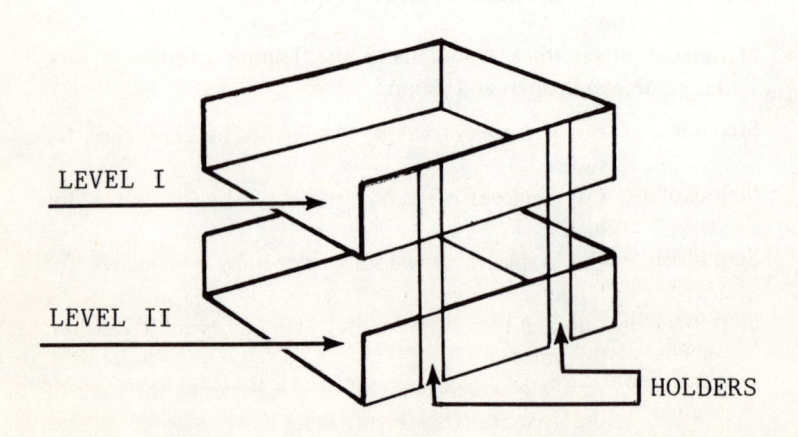

LEVEL I, LEVEL II, HOLDERS

Figure 9-4

Woodworking Equipment

1 - Workbench
2 - Bench vices
1 - 16-inch ten-point crosscut panel saw
1 - 20-inch ten-point crosscut panel saw
2 - 7-ounce nail hammers
2 - 13-ounce nail hammers
4 - 3-inch opening C clamps
4 - 5-inch opening C clamps
2 - 8-inch half-round cabinet files and handles
1 - hand drill
1 dozen - drill points, assorted sizes
1 - 6-inch try square
1 - 1-foot adjustable try square
2 - 2½-inch screwdrivers
1 - 6-inch slip joint pliers
1 - 6-inch needle nose pliers
1 - 6-inch adjustable wrench
2 - coping saws
2 - 6-foot carpenter's rule

Supplies for Woodworking

2 dozen - Coping saw blades
50 sheets - fine sandpaper
12 pints - Elmer's glue (in squeeze bottle)
3 pounds - nails (3/4 inch; 1 inch; 1¼ inch)
   Other sizes depending upon the project
12 - 1-inch paint brushes
Variety of wood stains
Variety of outside latex paints (for such projects as house signs, bird houses, and weather vanes.)

Construction Materials

1/4-inch plywood
1/2-inch plywood
1/8-inch masonite
1/2-inch pine, 6 inches to 8 inches wide
3/4-inch pine, 2 inches to 8 inches wide
9/16-inch Tri-wall (Manufactured by Tri-wall Containers, Inc., One Dupont Street, Plainview, New York) This is a relatively new product with excellent potential for classroom use. Tri-wall is a three-ply industrial cardboard strong enough to construct a variety of practical, creative classroom objects such as tables, screens, bookcases, movable carrels and rocking horses.

The integration of woodworking with academic areas is a vital factor in the acceleration of the transition-adjustment class students' total learning.

THE ROLE OF PLAY MATERIALS

Play materials rank high on a transition-adjustment class budget. Play means more to the transition-adjustment student than it does to other children. For him, it is one of the most important things in life. It is his escape from a world perceived as harsh; his way of bringing out his feelings, deep worries, and tensions; and his chance to express his potentials to create and to construct. Play is an essential component in his overall development.

An ample supply of play material is, therefore, available for use in the transition-adjustment class. All of the play materials that are not in use are kept under lock and key and distributed only at appropriate times. This material cannot be left visible and accessible in the room as it would distract the students during work periods and would soon be lost or destroyed.

Each transition-adjustment class has a corner of the room set aside for the children during "free time" or for one or two children during certain periods of the day. Activities like block building, with wooden or cardboard blocks, and making forts and model cars and trucks, take place in this corner with the younger children. A rug on the floor minimizes noise. The children are made aware of the limitations to be observed and rules to be followed when playing in this corner.

They are not to extend their buildings beyond the rug area. To do so would result in noise, interference with other activities, and danger because of possible tripping and falling over these projections. By setting "rug limits," the student is helped to develop inner controls.

Buildings are also limited "to the waist" in height. Thus, the crashing down of blocks, which could result in injury and fights among the children, is avoided. The impulse to destroy high towers is one they find difficult to resist. These children are helped to learn to control their impulses which frighten them when they get loose.

Materials to be used for play corner activities include:

1. Lincoln logs
2. Large cardboard building blocks
3. A half-set of large wooden blocks

MATERIALS AND EQUIPMENT

4. Boxes of small wooden blocks
5. Bags of soldiers, Indians, and cowboys
6. Plastic and wooden trucks, cars, and airplanes
7. Dolls
8. Dollhouse
9. Doll furniture
10. Play stove, refrigerator, sink, ironing board, and silverware

Also available in the classroom is a steel sand table. The students use this table for a number of activities. It is recommended that the table not be filled with sand until the class has learned to function as a group and to follow the rules governing play activity.

Play materials that children can use at their individual desks or at tables include:

1. Tinker toys
2. Checker and chess sets
3. Lego blocks
4. Mosaics
5. Puzzles (Teachers may shy away from puzzles since pieces invariably get lost. Allowing time for cleanup, together with close supervision, helps to avoid losses. By numbering each puzzle and its pieces with a magic marker, two or more puzzles can be easily identified if they are mixed together.)
6. Landscape peg sets
7. Cubical counting blocks and Cuisenaire Rods. (These materials are used in mathematics but the children also enjoy building with them at their desks.)
8. Puppets
9. Hammer and anvil sets
10. Anagrams
11. Bendable rubber families
12. Crayon and drawing paper
13. Modeling clay plasticine
14. "Space Maze" and "Shoot the Moon" games (These games increase concentration, perseverance, task completion, and visual-motor coordination. They have a built-in reward system in terms of the student's ability to manipulate a steel ball along a designated path towards a set goal. And the students enjoy the challenge the task presents.)

Play materials that are used for physical development and coordination include:

1. Bean bag games
2. Clayball (A teacher-developed game. A target is made out of plywood and the children knead clay to the point where it will stick when thrown at the target.)
3. Balancing board
4. Rocking boat
5. Play tunnel
6. Climbing ladder
7. Punching bags (One small bag permanently attached to the wall; one large bag—a mattress enclosed in a duffel bag.) An excellent release for aggression.
8. Chinning bar attached to the closet
9. Pogo sticks

Other materials that are used during free periods include:

1. Two painting easels (This permits four children to paint at one time.)
2. Woodworking activities
3. Various craft materials:
    a) Craft sticks
    b) Pipe cleaners
    c) Wood glue
    d) Material for leather craft projects such as comb cases, wallets, and pen holders
    e) Modeling clay
    f) Stencils for letters, animals, and designs
    g) Put-together-yourself kits
    h) Beads and laces

OTHER MATERIALS HELPFUL FOR LEARNING ACTIVITIES

Audio-visual materials serve a useful purpose with transition-adjustment class children. Academic materials involving sight, sound, and other sensory channels are valuable.

Here are some examples:

Audio-Visual Equipment

    1 Wallensak tape recorder

MATERIALS AND EQUIPMENT

1 Multiphone panel—rosebud
6 Headphones
1 Phonograph with external jack
1 Bell and Howell Language Master with card sets
12 Blank tapes
1 Controlled Reader Jr. with Filmstrip sets

School audio-visual equipment should be available for use in the transition-adjustment class. This includes a 16 mm movie projector, filmstrip projector, overhead projector, screen, duplicating machine, primary typewriter, and opaque projector.

SPECIAL ACADEMIC MATERIALS

These materials include a complete set of ditto master workbooks along with transparency workbooks for each grade level. They are available from the Milliken Publishing Company (St. Louis, Missouri), the Hayes School Publishing Company (Wilkinsburg, Pennsylvania), and the Continental Press (Elizabethtown, Pennsylvania). These workbooks cover all academic areas.

The following booklets from Education Service, Inc. (Stevensville, Michigan) describe games and activities to motivate and create interest in various academic areas;

a) *Spice* (Language Arts)
b) *Probe* (Science)
c) *Plus* (Arithmetic)
d) *Spark* (Social Studies)

Types of reading materials include:

Weekly Reader Practice Books
Eye and Ear Fun Workbooks (Webster Division, McGraw-Hill Book Company, New York)
New Practice Readers Books A, B, C, D (Webster Division, McGraw-Hill Book Company)
Webster Kit 20 (Webster Division, McGraw-Hill Book Company)
SRA Pilot Laboratories (Science Research Associates, Inc., Chicago, Illinois)
Barnell Loft's Specific Skill Series (Barnell Loft, Inc., Rockville Centre, New York)

MISCELLANEOUS MATERIALS

1. Safety-shear paper cutters (less dangerous than the lever type)
2. Planters (Economy Crafts, Flushing, New York)
3. Pet supplies
    a) 10-gallon aquarium
    b) animal cages
    c) fish, hamsters, gerbils, mice, and guinea pigs
4. Crayons
5. Rulers
6. Scissors
7. Paste
8. Glue
9. Masking tape (various widths)
10. Pencils (2 gross for each class—necessary due to misplacement, karate, and chewing)
11. Brushes (½-inch easel)
12. Colored chalk
13. Construction paper
14. Finger paints, water paints, and tempera paints
15. File cabinet with lock
16. Portable blackboard
17. Hot plate

As the students progress in their academics, they will be supplied with materials and books at their learning level. Therefore, money must be set aside for use during the year for these items as well as for science experiments, lumber, nails, pets, field trips, and class picnics.

The materials and equipment listed in this chapter do not include all of the materials or sources available. The teacher should, in the final analysis, select material according to his experiences and the specific needs of his students.

BUDGET AREA CONSIDERATIONS

So as to get a picture of the finances involved in the program, Appendix D details:

1. First Year Budget for Two Elementary Transition-Adjustment Classes: (1967-1968)

2. Summer Elementary Transition-Adjustment Class Budget for Three Groups of Eight Students Each (1969-1970)
3. Proposed Elementary Transition-Adjustment Class Budget for 1970-1971 Eight Classes (in Addition to Existing Equipment and Supplies for Six Present Classes)

CONCLUSION

Whatever the materials may be, or the equipment used, if they are part of the warp and woof of the student's play-learning experiences, they will serve a vital function in his total development.

TEN

Teaching Techniques

The teaching challenge presented by the transition-adjustment class is basically one of combining eight or nine "ungroupable," emotionally disturbed children into a functioning group in which they can be helped to develop academically, socially, and emotionally.

To understand the students better, the transition-adjustment class teacher reads the cumulative record folder data on each child and talks with his previous teachers. If he attended a summer camp or school, his progress is noted. The teacher continually meets with the school psychologist to discuss his findings.

By reviewing the student's records, and discussing his behavior patterns with those who have worked with him, the transition-adjustment class teacher is better able to anticipate what to expect from a particular child and to set his plans for the first weeks of school. Once the teacher has worked with the child, he can reformulate his educational plan of action.

Experience shows that the emotionally disturbed child may make a rapid adjustment to the transition-adjustment class. The behavior change, in some cases, has been dramatic. This does not mean that the basic personality picture has altered, but rather that the emotionally disturbed child is responding to a setting that he desperately needs.

TEACHING TECHNIQUES   143

THE FIRST WEEKS OF THE TRANSITION-ADJUSTMENT CLASS PROGRAM

During the first weeks of school, the teacher does not concentrate on academic instruction but attempts to develop insights into each child's behavior. Gradually, he determines the best ways to reach the child. The first few weeks are spent, therefore, in organized games, arts and crafts, films, and woodworking projects—along with opportunities for free play. The objective is to reduce the child's tensions by providing experiences which he can handle and enjoy (Figure 10-1).

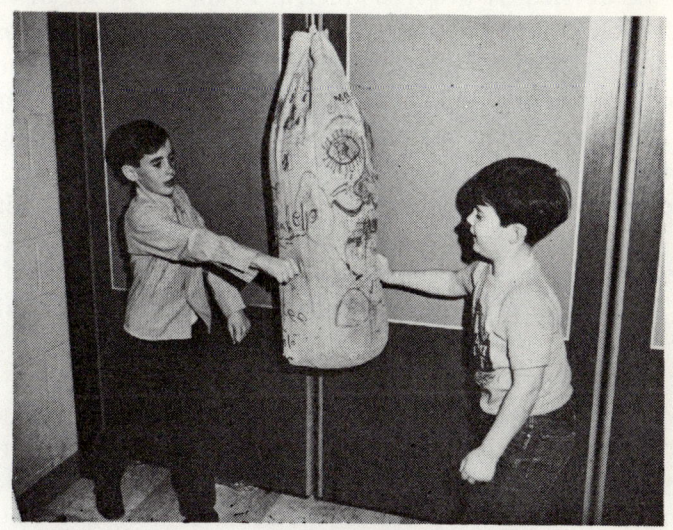

Figure 10-1
Letting Off Steam

The teacher is prepared and waiting for an opportunity to set a relaxed atmosphere. The first time the child draws a grotesque monster, for example, the teacher may print his own name on the drawing, with a comment like "I always thought I looked better than that." He then tacks the picture on the bulletin board. Soon the room may become a horror gallery of pictures of the teacher. Sometimes uncomplimentary phrases are attached to the drawings: "Mr. Richards is a pig," or "Mr. Richards is a slob." Each child tests the teacher in his own way. Each picture is a silent testimonial to a new relationship, a new kind of acceptance. In time, the drawings become less grotesque and the comments, "My best friend" or "The goodest teacher" begin to appear.

Perhaps one of the most startling discoveries to a new member of a transition-adjustment class is that he is permitted to engage in activities which before were considered taboo. He is allowed to participate in activities which formerly got him into trouble.

In the early stages of the year, one of the most fascinating experiments is the building of skyscrapers out of kindergarten blocks. The height is limited to waist high. Invariably, these structures are "accidentally" knocked over. Imagine their surprise when they are permitted to topple over the buildings—if they adhere to safety rules they themselves help to formulate. A game situation can then be devised. A tower is erected. From a distance of eight to ten feet, each child is permitted to slide a small block across the floor. The one who topples the structure over is the winner. The group and teacher participate together. Under these conditions, the children gradually come to accept the more stringent regulations to follow in the future.

Limits are placed on the student's behavior so as to help him develop a sense of where he stands in his environment. The structured approach is the most constructive in the growth of inner stability and group cohesiveness without which the class could not function.

The emotional problems the teacher encounters in the transition-adjustment class range from the extremely withdrawn to the aggressive, hyperactive, acting-out child. The withdrawn child presents relatively few problems in the initial stages of class organization. It is the living-out child who presents the greater obstacles. The basic technique to help to develop controls in the impulsive child is a quiet but firm approach, slowly moving along the road to a flexible yet structured school day.

Acting-out children are placed in the same class with withdrawn children as part of a mutually constructive experience. The withdrawn child tends to become more outgoing, while the hyperactive child tends to become calmer and to enjoy quieter activities as part of the group dynamic interaction—but this is the ideal and a long time coming.

Most transition-adjustment classes include more children who are disruptive. This is because the quiet child presents fewer problems in classroom management.

As school personnel become more aware of the symptoms of emotional disturbance, the withdrawn children who are marking time in regular classes will be referred for psychological evaluation as readily as those who act out, and will receive equal priority for transition-adjustment class placement (when enough special classes are available).

The starting-off period for the child and the teacher is a crucial one. Patience is the order of the day; slow and careful the motto. As the year rolls on, the students begin to settle into a learning groove. Changes in the child's attitude will manifest itself at home. He may become more buoyant in spirit and involved in learning. A child who formerly resisted school may now look forward to attending the transition-adjustment class.

THE ACTING-OUT CHILD

The acting-out child is the one most teachers find to be a severe challenge. He cannot accept limits. He may be no more disturbed than the withdrawn child but, in the regular class setting, he is harder to manage.

In order to help the acting out child in the special class, the teacher works to develop a positive relationship in the first weeks of school. This is the period of low pressure in which the child is presented with interesting activities. During this time, the teacher tries to find ways to help the child cope with his impulsive behavior. Techniques may range from sending him to another transition-adjustment class when he reaches the boiling point, to placing him in an individual study carrel, a cardboard enclosure that cuts down on outer stimuli and provides the child with a structured setting.

During the first few weeks, if the child is acting out but not significantly disrupting the classroom, intervention is kept to a minimum while the teacher searches for ways to work with him. Constant intervention in the early stages will result in frustration for both teacher and child and an oppositional struggle that will harden their positions.

Aggressive children want external controls to help them over their acting-out periods. They need to know that someone cares enough to set limits that will make them feel more secure. There are times when physical restraint (holding the child tightly) is necessary to prevent injury to himself or to others.

The structure of the class itself is a helpful aid in the struggle for control. The teacher is able to provide a closer one-to-one outer ego for the child than would be possible in a regular class.

The shorter school day with shorter work periods serves as a dampener on impulsive behavior, since the child is not as fatigued and on edge. Physically and mentally, there is a greater reservoir of control.

However, the task is difficult. The acting-out child will break many, if not all, of the rules set down by school authorities. He has to be helped, as does the regular class child, to try to conform to the regulations.

One approach is to review carefully, with the individual and the class, the reasons behind the rules that govern school and bus behavior. A group discussion with the children may iron out some of the confusion in their minds.

If the child is breaking the rules or conducting himself in such an antisocial manner that, in spite of the usual methods of enforcing the rules, he cannot respond, then he may be acting on something within himself that he cannot control.

Specific techniques to deal with the acting-out child develop as the teacher and child meet in the struggle for control.

Cursing within the classroom may best be met by ignoring it. It can become an attention-seeking device which is reinforced if the teacher reacts as the child wishes. Instruction as to why one does not use such language in places like the cafeteria must be given, since many of these children do not grasp that swearing overlooked in one situation is "off limits" in another.

Control of a situation is determined by the teacher's ability to control himself and to deal objectively with the child's behavior. The teacher does not want to become emotionally involved in the turmoil of the moment. His immediate goal is to produce a circumstance that will mitigate or alter the intensity of the outburst. For example, if George's frustration causes him to direct a volley of profanity at the teacher, the teacher's best retort might be to smile and say, "Where is that good paper we wanted to hang on the bulletin board?" Or, at another time, "Hey, don't call me by your first name. What happened to your hand?" Sometimes a recalcitrant student will put his body in an odd position as he expresses his anger. The teacher sits down and tries to duplicate the position. After a futile effort he says, "Boy, you're great, I can't sit that way. Would you teach me?" The objective is to accept the reality of the current situation while introducing a new element.

Hitting of other students and the teacher are behavior the teacher works to get under control as quickly as possible. Appropriate punishments are indicated. The child must learn this behavior cannot be tolerated; once he is more in command of his impulses he will feel that much better for it.

HOW A PUPPET GOT THROUGH TO A WITHDRAWN GIRL

The withdrawn child is gently helped to take a greater part in the class activities. The group is small enough so that the teacher can spend time to bring the withdrawn child back into the group activity when he begins to drift away. These children start to come out of their shell. They receive more attention than they received before. They do not have as much reason to retreat from reality because they do not have to grapple with subjects that are beyond their grasp and often empty of interest to them.

The children are given responsibilities within the classroom; for example, caring for the animals, running errands—activities which require them to come more into contact with their environment. They enjoy arts and crafts for it is an area in which they can express themselves and enjoy the activity. Initially, they are presented with projects that do not require sustained concentration to complete the task.

Through the medium of puppets, many children feel free to release their fantasy lives and to reveal their fears, hopes, frustrations, and conflicts. These projective materials help the teacher develop insights into the child.

One dramatic example of how puppets can serve to breakthrough a child's defense was experienced by a music teacher.

Mary had a history of withdrawn, nonverbal behavior in school by the time she was advanced to third grade. In the transition-adjustment class program, none of the staff was having success in getting her to talk. During a music class, the teacher gave each child a puppet, and a name for the puppet, for the purpose of acting out a song. Mary's puppet was called "Charlie." Each puppet was assigned a part to sing. When the teacher called on Mary she would not respond. The teacher finally asked "Charlie" if he was not feeling well since he was not singing. Mary shouted out, "No, Charlie's not sick. He's scared to death!" This experience served as an insight into her deep-rooted fears and provided the teacher with clues on ways to reach Mary. With puppets and tape recorder, Mary soon was able to talk to her classmates and her teachers to a limited degree.

THE ERRAND AS A TECHNIQUE

Another technique for developing confidence and responsibility is a hierarchy of errands. For example, the withdrawn child accompanied by another child, is asked to carry a message to an adjoining room. Through progressive stages, she then moves to the room at the end of the hall, to the cafeteria with the lunch count, and finally to the principal with a note. The same procedure is followed with an out going child to instill a sense of duty in carrying through with an assigned task.

In the initial stages of these outer-directed responsibilities, prearrangements are made with the teacher, nurse, cafeteria worker, or custodian who is to receive the note. The time that the child will arrive is specified. A withdrawn child might spend ten or fifteen minutes standing outside the door; an aggressive child might create havoc if provided the opportunity. The transition-adjustment class teacher suggests that the staff member reward the child with a compliment on the child's mission.

As a result of this technique, anxiety on the part of the withdrawn children in moving out into other school areas may be minimized or removed. On the other hand, aggressive children learn to carry out errands without incident. This responsible facet of behavior carries over to other school situations. Every small opportunity to help the child operate on his own, in an appropriate way, is a step towards independent, realistic functioning.

A DAY IN THE TRANSITION-ADJUSTMENT CLASS

There is nothing to take the place of an actual day in a transition-adjustment class to demonstrate the workings of the group. "Quiet days" for a transition-adjustment class teacher involve experiences that a person unfamiliar with the operation of the class would consider to be far from ordinary.

This is a description of an actual class day from 9:00 a.m. to 1:30 p.m. The children in this class range in age from eight to ten years.

>   When the teacher arrives at school, one hour prior to class time, he finds Charlie, one of the transition-adjustment class students, roaming the hall. "My mother brought me in early because she had to go shopping." *Charlie cannot go to the library or remain in the hall without supervision.* The teacher has Charlie accompany him to

class and gives him a written assignment to work on. He makes a note to himself to call Charlie's mother to explain to her that the school cannot be responsible for the child outside of class hours.

The teacher is called to the phone. A parent complains that her son was teased on the bus ride home the previous day. He came home crying and upset. She would not put him on the bus this morning. The mother was advised to bring her child to school by car, and the transition-adjustment class teacher assured her he would handle the matter.

At 8:45 a.m. the first bus arrives. The teacher meets his own bus. The bus driver states that she had difficulty with Ricky on the way home yesterday. He was yelling and cursing at people out the open window. The driver told Ricky that he will not be able to ride the bus if this behavior continues. "I understand that these children have problems, but I cannot tolerate the cursing." The teacher agrees with the driver and assures her he will have a talk with Ricky.

Ricky has been in the transition-adjustment class for two months. His behavior on the bus, and in the cafeteria, has created problems for everyone. Now Ricky has to be taken off the bus for a week to learn he must follow the rules.

At 9:00 a.m., the second bus rolls in with one child absent—an infrequent occurrence. In the classroom, the children put their belongings in the closet, turn in their homework, give the teacher their lunch money, and take their seats. Structure begins with the start of the school day. *When these children enter the transition-adjustment class program, they are not able to carry out simple tasks. Their belongings are all over the place, lunch money gets lost, and homework papers, if returned, disappear.* Lucy forgot her lunch money and Laurie said that Cathy stole hers on the bus. Cathy relinquishes the money at the teacher's request. She said she was "only borrowing it."

Ten minutes later, Sandra bursts into the classroom shouting, "I'm late. My mother forgot to wake me up." Sandra is a bright girl, with exceptional ability in some academic areas, but so disorganized that she cannot follow simple instructions. Her late arrival is taken for granted by the children and it does not upset the stability of the class.

Today, a principal and a psychologist from another school are visiting the class, at a prearranged time, after clearance with the principal and director. *When there is a work period, the teacher places a sign on the door, "Testing." An oak tag, appropriately decorated, is always in the door window so the students are not disturbed by other classes passing through the halls.*

The bulletin boards have the children's work sheets prominently *displayed, but there is a limit on other stimuli so as not to interfere with their attention. The room is situated if possible so that the class does not look out on the playground, or bus drop zone, for example, which are distractions to the students.*

Lunch count is next on the morning agenda. The menu is read to the children. They have a choice of peanut butter or bologna sandwiches. The trend is towards 100 percent bologna until Ricky makes the remark, "It comes from a dead pig." We now have 100 percent peanut butter.

The lights are put out. Confusion over the lunch count has caused some children to leave their seats. One boy is all set to play with the blocks. *Putting the lights out is a signal to the students that they are to return immediately to their seats and be quiet.*

During the flag salute, all of the children take part. One child leads the flag salute. *At the beginning of the year each student's name is placed on an oak tag strip, in alphabetical order, on the bulletin board. Later in the year, the children will make their own plywood name plates which are mounted on hooks on a finished panel of plywood. They also make their own name plates for their desks. The child at the top of the list is the one who goes on errands, leads the flag salute, heads up the line, and helps prepare and operate audio-visual equipment.*

The list is changed every fifth school day. Care is taken to ensure that each child receives five days at the top of the list. Adjustments are made for holidays or absences. At the end of the fifth day, the child who is first becomes last on the list.

Homework Is Checked

Following the flag salute, the homework is checked. Then it is discussed with the group and followed up on an individual basis, giving the children immediate reinforcement.

On the teacher's desk are two wire baskets: one labeled for classwork, the other for homework. Each child is given a homework folder, a file folder with his name on it. Inside the folder several sheets of composition paper are stapled. On this paper, the daily assignment is written by the teacher or the student. The folders are placed in the homework basket each morning by the children. After they are checked, a grade is recorded. The children are praised for good work. At this point, most of them look forward to homework—as do their parents.

One child "forgot" his work, another turned in a crumpled paper that he claimed his baby brother destroyed. These boys will have the opportunity to complete this work during the school day. *When a student does not turn in work that has been assigned, or if it is incomplete, he does not receive another assignment until the former one is finished.*

During homework checking time, one child reports to the class on *What's New*, a television program on National Education Television. Each student has a day assigned to watch the program and to report to the class on it. From the discussion that went on, it was apparent that many of the students were watching the show even though it was not assigned. The students select shows to watch for the coming week. A "Teacher's Guide to Television" is available from the National Education Association Magazine. Efforts are directed toward having the children watch worthwhile programs.

Science and Music

Following homework checking, the science period begins. The children have been learning about fire, its uses and its dangers. Today's lesson is on the elements necessary to make a fire. A transparency is ready for use with the overhead projector. To begin, the teacher reviews the previous materials. *The teacher never fails to be amazed at the retention exhibited by these children. If the material is presented clearly, simply, and meaningfully, they learn readily and retain factual information.*

At this point, Sandra wants to know if she can change her lunch order to a bologna sandwich. The teacher points out that it is too late. Sandra replies that she is going to get one anyway. The teacher ignores this remark and prepares to present the transparency. *The thought processes of these children are difficult to explain. The interjection of something irrelevant to the task at hand is common. Providing Sandra with the opportunity to pursue the bologna matter at this time would lead to a discussion apart from the scheduled science lesson.*

The science lesson goes well. Manipulative materials are not used in this lesson. The children are required to sketch a triangle showing the three elements necessary to make a fire. Their remarks relate directly to their life experiences. Two boys tell how they set the woods on fire. Their first attempt to get a fire going was by throwing firecrackers from high in a tree down onto the leaves. The dangers of these antics were pointed out to the children. The boys state how they went to a nearby house, took some gasoline from the garage, and poured it onto the leaves. They then climbed the tree again, lit rolled newspaper, and threw it down. The teacher pointed out that, in the second instance, the necessary ingredients for a fire were present. *Fortunately, a neighbor managed to extinguish the fire before there were any serious consequences.* As the music teacher arrives, the teacher makes a note to review the dangers of fire in the next science lesson.

Ricky, the newest member of the class, is not permitted to participate in music class today due to his disruptive behavior during the last music class. Ricky is sent to the other transition-adjustment class for the music period. Ricky must be made to realize that certain behavior is not tolerated in the transition-adjustment class. Therefore, he is excluded from the activity and the group. It is carefully explained to Ricky why he is being removed from music class.

There are times when the transition-adjustment class teacher may feel that the group is too unsettled to benefit from a special subject like music. He may stay with the class during the period or, through prearrangement with the special teacher, reschedule the period at a mutually convenient time.

Special subjects are scheduled, when possible, to break up the school day so that academic instruction periods are shorter. The goal is to increase attention span by gradually increasing work periods.

The Individual Work Period

There is a short break following music. The desks are then separated and individual assignments are distributed and explained to each child. The student has his own composition book and file folder; his daily assignments are placed in the book.

The teacher moves about the room guiding and helping each child. The children are not permitted to talk during this period. Any child who disrupts the class is not permitted to complete his work at this time. *Work now serves as a rewarding factor to the child.*

The children are provided with a "fun" seatwork activity if their assignments are completed before the period is over.

For this group, the work period lasts from forty-five minutes to an hour. Miss Roberta from the nearby university helps the teacher in working with individual students.

Following this period, the children usually go outside for a walk. These walks are taken around the school or playground. However, the day is rainy, and the children have a short recess instead in the classroom. After an exercise period, there is free time for approximately ten minutes.

Following this break, the children listen to a story read by the teacher. They are called upon to insert words they think will come next in the story. Their interest is high and they are kept on their toes because they do not know when they will be called on.

Time for Lunch

Preparation for lunch includes straightening the room and washing up. The children are encouraged to keep the room orderly throughout the day. They do not leave the classroom without cleaning off their desks and pushing in their chairs. They line up for lunch with the assigned leader at the head.

When walking in the hall, the transition-adjustment class children are expected to follow the same rules as the regular classes. Their teacher supervises them while they are going through the lunch line. The class takes the same tables every day, and their teacher remains with them throughout the lunch period.

In the cafeteria, the transition-adjustment class teacher helps to supervise the other classes. This action gains the appreciation and cooperation of the other staff members.

The transition-adjustment class children are allowed some leeway with regard to cafeteria rules until they learn to settle down. In order to avoid having milk containers stamped or straws blown through the cafeteria, the teacher allows them to bring the containers and bags back to the classroom where they may pop them. The class environment allows them ample opportunities to express themselves during the day; gradually their antagonism toward school rules subsides.

When they are ready, they may eat in the lunchroom without the teacher present as a special reward.

The After-Lunch Session

In some cases, following lunch, the children may be taken out for recess with the regular classes. Although the period is short and the transition-adjustment class teacher is present, this procedure has not generally been found to be of benefit to the children. The unstructured state of recess tends to upset the emotionally disturbed child. The "letting off steam" to permit the children to rid themselves of excess energy seems to work the opposite with many transition-adjustment class children. They become over-excited during recess and this behavior carries over into the classroom.

Today, following lunch, the class returns to their room where work in mathematics has been prepared for them. The children break up into groups. Two children work together on flash cards and their "daily accuracy sheets" with problems and computations they are able to perform. They are encouraged to aim for 100 percent on these papers.

Two other children work on individual assignments, while the remainder of the class receives group instruction on the board, followed by a seatwork assignment. The teacher walks around the room checking their work. This period lasts thirty minutes, and is followed by a group game. *The games vary from day to day.* The game today is Quizmo, which has constructive benefits in the mathematics area.

Following this period, both transition-adjustment classes join in one room for a film, an effective medium to teach these children. *By combining classes, they are provided with experiences in large group instruction.* Discussions take place prior to and following the film on how it relates to their own experiences. Some stare out the window or at the projector. Some suck their thumbs in the secrecy of the darkened room and seem to be in dreamland. Their lack of interest in reality is evident.

The Final Period

The final period of the day may include varied activities in class, in gym, or outside if the weather is warm. The day's events are discussed with each child. If the child has failed to complete an assignment, or has broken the rules, he is not permitted to take part in this period for as long as the teacher feels it is necessary. He is given the opportunity to complete work that he has not finished, and to discuss his feelings with the teacher.

If the period is to be outside, one teacher will take both classes while the other teacher remains with those children who have to complete their work or discuss their problems for the day. A teacher aide is invaluable at these times. When both teachers are outside with the classes, one can organize group games such as softball, kickball, and relays, while the other will supervise the general area where the children may wish to play with the playground equipment.

If the period is to be indoors, there is a wide variety of activities to engage in. A list on the bulletin board assigns each child to a particular activity for that day. They are not completely bound by the assignment but they are not permitted to interfere with any other child who is working in his assigned activity.

There is a rug in the corner of the room. If the younger children are playing with blocks, log cabins or soldiers, they are to do so on the rug where noise is kept to a minimum. Next to the rug is a fort made from Tri-Wall which the children assigned to this area may use. Two easels are kept in the room on which four children may paint.

Today, play is inside and the game closet is opened. Some children are permitted to choose the game of their choice; some are assigned to woodworking. *They are assigned for a week to ensure ample time to complete their woodworking projects—with the teacher supervising.*

One of the major purposes of the final period activities is to have the children leave school on a positive note.

Cleanup is begun twenty minutes prior to dismissal time. Cleanup assignments are listed on the board. The children should be given a five-minute warning that cleanup time is approaching. *Failure to clean up will lead to class restriction the following day.*

The room is cleaned, desks cleared, coats gathered, and the children are sitting at their desks when the lights go out to signal quiet time. They are reminded to take their homework. They line up for dismissal with the assigned leader at the head.

The dismissal time for the transition-adjustment classes should be separate from the regular classes so as to avoid the confusion and congestion that can result.

After the children are escorted to the bus, the transition-adjustment class teachers take an "unwinding period" over coffee.

The remainder of the teacher's day is spent in class preparations, parent conferences, or transition-adjustment class team meetings. During this time, by prearrangement with regular class teachers, children from regular grades may come to the transition-adjustment classrooms to use the special equipment or to complete woodworking projects. Also, certain students with areas of difficulty may recieve individual help from the transition-adjustment class teachers.

THE ADVANTAGES OF TEAM TEACHING IN THE TRANSITION-ADJUSTMENT CLASSES

One of the ideal arrangements for transition-adjustment classes is to set them up in such a way that the teachers may operate as a team. If there are only two classes in a district, it is advantageous to house them in the same school and to locate the classrooms adjacent to one another. Setting the classes up in this way allows the teachers to combine their talents while operating a flexible, dynamic program for the children.

The advantages of team functioning include:

1. Materials and equipment can be shared.
2. Individual student programs can be set up together.
3. Small and large group activities can be held simultaneously. During periods such as woodworking, when the group is limited to a few at a time, one teacher can work with the larger group.

4. An acting-out child can be sent to the other class for a cooling-off period.
5. Academics can be presented to the children who are ready while the other teacher works with the children who are not ready.
6. During large group instruction—science, for example—one teacher can circulate around the room helping individual children.
7. Many times a child placed in the older group can constructively help a younger child in academics or crafts.
8. An older child may profitably spend some time with the younger group. He may be emotionally younger, at an earlier academic level, or behind in his visual-motor coordination. On the other hand, a younger child may fit into the older group in a specific area.
9. Combining the classes for large group instruction enables the children to experience the type of structure they will eventually face in regular class.

There may also be a feeling of isolation for the transition-adjustment class teacher if he is the only special class teacher in the building. Team teaching presents the opportunity to discuss and solve problems that are unique to both teachers.

There are times when the teacher must get away from the class for a brief period. With the classes adjacent to one another, these breaks are possible. During a relief period one teacher can direct the two classes by moving back and forth. This procedure gives the class the chance to develop self-control.

THE INDIVIDUAL STUDY AREA

The designing of individual study areas, or carrels, in a transition-adjustment class serves as a creative structure for the emotionally disturbed child (Figure 10-2). An area where the student can be relatively free from extraneous stimuli is beneficial to the student's progress in personal organization and in academics (Figure 10-3). (A typical layout is shown in Figure 10-4.)

The carrels provide a feeling of security within limits. The areas also provide the children with the opportunity to vent their emotions without public display. Exterior organization is simplified for the student by limiting the area and the objects with which a pupil interacts. Academic progress is enhanced through quiet study. A

TEACHING TECHNIQUES 157

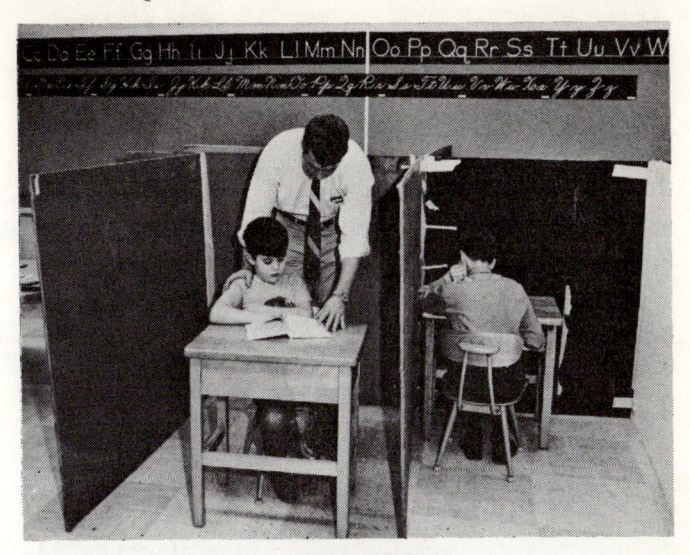

**Figure 10-2
The Individual Study Unit**

**Figure 10-3
Class Structure via Carrels**

student is able to concentrate more fully on his task instead of on the actions of the other students. The teacher can give individual instruction without distracting other students from their assignments. The students can work at their own level without fear of ridicule or criticism (real or imagined) since they work in private.

158　　　　　　　　　　　　　　　　　　　　　　TEACHING TECHNIQUES

THE USE OF TRI-WALL TO CREATE INDIVIDUAL STUDY AREAS

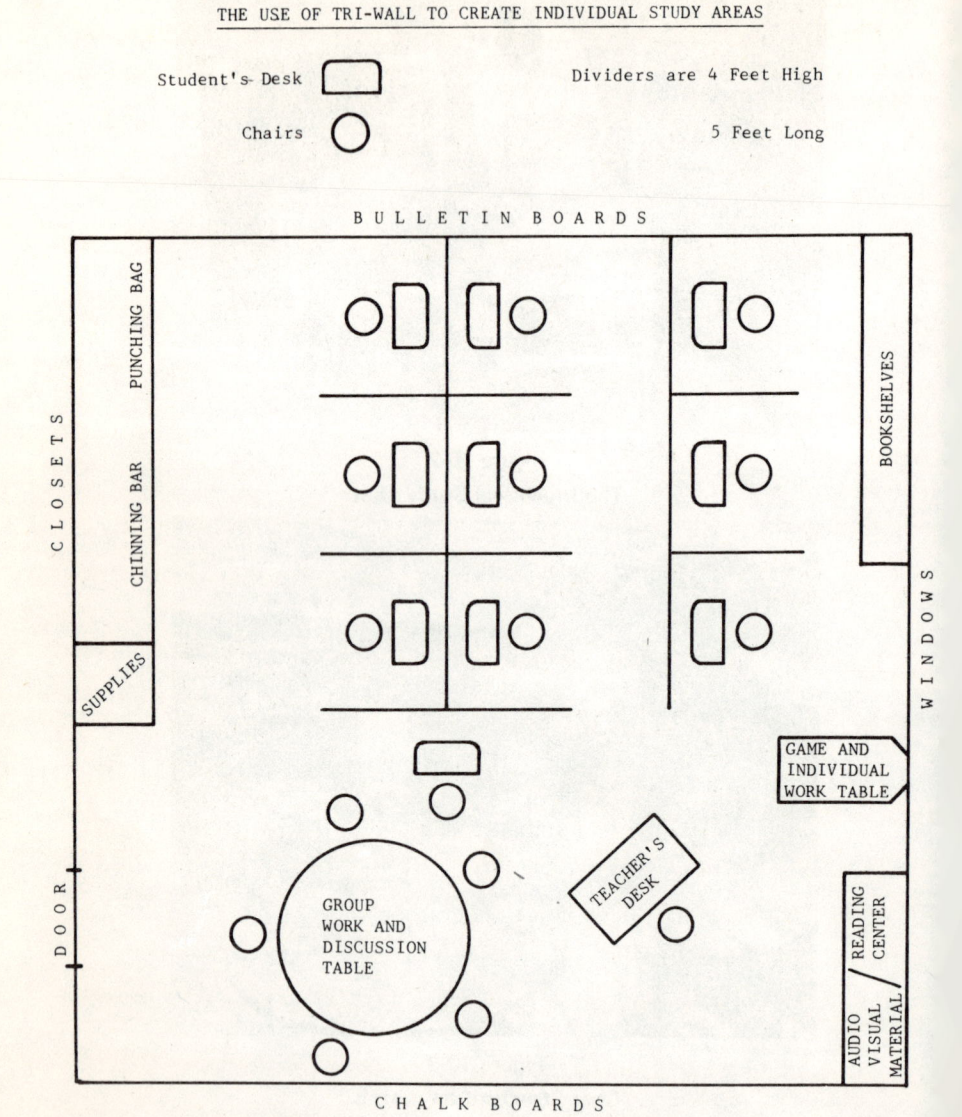

Student's Desk　▭　　　　　　Dividers are 4 Feet High

Chairs　○　　　　　　　　　　5 Feet Long

Figure 10-4
Designed by Mr. Robert McKee, Transition-Adjustment Class Teacher

Physical conflicts between students evolve to verbal conflicts, and eventually to coexistence and cooperation.

Finally, the individual study area gives each student a feeling of responsibility and involvement in the school because this area is "his."

ELEVEN

Farming Out

The term *farming out* is used to designate the procedure followed in reintegrating the student into the rest of the school community. In a sense, it begins the day the child enters the transition-adjustment class program.

In the transition-adjustment class, the child is never completely isolated from his peers in regular class. This program varies from others designed for the rehabilitation of disturbed children which are situated separate from the regular elementary building. In the transition-adjustment class program, for example, the child has lunch in the school cafeteria and participates in assembly programs, recess activities, and intramural sports. He is encouraged to take musical instrument lessons and to participate in band or chorus.

In the transition-adjustment class, the student finds a safer harbor in which to test his modes of behavior against the reactions of the group, and to grapple with ways to achieve his own felt needs in terms of the consequences of his actions. At the same time, he is surrounded by behavioral norms outside the classroom which provide pressure for more socially acceptable patterns of conduct. These norms offer the disturbed child opportunities for imitation and a yardstick by which he can evaluate his own actions. The accepted standards of behavior are reinforced within the ongoing structure of the transition-adjustment class.

Once a child has demonstrated by his attitudes, behavior, and academic achievement that he is ready to participate part time in a regular class, the farming-out process goes into operation. The recommendation to farm out is generally initiated by the transition-adjustment class teacher. However, the suggestion may come from any member of the school team who has observed and worked with the student.

REENTRY PROCEDURE

The first step toward farming out is an awareness of a change in the student's frame of reference, whether it is motivation, drive, academics, control of impulses, or social consciousness.

The data on the progress of the student is weighed by the transition-adjustment class teacher based on his perceptions and informal talks with other members of the school team. When it is clear that there has been observable improvement, the second phase begins.

This phase involves a team conference to discuss the pros and cons of several related questions:

> Is the change significant enough to warrant part-time placement in a regular class? If so, what are the child's chances of making the grade? Is the child's personal make-up such that part-time placement would tend to reinforce newly acquired attitudes and serve as motivation for further progress?

These considerations are vital. Premature placement and subsequent failure can result in a serious setback for the child. It would reemphasize his own feelings of frustration, defeat, and inability to function on a par with his peers. Rule of thumb is that the student be placed in a farm-out field where the educational cards are heavily stacked in his favor. For example, if he can barely read at the fourth-grade level but is sure of himself at the third, he will be placed in a third-grade reading class where he can handle the work with confidence.

TOUCHING BASES WITH THE CHILD

Once the school team feels the student is ready to be farmed out, the next step is to approach the child and assess his feelings about the proposed move.

In many cases, the answer is as direct as the question. "Yes, I want to," or "No, I don't want to." In either case, the positive or negative reply is not the final answer.

For example, a student who replies in the affirmative and works harder to improve himself is substantiating his "yes." He is ready.

On the other hand, the individual who replies "yes" but then shows a downhill pattern may be verbally going along with his parents' wishful thinking which he is eager to gratify so he can gain their approval and avoid their criticism. His overt actions reveal his true feelings and repudiate the verbal "yes." He is not ready.

If a child says "no," it may be his true feeling based on an appraisal of his own situation and current feeling level. He is not ready. But if the verbal "no" is followed by increased enthusiasm and progress, he may be set to make the move.

A "yes" or "no" is not taken at face value but is talked over in depth with the child to determine the true picture.

The decision to farm out is based on the school team observations and the reactions of the student to the proposal.

SELECTING A TEACHER

If the student meets the criterion for part-time placement, the next step is choosing the teacher who will best fill the needs of the child during the transition period. The building principal is the one with a thorough knowledge of the strengths, weaknesses, and personalities of his faculty; he and members of the school team who have worked with the child are in the best position to select the teacher. The selected farm-out teacher is then asked to cooperate in the rehabilitation program by including the child in her class for a specific period of time in a particular subject. The child will gradually stay for longer periods in that class or branch out into other ones. For example, if initially the "ice is broken" in a regular gym class, the next step may be placement in an art class or arithmetic in a regular class.

The choice of the teacher who will play a significant role during the farming-out period must be made with care. She is chosen in light of the child's needs and with her full cooperation. If the child is withdrawn, he may require a more friendly, freewheeling atmosphere while a more aggressive child may respond better to a highly structured setting.

The farming-out period is not only a crucial time in the life of the child, but it also carries emotional impact for the farming-out teacher, the transition-adjustment class teacher, and the students in his class.

The transition-adjustment class teacher and the regular class teacher are both involved with the child. The former, because of the implications of the student leaving the home base and taking a step forward to the mainstream; the latter, because of the responsibility shouldered in the move into her class. Both teachers have their own feelings riding on the farm-out move.

The other children in the transition-adjustment class react to the farming out of one of their members in various ways: angry it is not their lot; relieved that they do not have to face a situation they dread; spurred to try harder so they can get "promoted."

Parallel with the decision to farm out, the parents are called in for a conference to discuss the move. They are asked to note any feedback by the child that might result from the move.

Invariably, the parents are thrilled at the turn of events. Those parents who accepted the program if unwillingly become more friendly and cooperative. They see the farming out as a breakthrough of years of unhappiness and frustration brought about by their child's inability to cope with school, and their helplessness in dealing with the situation. A more relaxed attitude arising out of his achievement is reflected in their relationship with the child, and serves as a constructive ingredient in his development.

THE FARMING-OUT TRIAL PERIOD

As a general rule, the procedure is to first place the student in one of the special subject areas (art, music, physical education). There are two reasons:

1. Special subjects are given only once or twice a week. The child is given a breathing spell between his initial experiences in reentry. During this time, he has the opportunity to feel his own way; to analyze his position; to discuss his problems; and to get support from his transition-adjustment class teacher, the school psychologist, the farm-out teacher, and the parents. The more gradual the change, the more effective the end result.
2. Art, music, and physical education do not present the stress brought on by the pressures of academic achievement. The student is given an opportunity to adjust emotionally and socially to the new scene. Once this transition is accomplished, he is better able to cope with the tensions of academic subjects.

The first few days, or weeks, are regarded as the trial period. The term "trial" is not to be construed as meaning that the child is put under pressure either to perform to teacher standards or be "thrown out." On the contrary, it is a period in which the child "visits" a particular class. He has a chance to see how it goes and whether he is secure and capable of performing in the new setting. He makes the decision to remain or not. It may take several weeks for this decision to be forthcoming. By this time, the child is usually an integral part and accepted member of the farm-out class.

An organic process is at work. The student has been placed in a situation where he is developmentally ready to cope with the reality tasks at hand as part of a total program to build up his self-concept and ability to perform.

The transition-adjustment class teacher and the farm-out teacher work in close cooperation to provide a series of gratifying learning experiences for the child. The transition-adjustment class teacher is available to the student to give guidance, support, and tutoring—even when the child is in regular class full time. At the same time, the transition-adjustment class teacher is careful not to create a "teacher's pet" image that would arouse resentment among the others in his class.

The following report by a farm-out teacher presents some insights into the dynamics of a disturbed child and aspects of the rehabilitation process:

> It was very difficult for Frances to become accepted by the group. She came in late in the year (this is always difficult). She is much larger than the other students. She is very impulsive academically (answers questions before having thought them through, and so often is way off the mark), and is usually rather demanding of attention.
>
> Despite all this, she has been able to accept the rough spots; criticism and teasing from the children and admonitions from me. She does no more than blink to show her hurt, and picks up where she left off.
>
> She has learned to demand less. When I look quizzically at repeated requests, she will reflect—and then say, "but it's important," if it is.
>
> She has made a great effort to improve her handwriting and has succeeded. She has struggled with the new math and has not given up. She still has difficulty in all the above mentioned areas, but she is determined to keep her equanimity and sustain her effort, and is gradually gaining the respect of the class because of these qualities.

She has certainly gained my respect and affection; she is a valiant girl and a nice one.

This report concerns a girl who was placed in a transition-adjustment class at age nine. She was farmed out to a fourth-grade class at age eleven. When she entered the transition-adjustment group, she was not functioning in any academic area. Her speech was unintelligible. Her major activities alternated between crying and screaming, thumb-sucking, and starting fights with the other children. This had been the pattern throughout her school career. It had become progressively worse, so much so that the previous year's teacher had been forced to isolate the child from the group. The girl's desk had been placed in a corner. Now, in a transition-adjustment class two years later, in the farming-out stage, she is slowly finding her way. She *is* a "valiant girl and a nice one."

The progress made in a transition-adjustment class can only be determined by what the child was like when he entered and what he is like now. But the real test comes with his participation and achievement in the larger social setting. The farming-out phase of the transition-adjustment program provides the opportunities to build on the foundation of this program through gradual integration into the regular mainstream.

THE FARMING-IN PROCEDURE

An outgrowth of the farming-out program is a reverse procedure, *farming in,* which serves as an educational contribution to the rest of the school. When a child in a regular class is having situational problems, he is invited to spend a part of his school day in the transition-adjustment class after consultation among the principal, transition-adjustment class teacher, and regular class teacher.

Interestingly, these invitations are never refused.

So, for several days, or sometimes several weeks, the transition-adjustment group has a daily visitor. At some point, the visitor no longer appears. He gives a friendly "Hello" to members of the transition-adjustment class when they meet, or he may join them on the playground.

The visitor's problems? They appear resolved. Perhaps they would have cleared-up in any case. But visiting the transition-adjustment class spared him the painful procedure of trips to the principal's office and notes to his parents, and may have prevented the storing up of negative feelings towards school.

When the transition-adjustment class teacher has class from 9:00 a.m. to 1:30 p.m., for example, it is possible for him to see students from regular classes between 1:30 p.m. and 3:00 p.m. on certain days, to talk or tutor them on an individual basis.

CASE STUDY OF RON

The following case study shows in more detail the various stages in a disturbed youngster's progress from the vantage point of the principal and the transition-adjustment class teacher. The detailed planning that is involved before the child is placed in a transition-adjustment class is presented, together with the two-year transition program back into regular class.

Ron completed kindergarten with no particular problem recorded on his report card.

Something happened to Ron in first grade when he was faced with a more formal academic program. On his report card, his teacher observed that Ron has: "built up a small sight vocabulary, but he forgets words. He does not use word attack skills. He cannot do his number work. He cannot apply himself to any written work. He puts forth little or no effort. His attention span is extremely short and he finds it hard to concentrate on school work."

On the Gates Primary Reading Test, administered when he was six years, eleven months of age, he obtained a grade level score of 1.86 with the class median 3.0. He was twenty-ninth of thirty students in ranking.

Ron had few friends in his class. He treated the children roughly. Nevertheless, several children said that Ron would give them toys in an effort to win over their friendship.

The school team met to discuss various approaches to help Ron. The reading teacher evaluated his achievement and made suggestions to his teacher on how to work with him in this area. The school nurse-teacher found no record of any medical disabilities. A physical examination was negative. His vision and hearing were excellent.

The principal began working with Ron twice a week. During this time, he began to show more animation.

The principal worked with him in reading and arithmetic. After an academics and discussion period, they played tic-tac-toe, a game that Ron enjoyed because he was able to beat the principal. A slight smile would appear on Ron's lips whenever he played the game. His teacher reported that Ron settled down after these sessions with the principal and that he looked forward to them.

During this time, the art, physical education, and music teachers were attempting to break through to Ron. There was little progress, although the teachers were able to contain his outbursts. A great deal of staff time and effort was expended to accomplish this one goal.

In the meantime, the parents were consulted and agreed to a psychological evaluation. While he only obtained a stanine of 4 on the Stanford-Binet Intelligence Scale, Form L-M, with 60 percent of the scores above and 23 percent of the scores below this level, he was of a higher potential based on his ability to pass items above his age level. It was determined that Ron was emotionally disturbed.

His parents considered sending him to a military school where they felt he would be in smaller classes and would receive the military drill and training needed to help him get organized. The school team discussed with the parents the newly initiated transition-adjustment class program as an alternative, and the parents decided to accept his placement in this program.

Prior to Ron's entering the transition-adjustment class, the teacher met with the principal, Ron's regular class teacher, his special teachers, and the school psychologist. The transition-adjustment class teacher was provided with insights into Ron's behavior. He learned that in regular class Ron was not doing academic work. During instructional periods he would interrupt the teacher and disrupt the class by singing and uttering irrelevant remarks. He showed no overt response to reprimands by the teacher, either privately or in front of the group. It was clear that Ron, his classmates, and the teacher were at an impasse.

The teacher reported that Ron was physically harming other children and required constant supervision. It was necessary to keep him with her during recess or exclude him from the period. In the cafeteria, Ron would throw and spit food at the other children. He would pour soup, salt, sugar, or mustard on the other children's food. Most of the time he had to eat alone or with the teacher.

Substitute teachers noted that Ron was hard to handle. The teacher also had letters from parents of other children in her class, who were "shocked" at the stories their children were telling them about Ron's behavior.

In the latter part of October, Ron entered the transition-adjustment class on an "emergency" placement. The transition-adjustment class had its quota of children, but in Ron's case exception had to be made to the rule or Ron would have faced the prospect of exemption from school.

Prior to placement, Ron met with the transition-adjustment class teacher to discuss the reasons for the change.

FROM THE VIEW OF THE TRANSITION-ADJUSTMENT CLASS TEACHER

The first day Ron entered the transition-adjustment class he sat at his desk and followed directions with the group for about an hour. This was followed by what appeared to be a complete breakdown in behavior. He became hyperactive, noisy, roamed around the room annoying other children, and refused to sit down. He was placed in the back of the room away from the other students. He was given games to work with during the time the other children were occupied. The novelty of the equipment quickly wore off and Ron was soon sticking pencils in children or throwing things at them. An older student from the adjoining transition-adjustment class was assigned to sit with him and play games. This took the pressure off the transition-adjustment class teacher and allowed him to work with the class on academic subjects. The other children, annoyed that Ron could play games while they had to do their work, were reminded that they had the same opportunity their first week in the transition-adjustment class.

Ron continued to disrupt the class during the first day. While walking in the hall he would make funny noises and trip other students. In the cafeteria he went wild with his food, throwing and spitting. Limits had to be set, yet undue pressure was avoided in the early stages. The psychologist pointed out that Ron's aggressive impulses get away from him when he is under emotional stress, thereby increasing his anxiety. If he was on the verge of harming others, the teacher physically restrained him. When he started playing with his food, the teacher took it away from him and didn't give it back.

A conference was arranged with the parents on Ron's second day in the class. The mother presented the problems she was having with him at home and in the neighborhood. She was at her wits' end; she was thankful the school could offer the special placement to Ron. She believed the class would help to reduce the pressure on the family due to Ron's upset behavior. She stated that the neighbors would not allow their children to play with Ron. They even took turns meeting the school bus so that Ron would not have the opportunity to harm their children. Ron had the habit of hitting them at the bus stop with stones and sticks.

The mother said she would have the report on a recent visit to the doctors, sent to the school.

Plans were made for monthly conference meetings to discuss his progress. If anything came up before, the teacher and parent were to contact each other.

During those first days, Ron continued to have difficulty getting along with his classmates and adjusting to the new situation. However, Ron discovered that his attention-getting devices weren't getting the attention he sought. He also found that his new classmates were not so gentle themselves—they did not run to the teacher for help; they fought back. His classmates reprimanded him when he interrupted discussions and instruction periods. Ron soon gave up attacking the others when he realized he would get the same treatment back or his behavior would be ignored.

Ron made a dramatic adjustment to the class. He arrived on the fourth day happy and cooperative. He completed a handwriting assignment, sat quietly, and listened during story time. He actually enjoyed the stories once he sat still long enough to listen. The other children were encouraged to help Ron during free period and they soon had him started on a woodworking project. Ron was amazed when he saw that he was trusted with the tools. He continued to have difficulties, but not to the extent he experienced during the first three days.

On the first of November his day was exceptional. He got along with his classmates, had no difficulty in lunch, walked in the halls, and survived art and music without problems.

By November ninth, Ron had gone a full week without major difficulty. He was beginning to express interest in reading and he was taking part in other academic areas.

THE DIARY OF RON CONTINUED

December: Ron is still calm and doing well. He has serious difficulty in reading comprehension and can not grasp the simplest concepts in mathematics. He is reading on a primer level; although his sight vocabulary is good, he cannot understand what he reads. He enjoys playing with the younger children.

February: Ron is proud of his woodworking projects. He has made a sign for his front lawn as well as a birdhouse and a key holder. His parents are amazed at these accomplishments. His father has obtained some tools and is capitalizing on this interest by working with Ron at home. The father reported that Ron had rarely brought home work from school before or, if he did, it was a mess. Now he has so much work to hang up that his father had to erect a large bulletin board in Ron's room. The parents are so proud of his work that they have it also hanging in the kitchen.

In the classroom, Ron seems to be making a few friends, but he still gravitates toward younger children. He enjoys playing fantasy games with them; for example, acting out the *Wizard of Oz*.

Ron's attitude toward reading has improved. He appears interested in books, listens to stories, and is increasing his sight word vocabulary. He is using initial sounds to help unlock new words and, what is more important, he is attentive and willing to try during instruction periods.

Ron's progress in reading is discussed at a team meeting. The reading specialist, who previously had been unable to reach him, suggests that he may benefit from reading instruction at this time, due to the change in his attitude. It is decided to provide Ron with individual remedial reading instruction. He begins with bi-weekly sessions, gradually to be increased to twice-weekly periods.

March: Ron is attending remedial reading and he is moving along well in the sessions. He is attentive and responding to the one-to-one relationship. At another team meeting, his progress is evaluated. It is decided to place him in a small remedial reading class where he will participate in a group setting.

It is noted that Ron has been greeting his former teacher, Mrs. George, whenever he sees her in the hall or cafeteria. And he says "hello" to the other children in her class. As it turns out, Mrs. George's class has lunch at the same time as Ron's class. It is suggested that Ron eat lunch with his former classmates. There is ample supervision, for the transition-adjustment class teacher remains in the cafeteria with his class. Mrs. George is contacted and readily agrees. She prepares her class for his appearance.

It is mentioned at the team meeting that a recent teacher-parent conference indicates that Ron is improving at home in his overall behavior. He has reached the point where he can play in the neighborhood, but he still plays only with younger children.

April: Ron continues to do well in the reading group, and he is making definite progress in the acquisition of reading skills. He has not yet developed a sense of responsibility as far as academic work is concerned but he has developed self-control to the point where he can be trusted without constant supervision. Academics still do not come easily to him, and he will become frustrated over materials that may require more concentration than he is able to give at the time. He finds it hard to make a move without teacher guidance and encouragement. His attention-getting devices, however, are more appropriate than the ones he previously used.

It is decided to increase Ron's farming-out time. Ron is getting along well with his former classmates at lunch, and Mrs. George suggested that Ron join her class for a "fun" period every Friday afternoon. Ron is permitted to remain in school the full day on Friday in order to participate in this activity. He is dismissed with Mrs. George's class and goes home on a regular bus.

May: At the team meeting, it is clear that Ron is doing well in the transition-adjustment class, in regular lunch, and during Friday afternoon. The reading specialist reports that Ron is making such good progress in reading that she would like the opportunity to spend additional time with him. It is arranged for Ron to remain the full day in school on Mondays, Wednesdays, and Fridays. On two of these days, following dismissal of the transition-adjustment class, Ron reports to the reading specialist where he receives instruction until 2:00 p.m. He is then dismissed with Mrs. George's class at 2:15 p.m. On Fridays, he continues to spend the full afternoon, following lunch, with Mrs. George's class.

June: Ron has handled himself well. His reading progress has been excellent. He is selected as a candidate for the transition-adjustment class summer program and for continued placement in the transition-adjustment class in the fall.

July: In the summer program, Ron is able to maintain his school gains. The physical education teacher had previously reported that Ron was below average in skills and shied away from games and activities during the gym period. It is decided, therefore, that one of the objectives for Ron will be to develop coordination skills through increased individual help. Every day Ron receives instruction in throwing, batting, and kicking, and practice in the use of the playground equipment. At the beginning of the program, Ron would not play, catch, or hit a ball except when he was alone with the teacher; he did not want the other children watching him. Once Ron received daily instruction, got the hang of it, and started hitting the ball, he began to join in group games. One of Ron's assets is that he is a good runner. When he finally participated in relay races, he found that he frequently won. This helped to build up his confidence.

THE TRANSITION BACK

Ron spent a relaxing summer and experienced no great difficulty in the neighborhood, according to the parents.

September: During Ron's first weeks back in school, his attitude and behavior are closely observed by the transition-adjustment class team. Testing by the reading specialist indicates that Ron has progressed from a primer level to a second grade instructional level.

These findings are presented at the transition-adjustment class team meeting (Figure 11-1). It is decided that Ron should be farmed out to a regular third-grade class for reading and "specials." The transition-adjustment class teacher and the principal select a regular class teacher, based on their knowledge of the person best suited to meet Ron's needs. Ron is grouped for reading by the reading specialist.

Figure 11-1
School Team Conference on Farming Out a Student

The special teachers are contacted and arrangements are made for Ron to take music, art, and gym with the same class he is farmed out to.

Fortunately, all of the special area teachers are ones that Ron knew from the previous year.

The arrangements are concluded and Ron begins to spend more of the school day in regular class. He arrives at school at 8:20 a.m. for the regular special areas scheduled in the morning. Following the special subjects, he goes to the transition-adjustment class, which provides him with a home base and with support and additional instruction with the transition-adjustment class teacher. He leaves at 11:00 a.m. and takes lunch and recess with his third grade. He spends the afternoon with the third grade.

November: Ron continues to fit into the third grade, but there are times when he appears lonely and unhappy although he does not verbalize these feelings. He does not have any real friends in the class and he spends time alone when he is not involved in group activities. In the cafeteria, he requests to eat with the second-grade children, among whom he seems to have friends, and during recess he plays with them.

Parent conferences also indicate that Ron still plays with younger children in the neighborhood. Cub Scouts and Little League are recommended to the parents but Ron is not interested at this time.

May: At the team conference, it is decided that Ron, even though two years behind chronologically, should be placed in a regular third grade for the coming school year. It is evident that his social, emotional, and academic lags require placement at this grade level. He can handle average third-grade work without too many frustrations.

At the conference, the teacher for the next year is recommended. Once she is contacted and agrees to the placement, she is brought up to date on the situation.

A NEW START

Summer: Ron attended a private day camp as part of his assimilation back into a regular setting. The parents noted that Ron spent a happy, constructive summer in camp.

Fall: Ron is now functioning in the regular third grade. His progress will be followed by the team. The parents and regular teacher know that the resources of the transition-adjustment class team will be available during the year.

TWELVE

The Summer Transition-Adjustment Class Program

Summer can be a setback for emotionally disturbed children in the transition-adjustment classes if the school year ends and they are left without the structure and continuity the program provides. For this reason, summer classes are an integral part of the total transition-adjustment class program. They also serve as an initial preparation for children who are set to enter a transition-adjustment class in the fall.

The following program, developed by Mr. William Gilmer, transition-adjustment class teacher, ran one summer for five weeks. Nineteen children attended from 9:30 a.m. to 12:30 p.m. Transportation was provided by the parents. The cost of the program was included in the district summer budget.

For the most part, attendance was good. Two children were absent two weeks because of family vacations.

By the end of the first week, the program was running smoothly. Children were grouped according to ability. Sequential reading skills were taught to those who were able to benefit. Individualized reading was continued with the children who were in the transition-adjustment classes the previous year.

Mathematics was another area of study and one in which most of the children made progress.

Playground activities included relay races, small group games, softball, kickball, and "make-believe" games. The younger children enjoyed acting out stories they had read, such as *The Wizard of Oz* and *The Three Little Pigs.* Costumes to go with the stories were made during the arts and crafts periods. They played well outdoors as long as they were engaged in structured activities. "Free play" time was kept to a minimum.

The children looked forward to the varied arts and crafts activities scheduled during the last hour of the program. By having arts and crafts at the close of the day, the difficulty of settling them down following these activities was avoided. The children had woodworking, using the jig saw and other small power tools. Many fine projects were completed by the children, and they were proud of their work.

THE FIRST SUMMER

Most of the children enjoyed the summer program. Many, especially those new to the program, were reluctant to participate or were defiant during the first days. However, the children soon settled down. They were receptive to academic activities once they realized the program provided opportunities for "fun and games" and was not just "school work."

The younger children, five to seven years of age, gained structure from the program. They did, however, demand much teacher supervision.

One child, Barry, did not benefit from the program. He was defiant throughout and refused to take part in the activities. Barry had been doing well during the regular transition-adjustment class school year. The turnabout in his behavior caused concern. After discussing the situation with his father, it was found that Barry had not wanted to attend the program and was forced to do so by his parents. Barry was one of the children who was out two weeks on vacation, which was fortunate since he did not enjoy the class.

The experience with Barry points to the need to have the parents and the child clearly understand the program so as to avoid a frustrating, negative experience for the child.

Written reports on the students were given to the parents along with a parent evaluation form. The completed parent reaction forms, returned to school, were completely in favor of the program. All the parents indicated they would take advantage of the program for their child if it were offered again. Some made constructive recommendations for the future while others offered to volunteer their services.

What prompted the school district to decide on this program and how was the plan carried out?

FACTORS THAT WEIGH IN FAVOR OF A SUMMER PROGRAM

Experience has shown that emotionally disturbed children regress over the summer months if they are not provided with a structured setting. Some appear to go back to the point where they exhibit behavior patterns and academic levels similar to those which were present when they first entered the transition-adjustment class program.

Actually, there are few programs available for these children during the summer. Parents may enroll their child in a day camp or recreation program; a constructive move when the child is able to function in the summer setting. However, some may have difficulty adjusting to a camp situation not specifically geared to emotionally disturbed children.

What of the children who do not have outside activities in the summer? They may play alone in the street or in the backyard. They have few friends, physical outlets, or goal-directed activities. The family relationship that had started to build up begins to break down, over the summer, when the child has little to do and may get into trouble and upset his parents.

WHO SHOULD BE ENROLLED IN A SUMMER PROGRAM?

The children considered for the summer transition-adjustment program are those who are presently in a transition-adjustment class or set for placement in the fall. Team conferences determine the priority order of placement. (There are some children who are making good progress in a transition-adjustment class and would benefit more from a regular summer school program or day camp. Eventually, attendance at an away camp, first for a month, then for two months, may be a future developmental step.)

Children who are ready for part-time farming out are excellent candidates for the summer transition-adjustment program, together with students already farmed out. The summer program gives them the opportunity to continue their academic progress with teachers they know in an environment in which they are comfortable. It gives them an additional start toward regular class functioning, and the assurance that the skills they have acquired over the year will not be lost in the summer.

Children who are not able to function in regular day camps are prime candidates for enrollment in the transition-adjustment class summer program, as are the younger disturbed children who represent the potential for early organization.

Following the selection of candidates, a conference is held with each parent to explain the program. It is made clear to the parents that the program is an important step in their child's overall development. It is their decision as to whether or not the child attends.

THE SUMMER STAFF AND THE FACILITIES

The number of teachers required for the program depends upon the number of children enrolled. This, in turn, is contingent on district funds available. Two teachers and two teacher aides, for an enrollment of eighteen children, is a realistic goal. (There are usually college students in the community who have worked in summer programs and are sensitive to the needs of emotionally disturbed children who can serve as teacher aides.)

The two teacher aides in the program described here did an outstanding job. Not only did they assist in every way possible, but they showed marked resourcefulness and interest. They originated activities and brought in materials which they had prepared on their own time. Their attitude toward the children and the relationship they built up with them were important factors in the summer gains made by the children. (An additional aide would help to provide the eighteen children with even more worthwhile experiences.)

The coordinator of the program should be an experienced transition-adjustment class teacher who is acquainted with some of the children. The other teacher, if not in the transition-adjustment class field, should have a teaching background, a feeling for children, and an interest in special education.

The teacher aide applicants were carefully screened by a central administrator, the director of psychological services, and the coordinator of the summer transition-adjustment class program. It was helpful to have the aides observe the regular year's transition-adjustment classes in session.

One teacher taught a district transition-adjustment class. The other was to teach a transition-adjustment class in the fall, and the summer program served as an indoctrination to the transition-adjustment class program and the children.

It is recommended that the facilities used in the transition-adjustment classes be available for the summer program. An optimum setup includes classrooms near the playground, with bathroom and sink facilities. By utilizing the same facilities, the children operate in a familiar environment, and the teacher is able to use the materials and equipment that were part of the regular year's program.

Appendix D includes a proposed "Summer Elementary Transition-Adjustment Class Budget for Three Groups of Eight Students Each (1969-1970)."

THE SUMMER CURRICULUM

The curriculum is based on the child's level of academic functioning. Those children who had been in the transition-adjustment classes can continue the individual programs they had been involved with during the year. The curriculum helps to bolster their academic skills.

The younger children, with difficulties in organization, are directed towards a structured activity program. Games, arts and crafts, story time, plays, and dancing are all part of the daily program. Readiness materials are gradually introduced.

The summer program offers varied organized activities in all areas. Field trips are planned at least once weekly. These trips provide valuable experiences. The children then write experience booklets which are of value in reading motivation.

These booklets, which are an important aspect of the transition-adjustment program, are kept by each child. He dictates or writes his own stories, which are typed and placed in his booklet. A primary typewriter is used if the child is a beginning reader. The student makes appropriate drawings to go with the particular experience.

Another technique to develop interest in the booklets is to take snapshots on the trips, and reproduce enough copies so each child has a picture for his own booklet.

Children are grouped according to their needs and abilities before the program begins. During the six weeks, after the day's activities, the teachers and aides meet periodically with the director of the transition-adjustment class program to discuss the children and ways to work with them.

Structure is maintained, with the day's activities paced to the emotional climate of the class. The teacher aides circulate among the groups.

THE DAY'S SCHEDULE

Reading is usually during the first period. General reading skills are introduced on a group level, not only for the purpose of developing skills but also to give the children a group experience.

Individual work is then assigned, and the teachers and aides work with the children.

The first period is followed by a game, either inside or out. A quiet activity follows the game, such as story telling or discussion periods in small groups. For those children who are ready, further academics are scheduled. Activities for the rest of the children vary day to day: stories, plays, and arts and crafts. Some of the older children help with the younger ones.

A woodworking period is scheduled on a daily basis. During this period, an aide is present at all times. The children enjoy using the jig saw and hand tools in completing projects such as house signs and napkin holders. Necessary matterials are obtained from the local lumber yard.

POINTS TO CONSIDER

A summer transition-adjustment program is an organic development in the organization and implementation of district elementary transition-adjustment classes.

Once a summer transition-adjustment program is in operation, it can be expanded so that other disturbed students in the district can participate.

THIRTEEN

The Transition-Adjustment Class Teacher

Arnold sticks his tongue out at Bucky, Bucky responds with an obscene gesture. A small but bitter battle ensues. The teacher intervenes. Both student combatants emerge unscathed. The teacher's shins are bruised and sore. After Arnold's emotional state subsides, he begins to cry and says that he will be sent to the principal's office, kicked out of school, and get into trouble at home. The teacher sends Arnold to the nurse's office for Band-Aids. After a group discussion, the other members vote that it would be best to forget the whole incident.

Several days later, an enraged Bucky suddenly attacks the teacher—snarling, kicking, punching. Despite Bucky's attack, the teacher detects insincerity. In the corridor, a fearful Bucky relates that Arnold had called him "chicken" because he was afraid to attack the teacher.

> **Teacher:** Are you satisfied now that you've hit me, Bucky?
> **Bucky:** Well—you had to get two Band-Aids when Arnold hit you.
> **Teacher:** All right. Go to the nurse's office and get two Band-Aids—better make it three.
> **Bucky:** You won't ever tell the other kids?
> **Teacher:** Never.

With an appropriate limp, the teacher walks back into the classroom and displays three Band-Aids covering three imaginary wounds. At this point, hostilities which had caused almost daily warfare between Arnold and Bucky came to an end.

The transition-adjustment class teacher has many faces. To describe him properly, one needs several vantage points. He is viewed first by the teacher himself, then by the principal, and finally by the transition-adjustment program director.

AS SEEN THROUGH THE TEACHER'S EYE

The preceding illustration serves to point out one of the major characteristics of the successful transition-adjustment class teacher. He is an individual who attempts to seize every opportunity to develop an understanding; to project the germ of an insight; to generate a feeling of caring. Where does he start? Actually, he starts with everyone, everywhere, and at any time. There is no logical order in terms of points of departure or timing. He has learned to deal with the dynamic processes involved in human relations. He makes errors in judgment, but he is able to accept his own mistakes and to rectify them.

The transition-adjustment class teacher knows that the way to establish and maintain a class for disturbed children, within the framework of the regular school, is through good working relationships with his pupils, their parents, and the rest of the staff. The transition-adjustment class teacher must communicate frequently with the principal in order to make him aware of the philosophy, goals, and progress of the class. It is the principal's enthusiasm and involvement in the program that influence the staff's acceptance and cooperation. The transition-adjustment class teacher must have frequent conferences with parents. This may involve visits to the home. The parents must be made aware of the child's problems and their role in helping to overcome these difficulties. The transition-adjustment class teacher must be frank with the parents so that they are aware of the realistic picture.

As far as the relationships with the other teachers are concerned, the transition-adjustment class teacher must deal with them on an individual basis to gain their respect. An asset for the development of good rapport with fellow teachers lies in the fact that the teacher of a disturbed group has special techniques for handling discipline problems. He is, therefore, a natural resource person for other teachers having problems with some of their children. The transition-adjustment class becomes a desirable part of the school community in part because the teacher is willing and eager both to share experiences, skills, and materials with the faculty, and to ask for their help and advice. In the farming-out process, this cooperation is vital.

The transition-adjustment class teacher must consider the relationship of his class to the secretaries, the custodial staff, and the cafeteria help as well as to the faculty, for they, too, are a part of the child's world. Often, the first people to whom the disturbed child begins to relate, aside from the transition-adjustment class teacher, are the nonprofessional help.

The transition-adjustment class teacher works to build a positive image for his group with the other students. For example, when they help regular class children use the power tools, show them the projects they have made, or run the projector during assembly programs, they gain the admiration of their peers in regular classes. This respect does as much to develop a positive feeling of accomplishment within the child, as do compliments from the teachers.

Within the transition-adjustment class, the children influence one another. They form a social structure of their own and a group feeling of solidarity. The achievement of one child in farming out can stir within the others a feeling of, "Well, I can do it, too!"

In the class, the children are given opportunities to make the grade. They can then sit back, so to speak, and give themselves a pat on the back. The transition-adjustment class teacher capitalizes on this response, and provides opportunities to connect isolated series of good feelings so that the children can begin to think of themselves as being on a par with their contemporaries in regular class.

THE TRAINING VARIABLE

Selecting a teacher with the ability to accept children as they are, to relate to them, and to get them to relate back, is one of the most important factors in setting up the program

The teacher must possess the skills necessary to develop academic programs which motivate these children to struggle back onto the academic trail. The teacher with a background in regular class training and experience is familiar with various methods and techniques in teaching.

More graduate schools now offer programs in the special education of emotionally disturbed children. It is helpful for these teachers also to be exposed to a regular class experience. Students planning to enter the field of special education will benefit more if they have had regular class teaching prior to their graduate training. They can apply what they have learned in a regular setting to the special class, and be aware of the goals towards which the disturbed child must travel.

Some universities and colleges allow interested student-teachers to take their training in a transition-adjustment class. However, part of their training should include student teaching in the regular class.

It is helpful if the transition-adjustment class teacher is someone who gets along well with the other members of the staff. This will work to ensure their cooperation and involvement in the program. The teacher must be able to hit it off with the staff if the class is to find acceptance in the building.

AS SEEN THROUGH THE PRINCIPAL'S EYE

A transition-adjustment class teacher has to accept all the children in his class. He wants to teach them. He willingly takes a new student who needs placement as a new challenge.

The teacher enjoys working on special projects with the children. He constantly seeks new kinds of experiences for them. He sees to it that every child participates to his limit in all academic phases. It is evident that his children want to work for him.

He is consistent. Children know what he wants and what he expects of them. There is no guessing from day to day about how to act or what to do. He helps a student, as an individual, to organize plans to reach his goals. A rung-by-rung progression up the educational ladder is set in motion.

The teacher accentuates the positive. A type of behavior may not be approved and may need to be changed. However, the teacher is aware that the child needs time, and he is willing to work patiently with him.

TEACHING—A MANY FACETED AFFAIR

This teacher can make the child understand that he cares for him even though he may disapprove of his behavior. As one teacher put it to a student who loudly interrupted the class, "I love you, Sandy, but that behavior has got to go."

This person is guidance-oriented. In talking with him, it is evident that children come first. There is no question about his feelings with regard to a child-centered versus a subject-matter-centered classroom.

The teacher knows how to help these children to learn. He can diagnose academic weaknesses and correct them through sound remedial techniques.

His teaching is marked by appropriate subject matter at the level of the student he is teaching. Each child is totally involved in the classroom activities. Individualized attention alternates with group instruction. Each child works at correcting his own weaknesses.

Homework assignments are not given to the group at large. Each child's homework is geared to his level. It grows out of the daily classroom experiences and will lead to the child's successful completion of the assignment as well as his overall understanding of the unit of study.

The teacher is one who can work with parents. He is able to gain their confidence. They know he is working to help their child. And this parent-teacher teamwork is going to be an important factor in the long educational haul ahead.

AS SEEN THROUGH THE DIRECTOR'S EYE

The teacher is the most important part of the program. Age, training, and experience are factors in the teacher gestalt, yet a competent teacher of emotionally disturbed students may be young or old, well-trained in the field or not, and have a great deal of experience or little. How do you filter out specifics that are applicable to teaching disturbed children?

It is, first of all, a good idea if the teacher has taught in regular class. Here the basics of the teaching game are learned:

Lesson plans
Developmental teaching in a heterogeneous setting
Techniques to spark motivation and initiative
Separate learning groups
Ways to work with the whole class
Peer relations
Teacher-student contact
Parent-teacher communication
Standard operating procedures in an elementary building
Collaboration with other members of the staff

The overall implementation of the learning process in a regular class provides a basic teaching foundation. Like a player on Vince Lombardi's Green Bay Packer team, the teacher, experienced in regular class, has learned the educational blocking and tackling that are the heart of the teaching matter.

With this basic foundation in elementary teaching, whether there has been graduate college training in special education or not, the regular teaching framework essential to learning can be transferred to the transition-adjustment class setting. The goal is to organize disturbed students for realistic functioning in regular class. The teacher has a better grasp of the learning matrix and how to carry out the special class goals, when there has been prior training and teaching in a regular setting.

The transition-adjustment class is a regular class in miniature, with similar teaching aims, but with flexible alternatives due to the smaller group and the closer student-teacher contact.

Therefore, a master teacher in regular class can be a master teacher in the transition-adjustment class—if the teacher is geared toward working with emotionally disturbed students.

The regular class teacher who shifts to this field can be helped through participation in the transition-adjustment class team conferences, observation of the special classes, and supervision by the transition-adjustment class coordinator.

It is true that a teacher who has gained a master's in the field of emotionally disturbed, or one who has had prior experience with these special classes, has acquired a valuable asset in training and experience which is bound to be helpful. However, the regular class teaching experience is a good foundation to have under one's educational belt.

Besides, "remedial teaching skills in the basic tool subjects," it is well if the teacher is proficient in industrial arts; for example, "woodwork, art techniques, metal work."[13] Power tools are also a helpful adjunct in the class.

Musical instruments, photography, tape recorders, films and other audio-visual aids, art, plastics, ceramics, puppet-making, drama, sports, and games are techniques a skilled teacher can utilize to kindle learning—while they also serve as important sublimation channels for growth.

Teacher personality is a determining factor. First, the teacher must have a structured learning set if the students are to become organized for reality task functioning in the mainstream. Emotionally disturbed children have not developed self-regulation and inner autonomy. The structure must come from without until it can be gradually incorporated from within. The student must learn to play the game by the rules, withstand frustration, and cope with reality with the help of a teacher who has a structured frame of reference.

Other personality variables that form part of the teaching mosaic are:[13]

Resourcefulness

Physical and mental endurance

Emotional resiliency and the ability to bounce back

Empathy with the disturbed child, without vicarious identification with his antisocial feelings and behavior

Ability to withstand hostility without losing a feeling of self-confidence

It is helpful if the teacher is keen to learn and willing to take supervision. A friendly, honest, collaborative approach will go a long way.

And a sense of humor is essential!

At the root of teaching is the belief on the part of the teacher that the student can change and improve. No matter what the obstacles and the heartaches, or how high the odds, *they are going to make it together.* It is like winning a tennis match. No matter how far behind you are, play one point at a time and the games will take care of themselves.

It is important for the teacher to have a "normal range of human contacts outside the daily task of working with problem children."[13] It is hard for a teacher of emotionally disturbed students not to get more and more involved with the child and to identify with his disturbance. After constant work with these students, the teacher is burdened with the impact of the student's problems and has trouble shaking them off. He thinks about them, takes them home with him, and is weighed down by them.

Therefore, it is a good idea for a teacher of emotionally disturbed children to teach a regular class every three or four years so that he has the chance to operate as part of the regular mainstream. Refreshed, he is ready to tackle the transition-adjustment class and the challenge it represents.

The rewards of teaching emotionally disturbed children cannot be judged by outside standards. Those who have not been on the battlefield cannot know the total involvement of the teacher in a grueling task that moves slowly forward in the struggle to learn. Only the teacher can experience the satisfactions that make the journey worthwhile.

Teaching emotionally disturbed children requires unique person-

THE TRANSITION-ADJUSTMENT CLASS TEACHER 187

ality variables that defy description. At the core, however, the child instinctively feels the teacher cares and, in turn, respects and trusts him.

FOURTEEN

The Principal Looks at the Transition-Adjustment Program

The principal must be interested in helping emotionally disturbed children or he should not attempt to set up these classes in his building. He must be concerned with their problems as well as with their education. And he must ask himself certain basic questions before he has transition-adjustment classes in his building:

Am I able to put up with the disruption that may be caused by these classes at times?
Am I able to accept the odd behavior of some of these children?
Do I believe in the program strongly enough to help the school staff feel the way I do?
Can I give these classes priority over most other needs in my building?

Educators understand that there is no such thing as a hopeless child. There are only those who have grown hopeless about him.

The principal encourages teachers to look at children as individuals. The child is the important element in any group. Therefore, while there are broad objectives developed for all children, there are specific objectives sketched for each one.

The teacher, in working with children, realizes that success begets success. He must find ways to help each child succeed in some way and then must build upon that strength.

THE PRINCIPAL AS TEAM LEADER

When a student in regular class does not meet the teacher's expectations, the teacher begins to look for other ways to reach the child. The teacher is encouraged to discuss the achievement of the student with the principal. Together they plan a program for the youngster.

More data is collected by the teacher as she continues her search to understand the child. Anecdotal records help to illustrate daily social, emotional, and academic behavior.

The team concept has its roots in the initial meeting of the teacher and the principal to discuss the progress of a youngster and to plan a program of action. The team begins to expand as other areas of difficulty are uncovered.

The reading teacher will observe and test the child to determine the independent, instructional, and frustration levels. She will conduct a visual survey using the Keystone Telebinocular and an auditory survey using an audiometer. She will check phonic skills, word analysis, sight vocabulary, meaningful vocabulary, comprehension, oral and silent reading, and reversals, using such diagnostic reading tests as the Gray Oral Reading Paragraphs, Gilmore Oral Reading Test, Horst Reversal Test, and teacher-constructed Informal Reading Inventories (IRI). Visual perception is checked by administering the Frostig Developmental Test of Visual Perception. Auditory Discrimination is determined by the Wepman Auditory Discrimination Test. Dominance is checked by the Harris Tests of Lateral Dominance. Body image and balance are evaluated.

A team conference is scheduled. The school nurse provides information on the child's vision and hearing. She will also review his medical history. The physical education instructor explains the child's coordination development in team sports and individual skill areas. The art teacher relates the talents of the student, themes in his work, and his behavior in class. The music teacher presents her experiences with the child. If speech is involved, the therapist will explain her findings to the group.

THE TEAM DISCUSSES A SPECIAL BOY

A team conference on Roger, a new boy to the district, illustrates the team concept:

Classroom Teacher:
>He constantly complains about others. He broke several slides

during the microscope lesson. He hit Dan on the back without any provocation. He refuses to do anything by himself. He prefers to use crayons rather than pencils. Children refuse to play with him. He grabs them or takes their things away. He grabs adults who walk near him. A girl in the cafeteria was scratched on the arm when she did not sit down.

Physical Education Instructor:

He is very verbal. He is constantly thirsty. He always asks what time it is. His coordination is below average. He cannot sit still. He does not throw or catch a ball. Although he can walk forward on the balance beam, he has poor balance. He does not like to skip or run.

Art Teacher:

He loves the art class. He sits down and goes right to work. He draws heavily in crayon and uses black a great deal. He is afraid to try different media. He likes to draw "monsters."

School Nurse-Teacher:

He may have perceptual difficulty. His left eye seems to move inward. His vision is "20/25" in both eyes. His hearing is fine. A conference is scheduled with his mother to find out more about his vision and to complete the medical history.

Reading Teacher:

He is ambidextrous with no established dominance. He uses his right eye consistently. His laterality is poor. He reverses letters. His instructional level is reading readiness.

Principal:

Roger spent some time in a nursery school in California and was asked to leave. This same experience was repeated several weeks later. The next year he attended kindergarten. It was recommended that he repeat kindergarten. The family moved to New York City and the child was placed in first grade. After one month, the principal called the mother in and told her he was putting Roger back into kindergarten. The family then moved.

Following the team session, the principal arranges a conference with the parents to gain more information. Through the conference, the parents get a picture of the school team effort to help their child. The conference also provides the principal with more home data. Specific steps are planned that will help Roger in school and at home.

In a subsequent conference with the principal, the parents agree to have their son seen by the school psychologist.

THE PRINCIPAL WORKS WITH THE PARENTS

Unless the parents are cooperative, help for the emotionally disturbed child is a difficult process. The principal can set the groundwork with parents to help them understand the need for transition-adjustment class placement when it is necessary.

When the parents are in favor of the transition-adjustment class program they are invited to visit the class, once a program is in operation, and talk with the teacher.

Mr. and Mrs. Peters realized the difficulties their son Vernon was having in school. Year after year, teachers had been calling them to say that their son was not doing well. Vernon could not concentrate on his work. He had few friends. At times he said things that made little sense to his peers or to his teacher. The parents had trouble handling him at home.

A psychological evaluation pointed to an emotionally disturbed pattern.

In a conference with the parents, the principal and the psychologist explained the transition-adjustment class program that was to be set up in the district. The parents met with the teacher of the class.

At first, the parents hoped that outside tutoring might resolve the difficulties. When tutoring did not help Vernon to improve in school, or at home, Mr. and Mrs. Peters agreed to place him in the transition-adjustment class.

However, before the new school year began, Mr. and Mrs. Peters came up to see the principal. They were concerned about the "stigma" attached to the class and wanted to give him another chance in regular class. He was withdrawn from the program and replaced by another student on the waiting list.

After the year began, the same pattern repeated itself. His grades were poor; he had no friends; he took hours to do homework; and family life was constantly disrupted. Mr. and Mrs. Peters reconsidered their decision. They requested placement in the class stating, "You have to save our son."

Unfortunately, Vernon had to wait until the next school year for placement in the transition-adjustment class because there was no opening. Once in the class, he began to show gradual improvement.

THE PRINCIPAL'S ROLE WITH THE CHILD

The principal plays an important part with each student. He visits the classes, talks to the children, praises their accomplishments, and helps them with their work. They begin to see him as someone they can trust. He is not their "enemy."

Marvin was new to the district, entering in midyear. According to his records, it was recommended that he repeat a grade.

From the first day Marvin entered school, the staff knew he had problems. He struck out at other children. He could not establish peer relationships. One Friday afternoon, when his teacher led the class out of the building for dismissal, he returned to the room, stopped up the sink, and turned on the water. The classroom was flooded. At various times during the year, he would run out of the class unless physically restrained. He did not cooperate with the special teachers.

The following year, in the transition-adjustment class, his behavior began to change. One day Marvin noticed the principal was wearing glasses when he came into his room. This new awareness probably stemmed from the fact that Marvin had just received a new pair of glasses. The principal talked about glasses with Marvin and how they help people to see. Then he worked with him on arithmetic.

As he was about to leave, Marvin told the principal he could buy new glasses where Marvin bought his, and he would give him the name and address. The next day he came looking for the principal to give him the information. Every time he saw his "new-found friend" he asked if he had bought the new glasses, even though the principal explained to Marvin that he did not need new ones yet. It was just his way of expressing rapport.

This boy, as well as the other students in the class, began to realize that a principal was another member of the staff who was there to help him learn. A new relationship was established. A little progress was made.

HOW TO HANDLE PROBLEMS THAT MAY ARISE

Transition-adjustment classes affect the entire school. Therefore, a schoolwide attitude of acceptance must be established with the teachers, custodians, secretaries, kitchen staff, and other personnel. The degree of acceptance may relate to several potential problems.

The length of the transition-adjustment class is four and one-half hours. The reason for the shorter day is that these children have short attention spans and find it hard to concentrate. They reach a point of diminishing returns in their work, and their behavior begins to get out of bounds. The shorter day also allows the transition-adjustment class teacher to see parents or to complete other program responsibilities when the children go home. However, there may be teachers who resent the shorter working hours of the transition-adjustment class teachers. Orientation on this point helps them to understand the total picture.

Another potential problem revolves around the smaller class enrollment of usually eight children. Teachers may question the size of the group when they are not aware of the special needs of these children and the benefits they reap by not having to cope with a disturbed child in their class. The reasons for the smaller class size can be explained to the regular teachers.

Cafeteria workers will complain, at first, about the noisy, strange behavior of the transition-adjustment class children on the lunch line, or while they are eating at their tables. The staff soon learns that this is a temporary adjustment period. By having the transition-adjustment class teacher eat with his students, any management problems are kept under control.

Secretaries may not understand the behavior of the children when they come to the office for materials or information. However, they soon realize that these students crave attention. Then the secretarial staff can do their bit. When the children come to the office to show their papers to the principal, the secretaries can praise their work.

The bus driver is one who may complain about the emotionally disturbed children who ride his bus. He may find it hard to take their annoyances while driving. However, one may be able to enlist his sympathy once he understands more about the children.

At times, it may be necessary to keep a child from riding the bus for a period of time. Charles had a record of antagonizing bus drivers by yelling, throwing things out the window, and pushing smaller children. When he was assigned to the transition-adjustment class, and again acted up on the bus, he was told that he could not ride for a week. It was hard for him to accept, but he did. Afterwards, his behavior improved and he showed better control.

All members of the building staff get to know the transition-adjustment class children during the year and try to help them in some way. The librarian, for instance, may work with them to teach them to sit quietly in the library, a process that takes time and patience. The children know they can count on her in choosing a book. (Figure 14-1)

Figure 14-1
Story Time at the Library

The art, music, and physical education teachers set up special programs to help the children develop. In addition, as they are farmed out, the first class may be in a special area.

Mrs. Chase, a first-grade teacher with several years of experience, had George come to the playground with her class. George was able to show the first graders how to throw and catch a baseball. These activities gave George a chance to shine. He looked forward to these periods and began to succeed in other ways. He was now started on his way to regular class via the farming-out route.

THE PRINCIPAL AND FARMING-OUT

Farming-out procedures are extremely important. The principal has to be sure the child is ready to move into a regular class—even for one period. Generally, the child himself lets the teacher know when he would like to try it. He will be placed in a subject area he can handle well. The principal helps to find the right teacher and the right group of children before the child is farmed out. Once he is placed in the new setting, there is close communication between the principal, the transition-adjustment class teacher, and the farming-out teacher on the progress of the student.

The transition-adjustment classes can be supplied with a reading series that is different from that used in regular classes. Therefore, there is more flexibility at the time of farming out in reading because the child can be placed in a class without the concern that he may have read the book.

The reading teacher plays an important role in determining the proper group when the child is ready to be farmed out into a reading class.

THE PRINCIPAL AS THE BUILDING COORDINATOR

The principal is aware of the total aspects of the building program. He is in a position to identify a child who may need transition-adjustment class placement and to coordinate educational moves that may help him.

The principal sets the tone for his school which will pave the way to staff acceptance of the transition-adjustment class program.

FIFTEEN

Difficulties to Be Encountered and How to Approach Them

Difficulties are part of any new program, and transition-adjustment classes are no exception. To be aware of these potential reality obstacles is to prepare for them. The reality appraisal increases the chances for the success of the program.

AN INITIAL OBSTACLE

One initial difficulty is that of persuading the school district to institute a transition-adjustment class program. In some instances, administrators and school board members may feel there are not enough disturbed children to warrant the establishment of a special class program. District psychological services can identify the need for the program through evaluations and school team observations.

Many school districts are aware of the need for the rehabilitation of disturbed youngsters within their system, but they hesitate to inaugurate or to give high priority to such programs. The reluctance may be based partly on economic considerations, and partly on the limited data regarding the effectiveness of transition-adjustment classes.

How do you convince justifiably economy-minded educators that a class of eight children is, in the long run, more economical, both in money and human resources? How do you demonstrate to the district that a transition-adjustment class can provide the necessary elements to organize emotionally disturbed children for reality functioning?

HOW TO APPROACH DIFFICULTIES

The chief administrator and the board of education require data on the number of children in the district who need transition-adjustment class placement, and data substantiating the importance of the special class structure—if the program is to leave the ground.

If the director and teachers in the transition-adjustment class program have had previous experience in the development of district elementary transition-adjustment classes, the director can present these reality findings to point up the value of the program.

PARENT APPREHENSION

Facing the fact that their child is emotionally disturbed is an agonizing experience for parents. The child is an extension of the parents and a reflection of their own self-image. The parents may have deep guilt that the child's disturbance is somehow their fault, or they may feel there is a stigma attached to "emotionally disturbed." They do not want their child to be "different." They project their feelings onto other children who will "poke fun at him" in the transition-adjustment class. It is hard to accept their child's disturbance, as this raises the next question: "What does the future hold?"

Parents will explain away, deny, and escape from the realization that their child is disturbed. They will use wish-fulfilling thinking: "He has worked through his problems during the summer." "If he does not read at the first grade level, a tutor in second grade will clear up his trouble." "This year he is going to make a go of it."

It is important to put the cards on the table with the parents and let the chips fall where they may. If the parents are not clear on the reality picture when the child is placed in the transition-adjustment class, they will balk at a later date. At some point, they will precipitously remove the child from the special class when such a move will only magnify his difficulties. For example, they may demand at the end of one year in the transition-adjustment class that he go into regular seventh grade because he is the right age for junior high school and they do not want him to lose another academic year. They may insist on this move even though it is made clear that placement in sixth grade is a better alternative.

Parents will put their child in special class with trepidation. They will have difficulty grasping the nature of their child's disturbance and the need for continued placement—even after many conferences. A week before school is to start, they may place him in private school or they may ask to have him put in regular class because someone has told them "there is nothing wrong with your child."

Other parents, under severe pressure at home, and with a realization that their child is at the end of his rope in school, will eagerly accept placement in the transition-adjustment class as the last hope. They will cooperate right down the line. As one parent wrote:

> I have been waiting to respond to your letter until I was able to talk with Susan's teacher. We met yesterday and I feel that everything that can be done for Susan is being done. Mr. Robertson is a truly dedicated person with a deep concern for each and every child in his classroom. We both feel that Susan has made a great deal of progress this year and if we continue to work together as we have done in the past she will continue to do so.
>
> I shudder to think what would have happened to Susan and the other children in her class had they been placed in the average classroom. I feel that only those involved in this type of class can appreciate the benefits derived, and hope that this type instruction will be available for a long, long time to come.

Close parent-teacher conferences, once the child is in the class, will play an important role in helping the parents to see more clearly the realistic picture, understand the ways in which the class is vital to their child's organization, and clarify any misconceptions they may have on what is going on in class.

The parent-teacher conference is a team effort; closely involving the parents, helps them to understand and accept the placement. Parent-teacher conferences provide the staff with data on what is going on outside school, lead to ways to implement the school direction in the home, and serve as part of the step-by-step total development of the student.

If the parents do not accept placement in the transition-adjustment class, or if they remove the student while he is in the program, his progress in regular class is followed up.

Parents are human beings. Their decisions must be respected because they are the ones who will ultimately have to come to grips with what they are going to do with their child. Deep down they know their child has problems, but this is a difficult fact for them to face. If one tries to empathize with their predicament; if one considers what they go through with the child every day; then one is better able to understand their objections and determine how best to work with them in the long hard pull the child faces.

THE LONG STRUGGLE TO THE MAINSTREAM

The transition-adjustment class program is a long-term one since the screening has been utilized to place in the classes those students who have the severest difficulties in functioning, but are still capable of maintaining themselves in the public school setting.

Therefore, the most optimistic goals cannot be total assimilation back into the educational mainstream for all of the students. Seventy-five to eighty percent of the children will eventually find their way back to regular classes through gradual farming out. As to the others, it is not failure for the child, nor for the program, when he reaches his limits and can go no further academically. A firmer personality base of operations has now been set and he may, for example, be ready at fifteen to consider a vocational training program.

The goals are not to make the emotionally disturbed child like everyone else. Part of the core of his disturbance will remain untouched; he will tend to be different in some ways. The goals, rather, are to provide him with the inner equipment to build on top of the disturbance so that he can function more effectively in reality and cope with everyday tasks—whether in school or on a job.

The disturbed child may never marry or go to college. He will probably be more of a "loner." But in tackling society on his own, he has wrestled with the disturbance and come out ahead. He may not find a job commensurate with his intellectual potential, yet he will produce useful and creative work.

For those who have struggled with emotionally disturbed children, it is a rewarding experience to see the goal of total assimilation realized; to meet one day, one year, a former student coming down the hall with his regular class, and to say "hello" as he goes by.

THE PROBLEM OF SPACE

With growing districts, classroom space can be a serious problem. It may be neccessary to double team the classes on an overlapping schedule, sharing one classroom.

The available classroom may be smaller than a regular classroom due to room shortage, and smaller yet when double teamed on an overlapping schedule. It is helpful to have the time the two classes are together limited through special subjects, lunch, or a move to another available room for part of the day.

If only one classroom is available for two classes, it may be possible, for example, to devise a 9:00 a.m. to 1:30 p.m., and 10:30 a.m. to 3:00 p.m. overlapping schedule.

However, at 3:00 P.M. the buses may be engaged in taking regular class children home. Therefore, those children in the second session must live in the specific school area where the class is located and take the regular bus home. This is the best alternative when there is no other space available in a regular elementary school. To place the class in a building isolated from the regular class setting defeats the basic purpose of the program: gradual assimilation into the educational mainstream though a temporary necessity at times.

Double-team overlapping requires the dovetailing of two teachers who can work together in close harmony—particularly when the classroom is small. (An advantage of the double-teaming arrangement is the team-teaching flexibility.)

Another alternative is to schedule the hours of the two classes, for example, from 9:00 a.m. to 1:30 p.m. and from 11:45 a.m. to 4:15 p.m. There is now an overlap of only one hour and forty-five minutes, of which part can be broken up by alternate lunch periods and special subjects. One objection is the late hour the second class returns home—particularly in the winter months.

When space is scarce, another possibility is to utilize a temporary structure for a classroom when it is adjacent to the regular building.

At the beginning of each school year, it may be necessary to shift buildings due to district and elementary school area population changes. This interferes with building continuity so that a student, in three years, may be in three different elementary schools—though he may have the same teacher.

TRANSPORTATION

Transportation can create difficult problems which compound parent concern.

Buses may pick up children late or bypass those waiting, thereby unsettling the children and the parents.

At first, the bus drivers, not involved with the program, may balk at the behavior of disturbed children. It is helpful to have the transition-adjustment class teachers establish a liaison with the drivers so that when difficulties arise they will first discuss the problem together.

In matters of student conduct on buses, the teacher will call the director of the transition-adjustment class program and the building principal on difficulties that arise, or on other transportation matters. If a student continues to act up on the bus regardless of all that the teacher does to prevent it, the point may be reached where the principal or assistant principal, after consultation with the director, will contact the parents to explain the seriousness of the behavior and give a final warning. When there is one more incident, the student is removed from the bus for a stated period of time and the parents have to provide the transportation.

If another student goes into an opening in a transition-adjustment class, transfers in from another district special class, or moves into regular class full time, the bus route has to be revised. This is worked through the transportation officer to the bus company, and it is added work and inconvenience for both. The transportation officer will wonder why all the students from one area are not in that building's transition-adjustment class. The reasons why children are placed where they are must be explained in detail to the transportation coordinator.

It is better to have a clear understanding with transportation at the beginning of the program that changes in bus routes are inevitable in terms of the transition-adjustment class goals: gradual assimilation back into regular class.

Transportation is a vital factor in the program. Therefore, the director is wise to work as closely as possible with transportation since their cooperation is essential. One helpful step, when new students enter the program, is to arrange the new bus stop as close to the existing bus route as feasible. Other reasonable efforts to lessen the burden on transportation will help to insure a collaborative atmosphere.

THE SUBSTITUTE TEACHER AND THE TRANSITION-ADJUSTMENT CLASS

The substitute teacher is an important consideration. The following quotations are from reports submitted to the transition-adjustment class teachers by the substitute teachers and typify the problems that are encountered by the substitute.

> The absence of papers for Sandra is a mystery. Each day I'd check her work with her but her paper would disappear. She read aloud in the group once.
>
> Donald didn't produce much of anything, in fact he didn't do anything that he was supposed to do. However, he didn't cause much of a commotion either. His mother came to pick him up and she said she would have to praise him for not causing any trouble.

Alex was a lulu. He was very negative, refused to do anything, and taunted and teased everyone. Tony must have asked me a hundred times if I liked him. Freddy got in trouble with the bus driver but Tony was as much at fault. They both pushed everyone on the line.

Tony would't get his lunch. Harry flicked some sand into Donald's eye—purposely or not, I don't know. We had a pretty good day in general, but I'm not sure just how much we accomplished.

What a group! I swear I could have strangled Barry, I had to send him to the psychology office after he punched Harry in the eye. He looked like he was getting ready to punch me also. That was a good idea for me but the psychologist may not like it when he finds his pens are taped together, and that Barry hid some of his papers. The class is being docked from art next week—speak to the art teacher. All in all, I was happy to see the end of the day come. Actually, it's O.K. if you call me to substitute again. If possible do it on a day when Barry is absent.

These children take full advantage of a "day off" and seem to be proud of letting the substitute know that they are the "problem" students.

It is, therefore, important to prepare the substitute teacher for the class. One helpful move is to have the substitute teachers observe a transition-adjustment class before they substitute.

A list of four or more teachers who will substitute for transition-adjustment classes is optimum. Through special arrangement with the administration, they can be called directly by the transition-adjustment class teacher who is going to be absent. If they have already been called for another regular class, they can arrange for another substitute to cover so that they can take over the transition-adjustment class. These substitute lists should be set prior to or soon after the opening of school.

As the substitute teachers become familiar with the routine, and get to know the children, they can follow the transition-adjustment class teacher's plans to a greater degree. However, there is always an "Emergency Substitute Plan" on hand in the transition-adjustment class teacher's desk. The plan consists of review work, games the children enjoy, and structured activities. Special problems are noted in these plans so the substitute is alerted. These plans are periodically revised.

Candidates for substitute positions in the transition-adjustment class program should be interviewed by the transition-adjustment class teacher, the building principal, and the transition-adjustment coordinator and the director.

OTHER HURDLES TO PROGRAM ACCEPTANCE

Some administrators may not place a high priority on the transition-adjustment class program, and some principals may not be in favor of a class in their building. Some teachers may frown on the program.

Any new concept or direction will hit resistance. Inertia takes time to overcome. There will be those who are negative. However, this is par for the course and a factor to take in stride.

When the district principal and the board of education are behind the transition-adjustment class goals, the program is ready to roll. With a transition-adjustment class teacher who works with the staff in a teamwork effort, the proper climate is set for the total development of the program.

The transition-adjustment class program is, by its very nature, "low man on the totem pole." The district transition-adjustment class program is generally given a room assignment last, transportation arranged after the regular buses are set and special subject areas scheduled last. This is to be expected since it *is* a special program involving a minority of the students in the district.

The program is no better than the teacher. It is his or her skill and devotion that enables the children to climb the highest mountain. Programs and curriculum boil down to people. The growth of the program rests on how broad are the shoulders of the teacher and the school team, and on their involvement, enthusiasm, dedication, training, experience, and feeling for children.

The concepts and procedures for the transition-adjustment program must be clear or the program will not have a sturdy educational rudder. As a result, the classes may be unstructured so that the children do not get the organization they need; curriculum becomes hodgepodge, farming out is not gradually developed; children other than emotionally disturbed are placed in the class; and screening procedures are not set.

The program must be solidly built from the ground up. Every brick in the foundation must be part of the total pattern. The final structure is the design of the original blueprints with any necessary modification integrated into the overall developmental scheme.

SIXTEEN

Future Directions

The Report of the Joint Commission on Mental Illness and Health states that "Whereas the clinic occupied a pivotal position in the care of emotionally disturbed or mentally ill children, ideally it should be considered a part of a spectrum of community services, including 'special instruction for classroom teaching in the handling of emotional disturbances' and 'special public school classes for emotionally disturbed children....'"[16]

In line with the goals set by the Joint Commission on Mental Health, the organization and implementation of an elementary school special class program for emotionally disturbed students has been outlined.

As the New York State Education Manual on the training and supervision of teachers for emotionally disturbed children points out, "Providing educational opportunities for *all* children is a first duty of State government.[13] It is the responsibility of the school district to educate each student to his potential regardless of his handicap. As Judge Hand wrote, "The spirit of justice" is the "spirit that remembers that no sparrow falls to the earth unheeded."

The child writes:

> My life is an emty shadow
> Because I am so shy
> I sit alone and feel that way
> But I can't tell you why.

Transition-adjustment classes do not resolve all these troubled feelings, nor work out all the problems that hold the disturbed student back, but they do serve as an organizing catalyst for eventual assimilation back into the educational mainstream, and they are a springboard to realistic functioning in society.

There is a great range in theme and variations on the emotionally disturbed pattern—from the child who does not communicate and lives in a world of his own, to the brilliant student in ninth grade with all *A's* in honor subjects who is isolated from the rest of his class and cannot move out to make friends. All show, in varying degrees, difficulty in building a solid, integrated personality foundation; in differentiating reality from imagination; and in functioning independently in the gamut of human situations.

The children who are candidates for transition-adjustment classes stand halfway in between. They have enough development and reality orientation to enter public schools (though many stand out and are unable to make the grade from the beginning), yet they gradually drop further behind the functioning of the rest of the students in regular class.

If disturbed children are not organized in the early school years, they will crumble under inner and outer pressures in the stress of adolescence and later life crises. These classes, therefore, have a preventive goal that is a central force behind their organization. Certainly, there is abundant evidence to show that when this later collapse is prevented, what is really nipped in the bud are drug addiction, crime, human breakdown, and despair.

What of the many emotionally disturbed children who remain in regular class and do not get the preparation so necessary for their future? They drift along. They may not show behavior outbursts. They may not even be academically far behind their peers. But if they are not identified now, it is more difficult to help them later. And later, the need for that help will become apparent to all with whom they come in contact—perhaps at a point of no return.

To identify and set up transition-adjustment classes for disturbed children who are on the borderline is a vast undertaking in energy, time, personnel, and finances. Each school district will have to determine its degree of commitment to this kind of program.

What of the students who remain on the waiting list but may never have the chance to enter the transition-adjustment class because of the priority order? The teachers give their last ounce of energy to provide as much individual help as possible in the regular class but are faced with constant frustration in their inability to bring about constructive change. They are only too aware that the student is "dying in class" and "rotting away in his seat." They are helpless to cope with the solution, yet haunted by the child who is a living reminder of their "failure." And, if the student is a behavior problem disrupting class functioning, the teacher is faced with a constant stress factor.

What of the uncounted numbers of disturbed students who have not been identified and referred and who will have increasing difficulties with time? Here are brilliant potentials slowly going down the educational drain; creative waters carelessly spilled on the wastelands of society.

Massive, concentrated, crash programs are required in the public schools if emotionally disturbed children are to be identified in depth and provided with the necessary preventive-developmental, organizing experiences.

Intensified special class programs for emotionally disturbed children are a part of an educational trend toward homogeneously—smaller learning situations. These settings include, for example, extended readiness classes at the end of kindergarten for twelve to fifteen children with visual-motor lags, placed together for one or two years to permit their biological clocks to catch up; or a fifth-grade setup where one teacher has a smaller group of bottom learners. These are all evidences of a trend to help students make it in the regular setting through smaller class groupings.

The more one views the dynamics behind student progress in smaller class settings, the more one concludes that the close relationship between the teacher and the student is the human bridge to growth. Children develop inner strength through identification with the parents. The smaller class provides the student with a substitute parent figure with whom he can establish the emotional strength necessary to organize him for reality functioning.

Parents sense the importance of this relationship:

> Dear Mr. George,
>
> This has been Robert's happiest year in school. The notes of Robert's progress have been very encouraging to me and to Robert. School has taken on a new meaning to him. I feel this fine teacher relationship that has developed with you is responsible. This is apparent in his reference to school and his teacher. Many times when he is unsure of his position or a decision he decides to discuss it with Mr. George.
>
> He has come a long way in working with others and being with

> them socially. The year needless to say has also been a happier year for my husband and me. The entire family has been able to have a much better relationship.
>
> My husband and I wish to thank you. We deeply appreciate your efforts. It must be very rewarding to see the children come along. I wish you continued success in teaching and happiness.

The burden of living with an emotionally disturbed child, and its effect on the total family pattern, is becoming more apparent as one looks more closely into what goes on in the home. The disturbed child generates constant pressure on those around him. There is a continual circle of frustration, aggravation, and duress.

When the child is able to make progress in the transition-adjustment class, it helps to break this destructive circle. As the child becomes better organized in school through the continuity of the small class structure, he can be managed more easily at home. The parents can begin to reach him and to enjoy the relationship. There is a spark of hope for the future.

The essence of mental health is prevention. Educational steps in this direction are:

1. Increased community involvement.
2. The placement of disturbed students in transition-adjustment classes *at an early age*.
3. A district preschool evaluation service so that disturbed children, identified at three or four, or younger, can be placed in small group settings as part of a headstart organizing experience.

Yet, by the age of three or four, the child is, in a sense, "old" Dr. Peter B. Neubauer, Director of the Child Development Center in New York City, points out that children proceed from conflict to conflict; the younger the child the greater the pitfalls for pathological development. He suggests a comprehensive program geared to the first three years of life; not just family responsibility but community responsibility similar, for example, to the infant care programs now operating in Israel, North Carolina, and the Paris outskirts.[12]

Early studies are now in progress to observe and learn about the development of the infant from birth on so that the added knowledge can give us a better idea of just what goes on in growing up, what the variables are, and what we can do to help development take place.

Every effort by school districts and community resources to concentrate on the early development of children before they enter school will pay off in pure educational gold.

A step in this direction is the Center for Preventive Psychiatry in White Plains, New York. The "Cornerstone Project," directed by Dr. Gilbert Kliman, provides "individual psychoanalytic therapy...in a classroom setting for emotionally disturbed preschool children...."[9]

A district transition-adjustment class program can be successful only if there is a total school team effort. Once the elementary transition-adjustment classes have been established, along with a transition-adjustment class summer program, thought should be given to organizing a junior high school transition-adjustment class program.

Provisions also have to be made for older transition-adjustment class students who will not be able to make it back into the regular educational setting, and who will need work-study programs to prepare them for on-the-job functioning.

A seven-year-old disturbed student wrote:

>Mickey Wouse
>He got uq
>Wash his hand and face
>Them he went out
>He see a butterfly
>He tried to catch
>The butterfly
>Them he got lost
>Them he said which
>Way should I go
>Them he asked the
>Dog the (dog) said no
>Then he asked a robin yes
>I will take you home.

The elementary district transition-adjustment classes are one way to "take" the emotionally disturbed child "home."

Appendix A

Developmental History Form

Appendix B

Progress Report

Appendix C

Typical Physical Education Evaluations of
Transition-Adjustment Class Children

Appendix D

1. First Year Budget for Two Elementary Transition-Adjustment Classes (1967-1968)
2. Summer Elementary Transition-Adjustment Class Budget For Three Groups of Eight Students Each (1969-1970)
3. Proposed Elementary Transition-Adjustment Class Budget For 1970-1971 For Eight Classes (In Addition to Existing Equipment and Supplies For Six Present Classes)

APPENDIX A

DEVELOPMENTAL HISTORY

Date _____

NAME _____ BIRTHDATE _____
PRIOR SIBLINGS (BIRTHDATE) _____
PLANNED CHILD _____
PREGNANCY _____
    MOTHER'S HEALTH _____
HOSPITAL BORN _____ PLACE LIVING _____
LABOR _____
DELIVERY _____
    COMPLICATIONS _____
    BIRTH WEIGHT _____ FULL TERM _____
    DAYS IN HOSPITAL _____
CUDDLY, REACHING OUT _____ ACTIVE _____
    ALERT _____ SENSITIVE-NERVOUS _____
    CONTENT BY SELF _____ SMILING _____
BOTTLE - BREAST _____
    DEMAND - SCHEDULED _____ AGE WEANED _____
    FEEDING _____
    PACIFIER _____ THUMBSUCKING _____
    LATER EATING PATTERNS _____ COLIC _____
ROOM AT HOME _____
SLEEPING (INFANT) _____
LATER SLEEPING PATTERNS _____
FAMILY MOVES _____
ROOM CHANGES _____
PHYSICAL DEVELOPMENT _____
    WALKING _____
    TALKING _____

TOILET TRAINING _____

    URINE (DAY-NIGHT) _____

    BOWELS (DAY-NIGHT) _____

ENEMAS _____ SUPPOSITORIES _____

MASTURBATION _____

OTHER SIBLINGS BORN _____

MISCARRIAGES; STILLBORN _____

DATE OF BIRTH: MOTHER _____ FATHER _____

DATE OF MARRIAGE _____ OCCUPATION _____

OTHER RELATIVES IN HOME _____

    MATERNAL GRANDPARENTS _____

    PATERNAL GRANDPARENTS _____

SEPARATIONS _____

FRIENDS _____

OTHER EVENTS, ONE TO THREE _____

OTHER EVENTS, THREE TO FIVE _____

FURTHER PHYSICAL DEVELOPMENT _____

    RIDING A BIKE _____

    BALL PLAYING _____

    RIGHT OR LEFT HANDED _____

        CHANGES _____

PRESCHOOL DIFFICULTIES _____

TEMPER TANTRUMS _____

FEARS _____

DAY DREAMS _____

NIGHTMARES _____ SLEEPWALKING _____

WETTING (DAY - NIGHT) _____

SOILING (DAY - NIGHT) _____

LOW FRUSTRATION TOLERANCE _____

SPEECH _____

HOBBIES _____

CLUBS _____

SPORTS _____

MUSICAL INTERESTS _____

SUMMER DAY CAMP _____

AWAY CAMP _____

MEDICAL HISTORY

DISEASES _____

ILLNESSES _____

ALLERGIES _____

HIGH FEVERS _____

CONVULSIONS _____

OPERATIONS _____

INJURIES _____

HOSPITALIZATIONS _____

VISION _____

HEARING _____

AGENCIES CONTACTED _____

EDUCATIONAL DEVELOPMENT

NURSERY SCHOOL _____

KINDERGARTEN _____

FIRST GRADE _____

SECOND GRADE _____

THIRD GRADE _____

FOURTH GRADE _____

FIFTH GRADE _____

SIXTH GRADE _____

SEVENTH GRADE _____

EIGHTH GRADE _____

NINTH GRADE _____

TENTH GRADE _____

ELEVENTH GRADE _____

TWELFTH GRADE _____

SUMMER SCHOOL _____

TUTORING _____

DATE REFERRED _____

SCHOOL _____ GRADE _____ TEACHER _____

REFERRED BY _____

REASON FOR REFERRAL (I.E., ACADEMIC LEVEL; SOCIAL RELATIONSHIPS; DESCRIPTION

   OF BEHAVIOR) _____

_____

_____

SCHOOL SPECIAL SERVICES (I.E., MEDICAL; SPEECH; READING) DATA _____

_____

_____

APPENDIX B

PROGRESS REPORT
TRANSITION-ADJUSTMENT CLASS

Student _____Alfred_____   Date _____Midyear_____

Teacher _____Mr. Roger_____   School _____

I. Academic Progress

    A. Reading

        1. Level: Beginning

        2. Achievement: When Alfred joined us he was classed as a non-reader. He did not know the consonant sounds or vowel sounds. He knew only a small percentage of the basic sight vocabulary (220 words). At present Al is doing a good job in the areas mentioned above. He seems to be trying very hard.

    B. Mathematics

        1. Level: Beginning

        2. Achievement: Al does not know the basic number facts. However he can do reasonably difficult addition problems by counting on his fingers. The fact that he participates and attempts to be neat in his work is a good sign. In terms of attitude his progress is good.

    C. Penmanship   Al is making progress in the recognition and formation of letters.

Transition-Adjustment Progress Report

Name _____

D. **Language**

    1.   Verbal: No progress noted.

    2.   Written: Because of his problem in reading and spelling, Al has a problem with written language. However, he participates; writes good sentences with help in his spelling. In spelling, Al pays attention, answers questions, and shows an interest.

E. **Specials**

    1.   Art: Has learned to participate in group activities without starting fights.

    2.   Music: Shows greater listening interest but will not participate.

    3.   Physical Education: Excellent progress in developing large muscle coordination.

II. **Individual Development**

    A. **Work Habits**   At first Al did not pay attention, did not follow directions and handed in papers that were not very neat. He now makes a great effort to be correct and neat. At times if he feels that a paper is not neat enough, he will do it over without being told.

    B. **Health Habits**   Personal cleanliness has improved.

Transition-Adjustment Progress Report

                                      Name _____

C.   Emotional Adjustment

Alfred has shown improvement in the following checked (X) areas:

	Causes Disturbances
	Shows Off
	Boastful
X	Frequently gets into Fights
	Breaks Rules
X	Defiant toward Authority
	Lies to get out of Trouble
	Cheats in Games
X	Impulsive and easily Excited
	Uncooperative most of the Time
X	Little regard for personal or property rights of Others
	Has no real Friends
	Frequently Nervous

III. General Comments

In many of the other areas under "Emotional Adjustment" there will be little improvement until we first help him to gain a sense of self-respect.

In a sense it isn't a part of Al to be or do any of the things listed. He is just a little boy with a very low opinion of himself. He wants to be a "big shot." If we can help him raise his opinion of himself; show him that he is a capable worthwhile person, he will lose these anti-social ways for getting attention.

Transition-Adjustment Progress Report

Name _____

My judgment is based on school activities. It would be helpful if you would give me your impressions on progress in these and other areas

IV. <u>Parent Comments</u>

Appendix C

<u>Typical Physical Education Evaluations of Transition-Adjustment Class Children</u>

Phyllis seems to have improved a great deal this year in terms of her attitude toward participation. She is now more willing than ever to at least try something new and which she thinks she might not like to do. Her relations with the rest of the class have also improved to the point that there are now times when she becomes a group member rather than a loner. She has improved in terms of expressing herself. She talks much more now, and also lets her opinions and feelings be known. Her skills level is difficult to measure but it seems as though her general body coordination is "normal" for her age. In general, most of her improvement has come in the area of participation and interaction with the group.

Joan has probably made more overall improvement than anyone else in the class. Perhaps it may be due to the fact that she seemed to start off much lower than the others in the class, but nevertheless, her improvement has been genuine. Her general body coordination, although still requiring much work to bring it up to a suitable level, has improved greatly. On an aspect of coordination in which she was interested in (rope jumping) her progress could be observed on a day-by-day basis. She is not usually part of the group but can at times be a good team member. She seems to have a lot of fears and has no real idea of her body capabilities and limits. In general, Joan is progressing very nicely. She is less afraid of interacting with the rest of the group; she seems to be a much happier girl, and she is a much more willing participator in physical education activities.

Frank appears to be somewhere on the fringe of the group. He is not quite "in" with the group; yet he is not ostracized. He is usually in a group of two or three but not any larger. His skills ability is above average. He seems to have a good understanding of his capabilities and shies away from activities in which he is not too proficient. His behavior is no problem; he can follow directions, and he usually tries to do the right thing. He is one of the "followers" in the class and will go along with group thinking. There has been no great change in his functioning within the group. He gets along well with the rest of the group and has been no real problem.

Although George is still quite a problem, he has improved a great deal since the beginning of the school year. He has improved in his self-control but still needs a lot of work in this area. He is usually a loner but will team up with anyone if there is some mischief to get into. His skills level is above average and his coordination is good. In any of the games played he usually participates for his personal glory rather than that of the team. His performance and intensity of concentration (with activities he likes or is interested in) usually obtains for him acceptance as a team member. He seems to enjoy, very much, inflicting harm on others and also having others inflict harm on him. He is not in the least bit discriminatory in terms of who he antagonizes in the group. He will try to "bully" the biggest and strongest boys in the group as well as the meekest girls. He is not very honest and will usually find a way to cheat rather than be a loser. In general, George has improved in all phases of his behavior. He still, however, needs to improve a great deal more in order to function as a contributing member of the group.

Dick is a tough and aggressive class leader. Prior to about a month ago, Dick had been very difficult to manage and a disruptive influence in the class. Within the last month, however, he has made a great deal of improvement. He has become much more cooperative and now contributes to class order. He can be very cruel to the other children, and when reprimanded becomes very cold and aloof. His skills level and coordination are above average and he is usually a good participator. Dick seems to have better control of himself and, in general, is making good progress.

Margaret is usually a good participator who can be reasoned with and talked to. There are times when she has "bully fits" and she sulks, attempting to get her own way. These occasions are happening much less often now than earlier in the year, and she is more willing to go along with the consensus of the group. She is no behavior problem and seems to get along much better with the group than she did earlier in the year. This change in group interaction seems to have been brought about by her becoming more flexible and more willing to try new things. In general, Margaret is doing a good job in physical education and seems to be making good progress.

Toby has made a great deal of progress during the course of this year. He has achieved a greater amount of emotional control this year than he has had in the two years that I have known him. He is much more able to interact with the group, and now becomes involved in the activities of the group. He can become intensely interested in a game or other activity. In a competitive game atmosphere he is a better performer, and he is able to accept losing much better than he could earlier in the year. Under the same circumstances that would cause crying and striking out at objects around him, Toby now sulks, whines, and paces around. His skills level and coordination are below average and he could use a good deal of individual instruction in both of these areas. Although Toby seems to need more work and supportive help, he has made improvement in organizing himself and controlling his behavior.

Jack has been doing a very good job in physical education. He is a very good performer with above average skills, coordination, and strength. He seems to enjoy physical activity and he is a good competitor. He has been making great strides in terms of progress and seems to be trying very hard. Jack is a likable boy and seems to get along with most of the children in the class. He is willing to listen; he can be reasoned with, and he seems to understand the difference between right and wrong. His greatest shortcoming seems to be that he can be too easily led into wrongdoing. In general, Jack has made nice progress this year, and he is now at the point where he is a contributing member of the class.

APPENDIX D (1)

FIRST YEAR BUDGET FOR TWO ELEMENTARY

TRANSITION-ADJUSTMENT CLASSES

(1967-1968)

Teacher, Classroom and Art Supplies Obtained From School Supplies, Bid Item Approximately		$ 335.75
Attached Purchase Orders		2,764.25
	TOTAL	$3,100.00

1967-1968

TRANSITION-ADJUSTMENT BUDGET

White's
Jericho Turnpike
Middle Island, New York

2	3/8" Drill Kits @16.43	$	32.86
1	Drill Stand		22.95
1	Horizontal Drill Stand		4.95
1	Drill Set		3.47
1	Sander		19.99

$ 84.22

Science Research Association
259 E. Erie Street
Chicago, Illinois 60611

10   5-1521 A Book About Me @.55 $ 5.50

Scherer's & Sons
Waterside Road
Northport, New York

1	Undergravel Filter	$	3.00
1	Pump		8.00
8 ft.Tubing @.05			.40
20lb.Gravel			1.25
1	Heater		4.29
1	Cover		2.75
1	Light		4.60
1	Thermometer		.90
1	Net		.35
	Fish and Plants - Estimated Cost		10.00

$ 35.54

Education Development Laboratories
Huntington, New York

1	Story Filmstrips, Set 4g	3 Gr.	$	75.00
1	Story Filmstrips, Set D	4 Gr.		75.00
1	Story Filmstrips, Set E	5 Gr.		75.00

$ 225.00

1967-1968

TRANSITION-ADJUSTMENT BUDGET

American Book Company
300 Pike Street
Cincinnati, Ohio 45202

GRADE ONE, THIRD EDITION

5	The ABC On Our Way (first pre-primer) @.57	$	2.85
5	" " Time to Play (second pre-prim.) @.63		3.15
5	" " All in a Day (third pre-prim.) @.66		3.30
5	" " Up the Street and Down (Primer) @1.44		7.20
5	" " Around Green Hills (first reader) @1.62		8.10
1	" " Teacher Ed, Annoted. & keyed (first reader)		1.62

GRADE TWO, THIRD EDITION

5	The ABC Down Singing River (sec. reader 2^1) @1.80	9.00
1	" " Teacher's Ed. for above	1.80
5	" " Over a City Bridge (sec. reader 2^2) @1.80	9.00
1	" " Teacher's Ed. for above	1.80

GRADE THREE, THIRD EDITION

5	The ABC Beyond Treasure Valley (3rd reader 3^1) @2.04	10.20
1	" " Teacher's Ed. for above	2.04
5	" " Along Friendly Roads (3rd reader 3^2) @2.04	10.20
1	" " Teacher's Ed. for above	2.04

GRADE FOUR, THIRD EDITION

5	The ABC American Adventures (4th reader) @2.37	11.85
1	" " Teacher's Ed. for above	2.37

GRADE FIVE, THIRD EDITION

5	The ABC Adventures Here and There (5th reader) @2.43	12.15
1	" " Teacher's Ed. for above	2.43

GRADE SIX, THIRD EDITION

5	The ABC Adventures Now and Then (6th reader) @2.46	12.30
1	Teacher's Ed. for above	2.46
10	Websters New Elementary Dictionary @2.76	20.76
1	Teacher's Edition for above	2.76

$139.38

1967-1968

TRANSITION-ADJUSTMENT BUDGET

Creative Playthings, Inc.
Princeton, New Jersey

1	#AG490	Clown Punching Bag	$ 4.00
2	#AA358	Wood Telephones @3.25	6.50
1	#AB292	White Bendable Rubber Family Figures	6.50
1	#AD181	Stethoscope	2.95
1	#AT621	Inset Cylinders	5.95
1	#AA812	Asymmetric Space Construction Kit	9.95
1	#AT259	Box of 1000 ½" beads	8.00
4 doz.	#AT336	Black Laces @.70	2.80
2	#AT223	Landscape Peg Boards @2.50	5.00
1	#AT242	Color Cone	2.00
2	#AA813	Peg Board Play Tiles @4.00	8.00
1	#AN100	Graded Circles, Squares, Triangles	3.25
2	#AT330	Lincoln Logs @4.00	8.00
2	#AT248	Make-It Toy @3.00	6.00
1	#AT680	Set of 6 Beginner Puzzles	6.95
1	#AT269	Trucks Puzzle	1.95
1	#AT216	House Puzzle	1.95
1	#AT174	Doctor Puzzle	1.75
1	#AT172	Postman Puzzle	1.75
1	#AT171	Policeman Puzzle	1.75
1	#AT701	Teacher Puzzle	1.75
1	#AT704	Barber Puzzle	1.75
1	#AT040	Baseball Puzzle	1.75
2	#AN311	Day-By-Day Calendar @3.00	6.00
1	#AA370	Minute Minder (4245 NDEA)	3.00
1	#AA328	Clock	3.50
1 doz.	#AN750	Mini Clocks	3.50
1	#AN744	Phonetic Word Drill Set	2.25
1	#AA380	Letters and Numbers	3.50
1	#AB223	Introductory Set Blocks	29.50
1	#AB151	Flatbed Truck	15.95
			$167.45

J. L. Hammett Co.
2393 Vauxhall Road
Union, N. J. 07083

1	#9 Flannel Board, 36" x 48"	$ 10.95
1	H100 Number Frame	16.50
1	#571 Dremel Moto-Shop (Jig Saw)	33.95
1	#86 Aquarium	15.00
		$ 76.40

224

1967-1968

TRANSITION-ADJUSTMENT BUDGET

American Book Company
300 Pike Street
Cincinnati, Ohio 45202

GRADE ONE, THIRD EDITION
5	The ABC Study Book for all three pre-primers @.54	$ 2.70
5	" " " " (primer) @.54	2.70
5	" " " " (first reader) @.60	3.00
1	" " Teacher's Ed. Ann. & keyed, Study Bk, 1st Rdr	.60

GRADE TWO, THIRD EDITION
5	The ABC Study Book (2nd reader 2^1) @.60	3.00
1	" " Teacher's Edition for above	.60
5	" " Study Book (2nd reader 2^2) @.60	3.00
1	" " Teacher's Edition for above	.60

GRADE THREE, THIRD EDITION
5	The ABC Study Book (third reader 3^1) @.63	3.15
1	" " Teacher's Edition for above	.63
5	" " Study Book (third reader 3^2) @.63	3.15
1	" " Teacher's Edition for above	.63

GRADE FOUR, THIRD EDITION
| 5 | The ABC Study Book (fourth reader) @.69 | 3.45 |
| 1 | "   "   Teacher's Edition for above | .69 |

GRADE FIVE, THIRD EDITION
| 5 | The ABC Study Book (fifth reader) @.69 | 3.45 |
| 1 | "   "   Teacher's Edition for above | .69 |

GRADE SIX, THIRD EDITION
| 5 | The ABC Study Book (sixth reader) @.69 | 3.45 |
| 1 | "   "   Teacher's Edition for above | .69 |

$ 36.18

Educational Development Laboratories
Huntington, New York

2	Flash X @ 7.20	$ 14.40
2	Flash X Set X5 Sight Vocab. Gr. 1 @ 3.60	7.20
2	" " " X6 " " " 2 "	7.20
2	" " " X10 " " " 3 "	7.20
2	" " " X7 Basic Math + - @ 3.60	7.20
2	" " " X8 " " x ÷ "	7.20

$ 50.40

Science Research Association
259 E. Erie Street
Chicago, Illinois 60611

1 pkg. Pupil Analysis Sheet $ .75

225

1967-1968

TRANSITION-ADJUSTMENT BUDGET

F. A. Owen Publishing Co.
Instructor Park
Sansville, New York 14437

1	#500 Mathematics Concept Charts, Comp Series	$	12.00
1	#RRC803 For Primary Children		4.95
1	#RRC903 For Intermediate Children		4.95
1	#551 Good Health Charts Set 1		1.95
1	#552 " " " Set 2		1.95
1	#558 Community Helpers Posters		2.00
1	#711 Community Helpers Activities		3.00
1	#712 Community Helpers Activities		3.00
1	#559 Holidays and Special Days		3.50
1	#721 Outline Maps		3.00
1	#713 Color Charts		3.50
		$	43.80

Milton Bradley Company
Springfield, Mass.

1	#8039 Cubical Counting Blocks	$	4.00
4	#7615 Plastic Peg Boards @2.50		10.00
2	#7616 Plastic Counting Discs @1.00		2.00
2	#9315 Toy Money @1.25		2.50
1	#9312 Hundred Chart		1.50
1	#7611 Flash Cards, Addition		1.25
1	#7612 " " Subtraction		1.25
1	#7613 " " Multiplication		1.25
1	#7614 " " Division		1.25
2	#9102 Primary Number Line @1.50		3.00
1	#9309 Quizmo		2.00
1	#9310 "		3.00
1	#9004 Place Value Indicators		3.00
1	#9502 Alphabet Flash Cards		2.00
1	#4473 Ring Toss		2.00
		$	40.00

Hayes School Publishing Co., Inc.
321 Pennwood Ave.
Wilkinsburg, Pennsylvania 15221

1	Spec. Ed. Reading & Language Arts	$	3.00
1	85C Alphabet Wall Cards		1.00
1	85M Manuscript Writing Cards		1.00
1	Nip The Bear		3.25
1	Red Deer the Indian Boy		3.25
1	Scottie and His Friends		3.25
1	SS414 Social Studies Book 1		2.50
1	SS415 " " " 2		2.50
1	SU97 The Human Body		2.00
1	SU96 Hayes Our Solar System		2.00
		$	23.75

1967-1968

TRANSITION-ADJUSTMENT BUDGET

Milliken Publishing Company
c/o Martin Ader, 801 Richmond Road
East Meadow, New York

DUPLICATING BOOKS

1	Modern Arithmetic Grade 1 (1st part)	$ 3.25
1	" " " 1 (2nd ")	3.25
1	Number Exercises Grade 1 (1st part)	3.25
1	" " " 1 (2nd ")	3.25
1	Modern Arithmetic Grade 2 (1st part)	3.25
1	" " " " (2nd ")	3.25
1	Number Exercises Grade 2 (1st part)	3.25
1	" " " " (2nd ")	3.25
1	Arithmetic Word Problems Grade 2	3.25
1	Modern Arithmetic Grade 3 (1st part)	3.25
1	" " " " (2nd ")	3.25
1	Arithmetic Exercises Grade 3 (1st part)	3.25
1	" " " " (2nd ")	3.25
1	Modern Arithmetic Grade 4 (1st part)	3.25
1	" " " " (2nd ")	3.25
1	Arithmetic Exercises Grade 4 (1st part)	3.25
1	" " " " (2nd ")	3.25
1	Modern Arithmetic Grade 5 (1st part)	3.25
1	" " " " (2nd ")	3.25
1	Read & Do Pre-Primer A	3.25
1	Learning to Read Pre-Primer B	3.25
1	Starting to Read Grade 1 (1st half)	3.25
1	" " " " (2nd ")	3.25
1	Read and Do Primer	3.25
1	Starting Phonics Grade 1, Part 1	3.25
1	" " " " 2	3.25
1	Read and Think Grade 2 (1st Half)	3.25
1	" " " " (2nd ")	3.25
1	Learning Your Language Grade 2 (1st half)	3.25
1	" " " " (2nd ")	3.25
1	Learning Phonics Grade 2 (1st half)	3.25
1	" " " " (2nd ")	3.25
1	Learning to Spell Grade 2 (1st part)	3.25
1	" " " " (2nd ")	3.25
1	Read and Think Grade 3 (1st half)	3.25
1	" " " " (2nd ")	3.25

Milliken Publishing Company

1	Using Your English Grade 3 (1st half)	$ 3.25
1	" " " " " (2nd half)	3.25
1	Learning Phonics Grade 3 (1st part)	3.25
1	" " " " (2nd part)	3.25
1	Spelling Adventures Grade 3 (1st part)	3.25
1	" " " " (2nd part)	3.25
1	Reading Adventures Grade 4 (1st half)	3.25
1	" " " " (2nd half)	3.25
1	English Exercises Grade 4 (1st half)	3.25
1	" " " " (2nd half)	3.25
1	Learning Phonics Grade 4 (1st part)	3.25
1	" " " " (2nd part)	3.25
1	Growing in Citizenship Grade 2	1.75
1	Days We Like and Holidays	1.75
1	The Seasons Grade 2	1.75
1	Beginning Science Adventures, Part 1, Grade 2, 3	3.25
1	" " " Part II, Grade 2, 3	3.25
1	Science Adventures, Part I, Grades 3-4	3.25
1	" " " II, " 3-4	3.25
1	Indians of the Woods & Plains, Grade 3	3.25
1	Science Goals, Part I, Grades 4-5	3.25
1	" " Part II, " "	3.25
		$ 184.00

Audio-Visual Sales and Service
5 Franklin Avenue P.O. Box 302
Sag Harbor, New York   Att: Mr. Gettling

1	Wollensak 1500SS Tape Recorder w/cover N.C.	
1	Bell & Howell Language Master 711 - B	$ 250.00

Accessories for Language Master
4	Headphones @28.00	112.00
1	Dual Headphone Adapter	2.95
1	Multi-phone Panel	26.00
1	Interconnecting Cable for Multiphone	2.00
		$ 392.95

Educational Development Laboratories
Huntington, New York

1	Controlled Reader Jr. with case	$ 202.00

1967-1968

TRANSITION-ADJUSTMENT BUDGET

Audio-Visual Sales and Service
5 Franklin Avenue P.O. Box 302
Sag Harbor, New York

Att: Mr. Gettling

CARDS FOR LANGUAGE MASTER

2 sets	Blanks (100/per set) @6.00			$ 12.00
1	Vocabulary Builder Program - Set of 200			
	Grades 4-8	Set 1		35.00
		Set 2		35.00
		Set 3		35.00
1	Word Picture Program:			
	Pre-School	Set 1		35.00
	Kindergarten	Set 1		35.00
	Kindergarten	Set 2		35.00
	Grades 1-3	Set 1		35.00
		Set 2		35.00
		Set 3		35.00
1	Language Stimulation Program			
	Grades 4-8	Set 1		35.00
		Set 2		35.00
1	The Phonics Program			
	Pre-School	Set 1		35.00
	Kindergarten	Set 1		35.00
	Grades 1-3	Set 1		35.00
		Set 2		35.00
		Set 3		35.00
	Grades 4-8	Set 3		35.00

$ 607.00

Bardeen's, Inc.
543 East Genesee Street
Syracuse, New York 13201

2	#981 Double Panel Adjustment Easels @21.00	$ 42.00
1	#650K Easel Chalkboard	18.00

$ 60.00

1967-1968

TRANSITION-ADJUSTMENT BUDGET

J. L. Hammett Co.
2393 Vauxhall Road
Union, N.J. 07083

1	#1700 Bench Vise	$ 4.75
1	Half-Round File	1.70
1	#37 Ball Pein Hammer	2.30
1	#534 Hot Plate	10.00
4	#955 Planters @2.00	8.00
1	Ready to Read Puzzler Set	3.50
1	#286 Seasons Flannel Board	2.50
1	#51 Numerals, Words, and Symbols	1.50
1	#210 Counter Brush	1.36
1	#19 Dust Pan	1.00
4	#9220 Chart Tablets @1.70	6.80
1	Measurement Level 1 Duplicating Book	3.20
1	" " 2 " "	3.20
1	" " 3 " "	3.20
1	Time Level 1 Duplicating Book	3.20
1	" " 2 " "	3.20
1	" " 3 " "	3.20
1	U. S. Money Level 1 Duplicating Book	3.20
1	" " " 2 " "	3.20
1	" " " 3 " "	3.20
3	Craft sticks, undrilled, boxes of 1000 @1.50	4.50
2 doz.	#680 Leather Kit Comb Case @2.40	4.80
1	#1470 Slip Joint Pliers	.95
1	#54E End Cutting Pliers	3.65
1	5 lb. Poly-Mosaic Tiles	10.00
1	#S463 Door Bell, 2½"	1.50
1	#S462 Knife Switch	.45
2	#S466 Dry Cell Batteries @1.50	3.00
1	#S464 Receptacles	.50
1	#465 Light Bulbs	.50
1	#1418 Claw Hammer	2.85
1	#75 Plane	3.98
1	#2010 Saw Cross Cut	3.25
1	#651 Screw Driver	.60
2	#H200 Number Frames @2.60	5.20
2	#155 Colored Sticks (1000) @1.20	2.40
1 doz.	#780 Pupil's Number Line	1.00

$ 121.34

1967-1968

TRANSITION-ADJUSTMENT BUDGET

Bardeen's, Inc.
543 Genesee Street East
Syracuse, New York   13201

2	#AD-2A Flo-Master Pens @4.00	$ 8.00
1	#85 Coping Saw	1.40
1	#6L 6" Coping Saw Blades, pkg of 10	.35
3 doz.	Fine Sandpaper @.45	1.35
3 doz.	Medium Sandpaper @.45	1.35
1	#2500C Hand Drill	2.75
1	#403 Drill Points Set	.80
1	Medium Steel Wool	.65
4	#7200 Pipe Cleaner Art Kits @.85	3.40
2 doz.	#X34 Permoplast Modeling Clay @5.50	11.00
2	#175 Animal Cages @10.50	21.00
1	#987 Ideal Chart Stand	9.75
1	#270 Reading Readiness Charts	4.00
1	#271 Sequence Charts	5.00
1	#272 Initial & Final Consonant Charts	7.25
1	#273 Blends and Digraphs Charts	2.75
1	#274 Vowel Charts	5.00
1	#2011 Cut Out Letters	.75
1	#2015 Stencils	.50
1	#2084 Stencils	.50
1	#2204 Basic Sight Cards	1.10
1	#2200 Picture Word Cards	1.00
1	#2203 Group Word Teaching Game	1.59
1	#9850 ABC Picture Board	7.50
2	#108 Jumbo Anagrams @1.00	2.00
1	#54 Kinder City	7.00
2	#300 Deluxe Rig-A-Jig @3.00	6.00
2	#705 American Bricks @2.30	4.60
2	20 x 60 3 Panel Folding Screens @16.50	33.00
4	Checker Sets @2.00	8.00
1	#4751 Chinese Checkers	2.00
1	#S-735 Safe-T-Bat Set	2.25
4	#S-650 Fun Balls @.75	3.00

$ 166.59

231

APPENDIX D (2)

<u>SUMMER ELEMENTARY TRANSITION-ADJUSTMENT CLASS BUDGET</u>

<u>FOR THREE GROUPS OF EIGHT STUDENTS EACH</u>

<u>(1969-1970)</u>

Materials	$ 256.62
(See attached purchase orders)	
Field Trips	300.00
	$ 556.62

Note: Transition-Adjustment class equipment and supplies are utilized in the summer program.

SUMMER TRANSITION-ADJUSTMENT BUDGET

J. L. Hammett Co.
2393 Vauxhall Road
Union, New Jersey 07083

3	Cat. No. 92660,	Pennsylvania "Soft" Softball @2.15	$ 6.45
3	Cat. No. 92665,	Softball Bat @2.25	6.75
3	Cat. No. 92615,	Deluxe Playground Balls @6.10	18.30
6	Cat. No. 82700,	Jump Ropes @.30	1.80
3 doz.	Cat. No. 32014,	Crayola Crayons #241 @4.60	13.80
1 set	Cat. No. 9801,	Rubber Pitching Horseshoes	4.00
6 rolls	Cat. No. 24422,	Masking Tape 3/4" x 60 yds. @.57	3.42
30	Cat. No. 76551,	Permoplast Modeling Clay X-34 @.65	19.50
1 doz.	Cat. No. 21908,	Elmer's Glue-All 8 ounce @1.00	12.00
10	Cat. No. 44332,	Easel Brushes #1751 ½" @.35	3.50
12 doz.	Cat. No. 56500,	Pencils, Kendall #2 @.45	5.40
6 bxs.	Cat. No. 71165,	Craft Sticks, Undrilled @1.95	11.70
10 bxs.	Cat. No. 70775,	Pipe Cleaner Kits #200 @.80	8.00
30	Cat. No. 70838,	Pen and Pencil Holder #670 @.25	7.50

$ 122.12

Economy Crafts
47-11 Francis Lewis Blvd.
Flushing, New York 11361

2 Packs Wheelbarrow Planter @7.50	$ 15.00
2 Packs Horse Trough Planter @4.95	9.90
4 Lbs. Special Plastic Beads @2.50	10.00
12 Spools Beading Wire @.15	1.80
1 Cat. No. BN-100, Rainbow Beanies @14.95	14.95
1 Case Cat. No. 4097, Bulk Sheets (Styrofoam)	9.95

$ 61.60

Martin Ader
801 Richmond Road
East Meadow, New York

1 Cat. No. 703, Phonics Development Grade 3 TD	$ 5.95
1 Cat. No. 204, Heat, Light, and Sound TD	5.95

$ 11.90

SUMMER TRANSITION-ADJUSTMENT BUDGET

George Corsell
Route 2, Mayville
New Jersey 14757

1	Cat.	AD211, Arithmetic Drills, Grade 1	$	3.00
1	"	AD212 " " " 2		3.00
1	"	AD213 " " " 3		3.00
1	"	AD214 " " " 4		3.00
1	"	AD215 " " " 5		3.00
1	"	AD216 " " " 6		3.00
1	"	AD217 " " Junior High		3.00
1	"	0906, Human Body		7.00
1	"	0907, Our Solar System		7.00
1	"	0908, Magnets & Electricity		7.00
1	"	0909, Light and Sound		7.00
1	"	NS303, Flowers We Should Know		3.00
1	"	NS301, Birds We Should Know		3.00
1	"	NS304, Trees of the U.S.		3.00
1	"	NS307, Zoo Animals We Should Know		3.00

$ 61.00

APPENDIX D (3)

PROPOSED ELEMENTARY TRANSITION-ADJUSTMENT
CLASS BUDGET FOR 1970-1971 FOR EIGHT CLASSES
(IN ADDITION TO EXISTING EQUIPMENT AND SUPPLIES
FOR SIX PRESENT CLASSES)

Art Supplies - Bid	$ 462.79
Principals' Office Supplies - Bid	29.92
School Supplies - Bid	288.36
Attached Purchase Orders	5,184.94
TOTAL	$ 5,966.01

1970-1971

TRANSITION-ADJUSTMENT CLASS BUDGET

J. L. Hammet
2393 Vauxhall Road
Union, New Jersey, 07083

1	#61721 Flannel Board Set Community Workers	$	2.95
1	#61717 " " " The Community		2.95
1	#61719 " " " Members of the Family		1.25
1	#61528 " " " Seasons		2.50
1	#61536 " " " We Dress For the Weather		4.95
1	#66669 Picture Books, The Big Shoe Book		1.25
1	#83381 Helpmates, Button Model		4.50
1	#83380 " Zipper Model		5.75
1	#83382 " Buckle Model		4.50
1	#82510 Primary Games, The Childrens Hour		2.35
1	#82567 " " Deluxe Chutes and Ladders		2.15
1	#86515 " " Three Little Pigs		2.00
1	#60575 Kinesthetic Learning Numbers		2.50
1	#22486, Unit G, Small Organizer		2.00
1	#65610, Unit B, Political Globe 12"		9.95
1	#61896, Unit D, Kinesthetic Alphabet Cards		6.95
1	#61897 " " " " "		6.95
2	Harmon Walking Rails #9921 @33.00		66.00
2	Visual Target #9923 @6.50		13.00
6	Kaleidoscope Puzzles #6010 @2.50		15.00
6	Pyramid Puzzles #6036 @3.50		21.00
3	Stencils for Tracing #6021 @4.00		12.00
3 bxs.	Portable Study Corral #6259 @20.00		60.00
3 bxs.	Number rods #6300 @8.00		24.00
3	Liquid Measure #773 @7.50		22.50
6	Thermometer #759 @1.00		6.00
1	Alphabet Practice Cards, Capital Manuscript #6052		2.25
1	Lower Case Manuscript #6053		2.25
1	Gregory Peg Board Climb #92755		39.95
1	Celebar Stop Watch #92715		31.00
15	My First Dictionary #67553 @1.95		29.25
20	The Picture Dictionary For Children #67555 @3.95		79.00
2	Sorting Box #81506 @6.00		12.00
2	Mirror Box #81581 @5.00		10.00

$ 510.65

New Dimensions in Education, Inc.
131 Jericho Turnpike
Jericho, New York   11753

1	Alpha One	$	199.75
1	Teachers Guide for Alpha One		9.95

$ 209.70

1970-1971

TRANSITION-ADJUSTMENT CLASS BUDGET

William J. Scholtz & Son, Inc.
Sag Harbor, New York

1 Language Master	$ 250.00
8 Headphones for Language Master @28.00	224.00
1 Interconnecting Cable	2.00
1 Multiphone Panel	26.00
2 Word Picture Program Set 1 @35.00	70.00
1 Word Picture Program Set 2	35.00
1 Word Picture Program Set 3	35.00
1 Phonics Program Set 1	35.00
1 Phonics Program Set 2	35.00
1 Phonics Program Set 3	35.00
5 Blank Cards 3½" x 9", 100/bx @6.00	30.00
	$ 777.00

Premier Products
Rivervale, New Jersey

1 Training Bag #X142	$ 40.50
1 Spring & Swivel #X147	6.00
1 Medicine Ball #H215	24.75
	$ 71.25

Sport Craft
140 Woodbine Street
Bergenfield, New Jersey

1 Rubber Horse Shoe Set #08022	$ 6.50
1 American Made Wooden Darts #03212	2.70
	$ 9.20

Webster Division
McGraw-Hill Co.
340 West 42nd Street
New York, New York

50 Conquests in Reading @.90	$ 45.00
2 Teachers Edition @.90	1.80
30 The Magic Word of Dr. Spello @.90	27.00
	$ 73.80

1970-1971

TRANSITION-ADJUSTMENT CLASS BUDGET

Educational Development Lab.
Huntington, New York

1	Controlled Reader, Junior		$ 190.00
1	Carrying Case		12.00
2	Story Filmstrip Set 4E First Grade @90.00		180.00
2	" " " 4F Second Grade @90.00		180.00
1	" " " 4G Third Grade		45.00
2	" " " 3A Intermediate @99.00		198.00
1	" " " D Fourth Grade		55.00
1	" " " E Fifth Grade		55.00
20	Grade 1 Stories (Cat. #1-103)@.90		18.00
20	" 2 " (Cat. #1-105) @.90		18.00
20	" 3 " (Cat. #1-107) @.90		18.00
20	" 4 " and Lesson Plans (Cat.#1-109)@.90		18.00
20	" 5 " " " " (Cat.#1-111)@.90		18.00

$1005.00

Houghton Mifflin
55 West 43rd Street
New York, New York 10036

5	A Speller for Beginners, Grade Level 1, Code 1-21658 @1.28	$ 6.40
1	Teacher Edition Code 1-21659	2.72
10	Structural Arithmetic 1 Pupils W.B., Grade Level 1 @1.72	17.20
1	Kit 1 Starter Set, Structural Arithmetic Grade Level 1	52.00
1	Primary Reading Profiles, Grade Level 1	3.75
5	Come Along, Grade Level 2 @2.72	13.60
5	On We Go, Grade Level 2 @2.72	13.60
1	Inventory of Phonetic Skills, Grade Level 1	1.32
5	Workbook For Come Along, Grade Level 2 @.96	4.80
5	Workbook For On We Go, Grade Level 2 @.96	4.80

$ 120.19

Scott Foresman
99 Bauer Drive
Oakland, New Jersey 07436

<u>Invitation to Personal Reading</u>
1 set	Grade 1, Set A #2875-65	$ 51.00
1 set	Grade 1, Set B #2894-68	51.00
1 set	Grade 2, Set A #2876-65	51.00
1 set	Grade 2, Set B #2895-68	51.00

$ 204.00

1970-1971

TRANSITION-ADJUSTMENT CLASS BUDGET

Barnell Loft, Ltd.
111 South Centre Avenue
Rockville Centre, New York

40	GETTING THE MAIN IDEA, Level 1 (Bk A) @7.90 for 10	$ 31.60
40	USING THE CONTEXT, Levels 1-6 (Bks A,B,C,D,E,F) @7.90 for 10	189.60
2 pkg.	USING THE CONTEXT, Levels 3 and 4 @1.25 pkg/100	5.00
40	WORKING WITH SOUNDS, Levels 1-4 (Bks A,B,C,D) @7.90 for 10	126.40
2 pkg.	WORKING WITH SOUNDS, Levels 3 and 4 @1.25 pkg/100	5.00
40	FOLLOWING DIRECTIONS, Levels 1-6 (Books A,B,C,D,E,F) @7.90 for 10	189.60
2 pkg.	FOLLOWING DIRECTIONS, Levels 3 and 4 @1.25 pkg/100	5.00
40	LOCATING THE ANSWER, Levels 1-6 (Bks A,B,C,D,E,F) @7.90 for 10	189.60
2 pkg.	LOCATING THE ANSWER, Levels 3-4 @1.25 pkg/100	5.00
40	GETTING THE FACTS, Levels 1-6 (Books A,B,C,D,E,F) @7.90 for 10	189.60
2 pkg.	GETTING THE FACTS, Levels 3-4 @1.25 pkg/100	5.00
40	DRAWING CONCLUSIONS, Level 1 (Book A) @7.90 for 10	31.60
		$ 973.00

CCM School Materials, Inc.
2124 West 82nd Place
Chicago, Illinois 60620

1 set	Giant Wood Dominoes #05-133-0001	$ 9.95
1	Store Play Screen #27-003-0010	36.75
1	Wood Cash Register #27-001-0041	14.95
1	Contemporary Sink #27-003-0014	29.95
1	Contemporary Stove #27-003-0013	29.95
1	Contemporary Cupboard #27-003-0011	29.95
1	Contemporary Refrigerator #27-003-0012	29.95
1	Solid Wood Iron #27-001-0003	1.25
1	Wood Ironing Board #27-001-0002	9.95
		$ 192.65

Educational Materials Services
One DuPont Street
Plainview, New York.

100	4'x5' boards @1.33	$ 133.00

1970-1971

TRANSITION-ADJUSTMENT CLASS BUDGET

Sears, Roebuck and Co.
4640 Roosevelt Blvd.
Philadelphia, Pennsylvania 19132

12	Flexible Mask Goggles #9G1859 @1.49	$ 17.88
6	Tutor Typewriters #3G5267C @37.88	227.28
6	Typewriter Ribbons B/R @3 for 3.33	6.66
		$ 251.82

American Book Company
55 Fifth Avenue
New York, New York 10003

25	DOWN SINGING RIVER @3.00	$ 75.00
20	OVER A CITY BRIDGE @3.00	60.00
20	BEYOND TREASURE VALLEY @3.00	60.00
10	ALONG FRIENDLY ROADS @3.00	30.00

<u>WORKBOOKS</u>

50	UP THE STREET AND DOWN @.90	45.00
2	Teacher Editions @.90	1.80
50	AROUND GREEN HILLS @.90	45.00
2	Teacher Editions @.90	1.80
50	DOWN SINGING RIVER @.90	45.00
2	Teacher Editions @.90	1.80
50	BEYOND TREASURE VALLEY	45.00
2	Teacher Editions	1.80
50	ALONG FRIENDLY ROADS @.90	45.00
2	Teacher Editions @.90	1.80
		$ 459.00

TRANSITION-ADJUSTMENT CLASS BUDGET - 1970-1971

Houghton Mifflin Company
55 West 43rd Street
New York, New York 10036

1	Primary Let's Enjoy Poetry by Hughes	$ 4.75
1	" Set of Sixteen Read by Yourself #1-46392	23.85
5	Pre-Prim. I, TIP #1-37020 @1.00	5.00
1	Pre-Prim. Teacher Edition TIP #1-3782	1.00
5	Pre-Prim. II TIP and Mitten #1-3784 @1.00	5.00
1	" " " " " " Teacher Edition	1.00
5	Pre-Prim. III, The Big Show #1-37030 @1.00	5.00
1	" " " " " Teacher Edition	1.00
5	Primer, Janet & Jack #1-37035 @2.32	11.60
1	" " " " Teacher Guide #1-3788	2.32
5	First Reader Up and Away @2.32	11.60
1	First Reader Teacher Edition	2.32
1	Duplicating Masters for Tip, #1-37180	5.20
1	" " " " Tip and Mitten #1-37181	6.24
1	" " " " The Big Show #1-37182	5.48
1	" " " " Janet & Jack #1-37183	13.08
1	" " " " Up and Away #1-37184	10.08
1	" " " " Come Along #1-37185	12.48
1	" " " " On We Go #1-3186	13.92
5	Grade Level 2, Come Along #1-37045 @2.72	13.60
1	" " " " " Teacher Guide #1-37092	2.72
10	" " " Workbook for Come Along #1-37136 @.96	9.60
1	" " " Teacher Guide for Workbook #1-37161	.96
5	" " " On We Go #1-37050 @2.72	13.60
1	" " " " " " Teacher Guide #1-37094	2.72
10	" " " " " " Workbook #1-37138 @.96	9.60
1	" " " " " " Workbook Teacher Guide	.96
		$ 194.68

BIBLIOGRAPHY

1. Bentzen, Frances. "Sex Ratios in Learning and Behavior Disorders," *National Elementary Principal,* 1966, 46, pp.13-17.
2. Bisgyer, Jay L., Carl L. Kahn, and Vernon F. Frazee, "Special Classes for Emotionally Disturbed Children," *American Journal of Orthopsychiatry,* 1964, 34, pp. 696-704.
3. Bower, Eli M. *Early Identification of Emotionally Handicapped Children in School.* Illinois: Charles G. Thomas, 1969.
4. Ekstein, Rudolf. *Children of Time and Space, of Action and Impulse.* New York: Appleton-Century-Crofts, 1966.
5. Freud, Anna *Normality and Pathology in Childhood, Assessments of Development.* New York: International Universities Press, Inc., 1965.
6. Furman, Robert A. and Anny Katan. *The Therapeutic Nursery School.* New York: International Universities Press, Inc., 1969.
7. Haring, Norris G. and E. Lakin Phillips. *Educating Emotionally Disturbed Children.* New York: McGraw-Hill Book Company, 1962.
8. Hewett, Frank M. *The Emotionally Disturbed Child in the Classroom.* Boston: Allyn and Bacon, Inc., 1968.
9. Kliman, Gilbert, "Survey Finds Needs of Children Unmet"; "N.Y. Preschoolers Receive Psychoanalytic Therapy," *Psychiatric News,* 1968, 3, p. 7.
10. Magary, James F., ed. *School Psychological Services: In Theory and Practice. (a Handbook).* New Jersey: Prentice-Hall, Inc.,1967.
11. Mahler, Margaret S. *Of Human Symbiosis and the Vicissitudes of Individuation,* Vol. I, Infantile Psychosis. New York: International Universities Press, Inc., 1968.
12. Neubauer, Peter, B., Josephine Pell, Kathryn Bobbins Memorial Lectures, Series No. 4, 1969, North Shore Child Guidance Center, Manhasset, New York.
13. Rabinow, Barney. *The Training and Supervision of Teachers for Emotionally Disturbed Children.* Albany, New York: The State Education Department, 1964.
14. Strunk, Betty Bliss. "Helping the Disturbed Child," *School Management,* 1969, pp. 53-58.
15. Weil, Annemarie P. "Some Evidences of Deviational Development in Infancy and Childhood," *The Psychoanalytic Study of the Child,* Vol. XI. New York: International Universities Press, Inc., 1956.
16. *Action for Mental Health,* Final Report of the Joint Commission on Mental Illness and Health 1961. New York: Basic Books, Inc., 1961.
17. *What Are the Facts About Mental Illness in the United States?* National Committee Against Mental Illness, Inc. Washington, D. C., 1966.

Index

A

Achievement tests, 38, 39
Acting-out child, 144-146
Adolescence:
 biological stresses, 41
 dynamics, 52
Aides, teacher, 58, 176
Anecdotal records, 189
Aptitude tests, 38
Arithmetic level, test, 39
Art education:
 ability, 122
 behavior favorable for child, 122
 breakthroughs, 120-122
  examples, 121
  work of art speaks, 121-122
 choice of materials, 124-126
  advantage in several choices, 124
  attention span, 126
  building and manipulative skills, 126
  colored chalk, pencils, 125
  colored sticks, pipe cleaners, wire, 125
  crayons, cray-pas, charcoal, 125
  directions, 126
  drawing, 126
  farming-out, 127
  freedom, 126
  introduce new lesson or material, 126
  painting media, 125
  reality limitations, 126
  recognition to work, 126
  satisfy immediate needs, 125
  storage shelf, 126
  structural materials, 125
  two-dimensional expression, 125
  water colors, tempers, finger paints, 125
  wide variety, 125
 clay, 123-124
  all achieve degree of success, 124
  countless opportunities to use, 124
  manipulative motor skills, 123
 different from regular art classes, 120
 farming out, 122
 goals, 126-127

INDEX

Goals (*continued*)
    creative direction for drives, 127
    experimenting with materials, 127
    farming-out, 127
    feeling of accomplishment, 127
    feeling that they can achieve, 126
    inner aspirations and hope, 127
    meaning in environment, 127
    means to growth, 127
    self-esteem, 127
    self-identity, 126
    sense of pride, 127
  inner self exposed, 122
  listen to child, 122
  means to emotional end, 120
  opportunity to communicate, 122
  placement in regular art class, 122
  reflection of personality, 122
  summer program, 174
  wood, 122-123
    impractical in large regular class, 123
    mechanical ability, 123
    practical for class of eight, 123
    released emotions, 123
    small class, 123
    tools, 123
    worthwhile, 123
Attention span, 126
Attitude, black and white, 48
Audio-visual equipment, 137-138
Auditory discrimination, 188
Autistic shell, 49

B

Bender-Gestalt designs and human figure drawings, 39
Biological stresses, 41
Board of education, 59-60
Body image and balance, 188
Brain damage, term, 25, 36
Brain dysfunction, 25, 36
Budget:
  economic considerations, 195
  finances of program, 139-140
  summer program, cost, 173
Building, 64
Building coordinator, 194
Building skills, 126
Bus driver, 58, 66, 193
Buses. 66-69, 173, 199-200

C

Cafeteria workers, 192

Causal factors, 40
Center for Preventive Psychiatry, 208
Children:
  acting-out, 144-146
  candidates for class, 204
  disturbed, in regular class, 204
  dynamics behind progress, 205, 206
  entering fall class, 174
  goals, 198
  long struggle to mainstream, 197-198
  not identified and referred, 205
  number in system, 195
  objectives for, 187
  organized in early school years, 204
  placement, 55
  success begets success, 187
  summer program, 175-176
  theme and variations on disturbed pattern, 204
  transportation, 199-200
  waiting list, 204-205
  withdrawn, 146
Children's Apperception Test, 39
Class organization, 63-64
Class schedule, daily, 55
Class, smaller enrollment, 192
Classroom, 64-66
Clay, art education, 123-124
Community groups, 60
Comprehension, 188
Conferences:
  parent, 41, 55, 103, 162, 180, 189-190, 197
  postevaluation, parent, 76-77
  team, 38, 160, 175, 188-190
Consulting services, 55
"Cornerstone Project", 207
Cost, summer program, 173
Curriculum:
  case history, 86-88
  elementary, 88-103
  evaluating student progress, 103
  handwriting, 95-96
  junior high school, 103-105
  materials, 91-93
  mathematics, 98-99
  motivation and attitude, 82-84
  need to build interest, 84-85
  optimistic attitude of teacher, 85
  parents can help, 90-91
  pressure from parents, 89-90
  rapport between student and teacher, 86
  reading, 89
  reading specialist, 93-95

INDEX

Curriculum (*continued*)
    reporting to parents, 103
    science, 99-103
    spelling, 96-97
    standard operating procedure, 55
    success in any area, 85
    summer program, 177
Custodians, 58

D

Daily class schedule, 55
"Developmental delay," 36
Development:
    history, 40, 41
    interferences, 48-49
        autistic shell, 49
        black and white attitude, 48
        clumsy and rough in movements, 48
        inappropriate behavior, 48
        sleep, 48
        toilet training, 48
        walking or talking, 48
Diagnosis, determining, 40
Difficulties:
    curriculum hodgepodge, 202
    demonstrating value of class, 195
    economic considerations, 195
    farming out not gradually developed, 202
    goals for children, 198
    initial obstacle, 195-196
    low man on totem pole, 202
    limited data on effectiveness of classes, 195, 196
    long struggle to mainstream, 197-198
    number of disturbed children, 195
    parent apprehension, 196-197
        conferences, 197
        facing facts, 196
        future, 196
        guilt, 196
        nature of child's disturbance, 196
        need for continued placement, 196
        not accepting placement made, 197
        not clear on reality picture, 196
        removal of student, 197
        stigma, 196
        under pressure at home, 197
    persuading school district, 195
    principals, 203
    program no better than teacher, 202
    resistance to new concept, 202
    screening procedures not set, 202
    space, 198-199
        (*see also* Space)
    substitute teacher, 200-201
    transportation, 199-200
    unclear concepts and procedures, 202
    unstructured classes, 202
    wrong children in class, 202
Director, 54-55, 56-57, 58, 59
    (*see also* Organizing district program)
District program, organizing, 54-72
    (*see also* Organizing district program)
Ditto master workbooks, 138
Dominance, 188
Drawing, 125, 177
Dynamics:
    adolescence, 52
    blamed and blameless, 50-51
    causes, 44-45, 49-50
    clinging to mother, 44-45
    developmental interferences, 48-49
        (*see also* Development)
    effects on family life, 45-46
        constant surveillance, 45
        energies drained, 45
        lack of pride, 45
        parents disturbed, 45
        potential lifetime burden, 45
    goals, 51-52
        bring closer to reality, 51
        coping with demands of reality, 52
        organize for life functioning, 51
        regular class, 51
    illusion of environmental cause, 49-50
        cumulative traumas, 49
        feeling of being "different," 50
        nonenvironmental factors, 49
        operations and hospitalizations, 49
        pathology lurking beneath surface, 49
        predisposition, 49
        separations, 49
    infant, 44
    infantile manifestations, 45
    jet-propelled behavior, 45
    parents must understand, 52-53
        adolescence, 52
        goals of program, 53
        school psychologist, 52

Parents must understand (*continued*)
    teacher and principal, 52
    years of regular class lost, 52
  personality, 39
  portrait, 46-48
  public school, role, 51
  rejection of or by mother, 14
  shied away from contact, 44
  varying patterns, 44
  when pattern emerges, 44

E

Education Manual, New York State, 203
Electroencephalogram, 36-37
Elementary classes, 88-103
  (*see also* Curriculum)
Emotional development, visual-motor and, 39
"Emotionally disturbed":
  behavior patterns, 17
  characteristics, 24-25
  determining diagnosis, 40
  dynamics, 43-53
    (*see also* Dynamics)
  identification, 31-42
    (*see also* Identification of emotionally emotionally disturbed child)
  in regular class, 204
  not identified and referred, 205
  profile, 20-21
Enrollment, smaller, 192
Environmental cause, illusion, 49-50
  (*see also* Dynamics)
Equipment and materials, 128-140
  (*see also* Materials and equipment)
Errands, 147
Evaluation:
  preschool level, 36-37
    (*see also* Preschool level)
  psychologist, 75-76
  student progress, 103

F

Family life, 45-46, 206
  (*see also* Dynamics)
Farming-in procedures:
  invitations never refused, 164
  resolution of problems, 164
  service to rest of school, 164
  several days or weeks, 164
  time to see students, 165
Farming out:
  art education, 122, 127
  both teachers involved, 162
  case study, 165-172
    diary continued, 168-171
    introduction, 165-166
    new start, 172
    transition back, 171-172
    view of transition-adjustment teacher, 167-168
  part time in regular class, 160
  principal, 193-194
  recommendation, 160
  reentry procedure, 160
    changed frame of reference, 160
    data on student progress, 160
    first step, 160
    premature placement, 160
    team conference, 160
  selecting teacher, 161-162
    emotional impact for teacher, 161
    feedback by child, 162
    friendly, freewheeling atmosphere, 161
    highly structured setting, 161
    parents called for conference, 162
    principal knows faculty, 161
    reactions of other children, 162
  significant role, 161
  standard operating procedure, 55
  term, 159
  touching bases with child, 160-161
    approaching child, 160
    assessing child's feelings, 160
    decision to farm out, 161
    positive or negative reply, 160-161
  trial period, 162-164
    art, music, physical education, 162
    decision made by child, 163
    first few days or weeks, 163
    gratifying learning experiences, 163
    organic process at work, 163
    report by farm-out teacher, 163-164
    special subjects, 162
    "visits" to class, 163
Family life, 45-46
  (*see also* Dynamics)
Final period, 153-154
"Free play", summer program, 174
Frostig Developmental Test of Visual Perception, 188

INDEX

Future directions:
    candidates for classes, 204
    Center for Preventive Psychiatry, 207
    class as organizing catalyst, 204
    "Cornerstone Project," 207
    crash programs, 205
    disturbed children in regular classes, 204
    dynamics behind progress, 205
    early organization of disturbed child, 204
    early placement, 206
    essence of mental health, 206
    family pattern, 206
    frustration, aggravation, duress, 206
    homogeneously smaller learning situations, 205
    identify and set up classes, 204
    increased community involvement, 206
    infant care programs, 206
    junior high school program, 207
    New York State Education Manual, 203
    older students, 207
    parents, 205-206
    preventive goals, 204-206
    Report of Joint Comission on Illness and Health, 203
    studies, 206
    substitute parent figure, 205
    total school team effort, 207
    uncounted disturbed students, 205
    waiting list, 204
    work-study programs, 207

G

Gilmore Oral Reading Test, 188
Gray Oral Reading Paragraphs, 39, 188

H

Handwriting, elementary, 95-96
Harris Tests of Lateral Dominance, 188
Homework, checking, 149-150
Horst Reversal Test, 188
Hospitalizations, 49
Hours for class, 191-192
Housing of classes, 55
    (see also Space)

I

Identification of emotionally disturbed child:
    clues, 32-33
    description of one student, 31-32
    evaluating test results, 40-41
        (see also Testing, individual)
    events preceeding, 33-34
    individual testing process, 39-40
        (see also Testing, individual)
    need for diagnostic action, 34-35
        before preadolescence, 35
        corrective measures, 35
        early identification, 35
        "quiet period," 35
        role of school, 35
        school as model, 34-35
    preschool level, 36-37
        (see also Preschool level)
    school, 38-39
        aptitude and achievement tests, 38
        children referred for testing, 39
        classroom teacher, 38
        evaluation, 38
        previous teachers, 38
        principal, 38
        psychological testing, 38
        specialists, school, 38
        team, 38
        team conferences, 38
    summarized, 41-42
Illinois plan for special education of exceptional children, 103
Inappropriate behavior, 48
Individual work period, 151
Infant, 44, 206
Infantile manifestations, 45
Informal Reading Inventories, 188
Intelligence Test, 39
Interferences in development, 48-49
    (see also Development)

J

Joint Commission on Mental Illness and Health, 203
Junior high school, 103-105, 207

K

Kliman, Dr. Gilbert, 19, 207

L

Lateral dominance, 188
Length of class, 191-192
Librarian, 192
Lunch and after-lunch, 152-153

M

Manipulative skills, 123, 125
Materials and equipment:
    art, 124-126
    budget, 139-140
    ditto master workbooks, 138
    miscellaneous, 139
    play, 135-137
        (see also Play materials)
    power tools, 128-133
        (see also Power tools)
    reading, 138
    right ones at right time, 91-93
    standard operating procedure, 55
    transparency workbooks, 138
    woodworking, 134-135
        construction materials, 134-135
        equipment, 134
        supplies, 134
Mathematics:
    elementary, 98-99
    summer program, 173
Meaningful vocabulary, 188
Mechanical ability, 123
Meetings, standard operating procedures, 55
Mental health facts of life, 18
Merrill-Palmer Scale of Mental Tests, 39
Methods, Teaching, 141-158
    (see also Techniques, teaching)
Mother:
    clinging to, 44-45
    parents disturbed, 45
    parents must understand, 52-53
        (see also Dynamics)
    rejection of or by, 14
Moments, clumsy and rough, 48
Music and science, 150-151

N

Neubauer, Dr. Peter B., 206
Neurological factor, 25, 36
New lesson or material, art, 126

O

Operation 149
Oral reading, 188
Organizing district program:
    acceptance, class, 69
    building, 64
    class organization, 63-64
    community groups, 60
    director, 54-55, 56-57, 58, 59
        board of education, 59
        centrally coordinates program, 55
        collaborates with teachers and administrators, 57, 58
        data through parent conferences, 57
        documents needs for special classes, classes, 59
        final recommendation on teacher, 56
        findings of psychological services, 57
        learns from teacher, 57
        priorities, 55
        psychological services, 54
        pupil personnel services, 54, 55
        reading specialist, 58
        relationship with principal, 58
        responsibilities, 56-57
        school nurse, 58
        selection, 54-55
        serves teacher, 57
        special teachers, 58
        speech therapist, 58
        standard operating procedures, 55
        student placement, 56
        team member, 57
    documenting the need, 59
    initiation, 69-71
    model, 55-56
    parents as part of team, 71
    referred student, 59
    room for class, 64-66
    setting up, 60-61
    summarizing, 72
    summer and secondary programs, 71-72
    teacher, selection, 61-63
    transportation, 66-69
Outdoors, summer program, 174

P

Parent-teacher associations, 60

INDEX

Parents:
    apprehension, 196-197
    (see also Difficulties)
    conferences, 41, 103, 162, 180,
        189-190, 197
    curriculum, 89-90, 90-91
    (see also Curriculum)
    not to blame, 22-23
    part of team, 71
    post evaluation conference, 76-77
    relationship between student and
        teacher, 205
    screening process, 79-81
    written reports, 103
Patterns of behavior, 17
Pediatric-neurologist, 25, 36, 40
Personality dynamics, 39
Phonic skills, 188
Physical education:
    activities, program, 113-116
        games for different groups, 115
        middle group, 114-115
        oldest group, 115
        younger group, 113-114
    class composition, 110
    class organization, 111-113
        brief exercises, 111
        "catching their breath," 112
        day's activities begin, 113
        decision-making process, 112
        dismissal, orderly, 113
        equipment, 113
        orderly dismissal, 113
        specific place to go, 111
    difficulties likely to arise, 116-117
    individual attention and special
        help, 110-111
    mental objectives, 107-108
        analyze and understand game
            strategy, 108
        complying with rules and
            regulations, 108
        concentration on task, 107
        determination and self-motivation,
            108
        involvement in activities, 107-108
        understanding rules and
            regulations, 108
    physical objectives, 107
        body strength and flexibility, 107
        cardio- vascular fitness, 107
        general body coordination, 107
    socio-emotional objectives, 108-109
        ability to accept losing, 109

        getting along with others, 108-109
        self-control, 109
        summary, 117-119
    time allotments, 109-110
Play materials:
    free periods, 137
    individual desks, 136
    physical development and co-
        ordination, 137
    play corner, 135-136
    role, 135-137
    steel sand table, 136
Playground activities, summer, 173-174
Power tools:
    before hand tools, 128-129
    implementation, 130-131
        goals, 130
        indoctrination in safety, 130
        introducing machinery, 130
        procedures, 130-131
        safety guides, 130-131
    list, 129-130
    simple projects, 131-133
        free form name plate, 132
        paper tray, 132
        puzzle, 131-132
    summer program, 174
Preadolescence, 35
Predisposition, 49
Preschool level:
    evaluation, 36-37
        "brain damage," 36
        brain dysfunctioning, 36
        "developmental delay" 36
        electroencephalogram, 36
        gross evidence of brain injury, 37
        pediatric neurologist, 36
        school psychologist, 36
        symptom picture, 36
    help to family, 37-38
        home and nursery school, 37
        identifying children, 37
        kindergarten registration, 37
        private day setting, 37
        structure environment, 37
Primary brain dysfunctioning, 25, 36
Principal:
    area of special interest, 55
    asks himself certain questions, 187
    board of education, 59
    building coordinator, 194
    children as induviduals, 187
    concerned with problems, 187

Principal (*continued*)
  conference with parents, 189-190
  director, 58
  farming-out, 193-194
  helps clarify child's difficulties, 52
  meeting educational goals, 55
  must be interested in helping, 187
  not in favor of class, 202
  objectives for children, 187
  priorities, 55
  problems, 191-193
    bus driver, 192
    cafeteria workers, 192
    length of class, 191-192
    secretaries, 192
    smaller class enrollment, 192
    unique to building situation, 55
  role with child, 191
  rules and regulations, 55
  success begets success, 187
  team conference, 188-190
  team leader, 188
  working with parents, 190
Problem:
  drains teacher and class, 21-22
  "emotionally disturbed," 24
  parents not to blame, 22-23
  patterns of behavior, 17
  profile of disturbed child, 20-21
  special class, value, 22
  transition and adjustment, 23-24
  where it begins, 18-20
Profile of disturbed child, 20-21
Prognois, 39
Program for district, organizing, 54-72
(*see also* Organizing district program)
Projective tests, 39-40
Psychological testing, 38, 39-41
(*see also* Testing; induvidual)
Psychologist, school, 52
Public school, role, 51

R

Rapport, teacher-student, 86
Reading:
  elementary, 89
  materials, 138
  oral, 188
  recognition, 39
  silent, 188
  specialist, 93-95
  summer program, 173-178
  test of level, 39
Records, anecdotal, 189

Referral form, preparation:
  classroom teacher fills out, 73
  evaluation, 74
  parent awareness, 73
  pertinent data, 73
  physician, 74
  principal, 74
  psychologist, 74
  reasons, 73, 74
  school nurse, 74
Reporting to parents, 103
Reuben, Dr. Richard, 36
Reversals, 188
Rooms for classes, 64-66
Rorschach, 39, 40

S

Schedules, daily class, 55
School psychologist, 52
School, public, 51
Science:
  elementary, 99-103
  teaching techniques, 150-151
Screening:
  informing student, 81
  parent and program, 79-81
  post evaluation parent conference, 76-77
  psychologist's evaluation, 75-76
  referral form preparation, 73-74
  (*see also* Referral form, preparation)
  standard operating procedure, 55
  student priorities, setting, 74-75
  teacher, 55
  transition-adjustment class priority, 77-78
Secondary and summer programs, 71-72
Secretaries, 58, 192
Separations, 49
Sight vocabulary, 188
Silent reading, 188
Sleep, 48
Space:
  buses, 198-199
  double-team overlapping, 198, 199
  less than regular class, 198
  sharing classroom, 198
  shifting buildings, 199
  temporary structure, 199
Spelling, elementary, 96-97
Stanford-Binet Intelligence Scale, 39
Structural materials, art, 125
Structured activities, summer program, 174
Studies, 206

INDEX

Study area, individual, 155, 158
Substitute teacher, 200-201
Summer program:
  acting out stories, 173-174
  advantages, 71-72
  arts and crafts, 174
  can be expanded, 178
  children enrolled, 175-176
    farmed out students, 175
    presently in special class, 175
    priority order of placement, 175
    ready for part-time farming out, 175
    set for fall placement, 175
    team conferences, 175
    unable to function in regular camp, 176
    younger disturbed children, 176
  cost, 173
  cirriculum, 174
    bolsters academic skills, 177
    experience booklets, 177
    field trips, 177
    level of academic functioning, 177
    primary typewriter, 177
    readiness materials, 177
    structured activity program, 177
    teacher aides circulate, 177
    various organized activities, 177
    younger children, 177
  day's schedule, 178
  difficulty with camp situation, 175
  drawings, 177
  factors in favor, 175
  few other summer programs, 175
  first period, 178
  first summer, 174-175
  "free play" time, 174
  game, 178
  helps preserve family relationship, 175
  individualized reading, 173
  indoctrination of teacher, 176
  integral part of total program, 173
  mathematics, 173
  need for outside activities, 175
  offsets regression, 175
  older children help younger, 178
  periodical meeings, 177
  playground activities, 173
  points to consider, 178
  power tools, 174
  preparation for fall class, 173
  quiet activity, 178
  reading, 178
  sequential reading skills, 173
  snapshots, 177
  staff and facilities, 176-177
    activities originated, 176
    attitudes to staff members, 176
    bathroom and sink facilities, 177
    coordinator, 176
    district funds, 176
    eighteen children, 176
    materials brought, 176
    number of teachers, 176
    optimum setup, 177
    relationships with children, 176
    rooms near playground, 177
    teachers and aides, 176
    transition-adjustment classrooms, 177
  structured activities outdoors, 174, 175
  woodworking, 174, 178

T

Talking, 48
Teacher:
  children on waiting list, 204-205
  constant stress factor, 205
  farm-out, 161-162
  final recommendation on, 56
  (see also Organizing district program)
  helps clarify child's difficulties, 52
  may frown on program, 202
  personality, 184-185, 185-186
  screening, 55
  seen through director's eye, 183-186
  seen through principal's eye, 182
  seen through teacher's eye, 180-181
  selection, 61-63, 161-162
  substitute, 200-201
  substitute parent figure, 205
  selection, 61-63
  summer, 176-177
  teaching, 182-183
  training and supervision, 181-182, 203
Teacher aides, 58, 176
Teaching techniques, 141-158
(see also Techniques, teaching)
Team:
  communication, 29

Team (*continued*)
    concept, 188
    conference, 38, 175, 188-190
    leader, 188
    teaching, 154-155

Techniques, teaching:
    acting-out child, 144-146
    actual day in class, 148-155
    after-lunch session, 152-153
    errand, 147
    final period, 153-154
    first weeks of program, 142-144
    homework is checked, 149-150
    individual study area, 155, 158
    individual work period, 151
    lunch, 152
    science and music, 150-151
    team, 154-155
    withdrawn child, 146

Testing, individual:
    achievement test, 38, 39
    Bender-Gestalt designs and human figure drawings, 39

    Children's Apperception Test, 39
    diagnosis and prognosis, 39
    evaluating results, 40-41
        contributing causal factors, 40
        corrective measures, 40
        degree of symptoms, 40
        determining diagnosis, 40
        developmental history, 40, 41
        developmental interferences, 41
        outside resources, 40
        parent conferences, 41
        pediatric neurological examination, 40
        psychological battery, 40

    Gray Oral Reading Paragraphs, 39
    intelligence test, 39
    Merrill-Palmer Scale of Mental Tests, 39
    personality dynamics, 39
    projective measures, 39-40
    qualifications to use of Rorschach, 40
    reading and arithmetic level, 39
    reading recognition, 39
    Rorschach, 39, 40
    Stanford-Binet Intelligence Scale, 39
    Thematic Apperception Test, 39

    visual-motor and emotional development, 39
    Wechsler Adult Intelligence Scale, 39
    Wechsler Intelligence Scale for Children, 39
    Wechsler Preschool and Primary Scale of Intelligence, 39
    Wide Range Achievement Test, 39
Thematic Apperception Test, 39
Transition-adjustment class:
    admission upon entering school, 37
    board of education, 59-60
    cafeteria workers, 192
    candidates, 204
    community groups. 60
    data on effectiveness, 195-196
    director, 54-58
        (*see also*
            Organizing district program)
    documenting need, 59-60
    four and one-half hours, 191
    funds, 59-60
    future directions, 203-210
    homogeneously smaller learning situations, 205
    identify and set up, 204
    Joint Commission on Mental Health, 203
    junior high school program, 207
    librarian, 192-193
    older students, 207
    organizing catalyst, 204
    organizing district program, 29-30, 54-72
        (*see also* Organizing district program)
    preventive goal, 204
    problems, 191-192
        bus driver, 192
        cafeteria workers, 192
        secretaries, 192
    program presented to administrators, 59
    referred student, 59
    reading specialist, 58
    school nurse, 58
    screening procedures, 73-81
        (*see also* Screening)
    secretaries, 192
    smaller class enrollment, 192
    space. 198-199
        (*see also* Space)

INDEX

Transition-adjustment
   class (*continued*)
     special teachers, 58
     speech therapist, 58
     substitute teacher, 200-201
     summer program, 173-178
        (*see also* Summer program)
     teacher, 61-63, 179-186
        (*see also* Teacher)
     teacher aides, 58, 176
     term, 23
     total school team effort, 207
     waiting list, 204-205
Transparency workbooks, 138
Transportation, 55, 66-69, 173, 199-200
Traumas, cumulative, 49

V

Visual-motor and emotional development, test, 39
Visual perception, 188

Vocabulary, sight and meaningful, 188
Vocational training, 198

W

Waiting list, 204-205
Walking, 48
Wechsler Adult Intelligence Scale, 39
Wechsler Intelligence Scale for Children, 39
Wechsler Preschool and Primary Scale of Intelligence, 39
Wepman Auditory Discrimination, Test, 188
Wide Range Achievement Test, 39
Withdrawn child, 146
Wood, art education, 122-123
Woodworking, 134-135, 174, 178
Word analysis, 188
Work-study programs, 207
Workbooks, 138